Reinventing the
Community College
Business Model

ABOUT *THE FUTURES SERIES ON COMMUNITY COLLEGES*

The Futures Series on Community Colleges is designed to produce and deliver books that strike to the heart of issues that will shape the future of community colleges. *Futures* books examine emerging structures, systems and business models, and stretch prevailing assumptions about leadership and management by reaching beyond the limits of convention and tradition.

Topics addressed in the *series* are those that are vital to community colleges, but have yet to receive meaningful attention in literature, research, and analysis. *Futures* books are written by scholars and practitioners who deliver a unique perspective on a topic or issue—a president or higher education consultant bringing expert and practical understanding to a topic, a policy analyst breaking down a complex problem into component parts, an academic or think tank scholar conducting incisive research, or a researcher and a practitioner working together to examine an issue through different lenses.

Futures books are developed on the premise that disruptive innovation and industry transformation are, and will be, an ongoing challenge. Gradual improvement is, understandably, a natural preference of leaders. It will not be enough, however, to position our colleges for the future. The future will be about transformation and, to perform optimally, our colleges will need to become capable of large-scale change. As leaders come face-to-face with digital forces and rapidly changing social, economic, and public policy conditions, they will have no choice but to get ahead of change or relinquish market position to competitors. *Futures* books are a vehicle through which leaders can learn about and prepare for what's ahead. Whether it's through analysis of what big data will mean in the next generation of colleges or which business models will become the new normal, *Futures* books are a resource for practitioners who realize that the ideas of out-of-the-box thinkers and the innovative practices of high performing organizations can be invaluable for answering big questions and solving complex problems.

Richard L. Alfred, Series Founding Editor, Emeritus Professor of Higher Education, University of Michigan

Debbie L. Sydow, Series Senior Editor, President, Richard Bland College of the College of William and Mary

Kate Thirolf, Series Editor, Dean of Business & Human Services, Jackson College

Books in *The Futures Series on Community Colleges*

Developing Tomorrow's Leaders: Context, Challenges, and Capabilities
By Pamela Eddy, Debbie L. Sydow, Richard L. Alfred, and
Regina L. Garza Mitchell

This book provides a template for leadership development in the community college sector. The theme of the book focuses on the need to move beyond hierarchical leadership to networked leadership that taps talent throughout the institution. The transformational change required in the two-year sector demands new approaches to leading, including tolerance for risk, use of data analytics, and a focus on relationships. New and alternative means for leadership development are presented.

The Urgency of Now: Equity and Excellence
By Marcus M. Kolb, Samuel D. Cargile, et al.
    The Urgency of Now asserts that in addition to being granted access to the community college, all twenty-first-century students need uncompromised support to succeed. Success means demonstrating relevant learning for transfer and employment, and timely completion of credentials. Looking to the future, the authors contend that community colleges, both by their past successes and future challenges, are at the epicenter for determining the essential ingredients of a new student-centered system that guarantees equity and excellence.

Unrelenting Change, Innovation, and Risk: Forging the Next Generation of Community Colleges
By Daniel J. Phelan
    In this book, thirty-five-year veteran Dan Phelan shares key insights from his personal and professional journey as a transformational, entrepreneurial community college leader. The book's wisdom and insights are amplified by observations gleaned from interviews and visits with dozens of leading practitioners. Drawing upon his sailing experiences, Phelan argues that leaders should stop playing it safe in the harbor because the real gains driving institutional and student success are found in uncharted waters. *Unrelenting Change, Innovation, and Risk* dares community college leaders to innovate and provides them with a toolkit for understanding changing conditions, assessing risk, and successfully navigating change.

Financing Community Colleges: Where We Are, Where We're Going
By Richard Romano and James Palmer
    Grounded in an economic perspective, *Financing Community Colleges* helps college leaders make sense of the challenges they face in securing and managing the resources needed to carry out the community college mission. Finance has perpetually been an Achilles heel for leaders at all levels of management. With the premise that leaders are better at winning battles they know something about, this book equips leaders with an understanding of the fundamentals and the complexities of community college finance. It tackles current and emerging issues with insight that is analytic and prophetic—a must read for current and prospective leaders.

The Completion Agenda in Community Colleges: What It Is, Why It Matters, and Where It's Going
By Chris Baldwin
    This book is intended to improve understanding about the complex issues surrounding the national college completion agenda. By highlighting

the origins of this agenda and the dilemmas and opportunities it creates for community colleges, the text describes the many innovations underway nationally. The book is an effort to bridge gaps between practice, policy, and research to provide the reader with a holistic view of community college response to the completion agenda.

Competing on Culture: Driving Change in Community Colleges
By Randall VanWagoner

Community colleges are under intense pressure to change in response to shifts in an increasingly complex environment. Stakeholders are placing simultaneously contradictory demands on colleges for more and better service, increased accountability, and more efficient use of resources in order to get the most from colleges in tough economic times. These demands have contributed to cultural fragmentation in community colleges as staff are pulled in competing directions by events beyond their control.

The upshot is a circumstance in which leaders are finding that culture is perhaps the most powerful element affecting organizational performance and change. The old saw "culture eats strategy for breakfast' epitomizes the importance of culture as a means for enhancing the long-term viability of an organization. This book provides fresh analysis of organizational culture in the community college context with a critical examination of the relationship between organizational culture and change. Readers will benefit from frank advice with insights to drive change by transforming and leveraging culture to shape the future of community colleges.

Previously Published Books in *The Series on Community Colleges*

Minding the Dream: The Process and Practice of the American Community College, Second Edition
　By Gail O. Mellow and Cynthia M. Heelan
First in the World: Community Colleges and America's Future
　By J. Noah Brown
Community College Student Success: From Boardrooms to Classrooms
　By Banessa Smith Morest
Re-visioning Community Colleges
　By Debbie Sydow and Richard Alfred
Community Colleges on the Horizon: Challenge, Choice, or Abundance
　By Richard Alfred, Christopher Shults, Ozan Jaquette, and Shelley Strickland

Reinventing the Community College Business Model

Designing Colleges for Organizational Success

Christopher Shults
Series Founding Editor: Richard L. Alfred
Series Senior Editor: Debbie L. Sydow

AMERICAN ASSOCIATION OF COMMUNITY COLLEGES

ROWMAN & LITTLEFIELD
Lanham • Boulder • New York • London

Published by Rowman & Littlefield
An imprint of The Rowman & Littlefield Publishing Group, Inc.
4501 Forbes Boulevard, Suite 200, Lanham, Maryland 20706
www.rowman.com

6 Tinworth Street, London SE11 5AL, United Kingdom

Copyright © 2020 by Christopher Shults
All images created by the author unless otherwise stated.

All rights reserved. No part of this book may be reproduced in any form or by any electronic or mechanical means, including information storage and retrieval systems, without written permission from the publisher, except by a reviewer who may quote passages in a review.

British Library Cataloguing in Publication Information Available

Library of Congress Cataloging-in-Publication Data

Names: Shults, Christopher, author.
Title: Reinventing the community college business model : designing colleges for organizational success / Christopher Shults.
Description: Lanham, Maryland : Rowman & Littlefield, 2020. | Series: The futures series on community colleges | Includes bibliographical references and index. | Summary: "This book defines and explores the four fundamental elements of a community college business model, demonstrates the necessity and impacts of the model, and provides guidance on managing within, effectively developing, and successfully implementing an operational framework structured to enhance student learning and success"—Provided by publisher.
Identifiers: LCCN 2019047499 (print) | LCCN 2019047500 (ebook) | ISBN 9781475850727 (cloth) | ISBN 9781475850734 (paperback) | ISBN 9781475850741 (epub)
Subjects: LCSH: Community colleges—United States—Administration. | Community colleges—United States—Planning.
Classification: LCC LB2341 .S468 2020 (print) | LCC LB2341 (ebook) | DDC 378.1/5430973—dc23
LC record available at https://lccn.loc.gov/2019047499
LC ebook record available at https://lccn.loc.gov/2019047500

∞™ The paper used in this publication meets the minimum requirements of American National Standard for Information Sciences—Permanence of Paper for Printed Library Materials, ANSI/NISO Z39.48-1992.

Contents

List of Figures and Tables	ix
Foreword	xi
Preface	xiii
Acknowledgments	xix

SECTION I: BUILDING THE CASE FOR A COMMUNITY COLLEGE BUSINESS MODEL — 1

1	Introducing the Community College Business Model	3
2	The Increasingly Dynamic Higher Education Industry	19
3	Operational Management in a Community College Business Model	41

SECTION II: CREATING THE CONDITIONS FOR A NEW COMMUNITY COLLEGE BUSINESS MODEL — 53

4	Organizational Culture, Organizational Change, and the Business Model	55
5	Administration, Governance, and Leadership	71

SECTION III: EXPLORING THE COMMUNITY COLLEGE BUSINESS MODEL — 91

6	The Student Value Proposition	93
7	Managing Key Resources	115
8	Delivering the Product	147
9	The Profit Formula	175

Conclusion	195
Bibliography	201
Index	215
About the Author	227

Figures and Tables

FIGURES

4.1	Institutional Culture and Subcultures in Community Colleges	58
5.1	Continuum of Organizational Business and Management Approaches	72

TABLES

1.1	Business Model Difference between Community Colleges and For-Profit Colleges	7
1.2	Translation of Business Model Concepts to Higher Education Questions	10
2.1	Impact of Changing Compliance Expectations on Community Colleges	33
3.1	Limitations of Standard Management Techniques in Driving Organizational Effectiveness	43
3.2	Student Value Proposition in a Traditional Business Model and CCBM	47
3.3	Key Resources in a Traditional Business Model and CCBM	49
3.4	Product Delivery in a Traditional Business Model and CCBM	50
4.1	Culture Type by Decision-Making Category and Institutional Orientation	60

4.2	Methods in Which Institutional History is Used to Impact Organizational Change	63
4.3	Inventory of Cultural Factors that Impact Organizational Change Efforts	64
5.1	Leadership Styles and Culture Type Alignment	79
5.2	Leadership Principles and Practices Central to Distributed Leadership	83
6.1	College Expectations by Different Student Populations	96
6.2	Benefits, Problems, and Needs by Mission Type	97
6.3	Data Usage and Evaluation of the Student Value Proposition	101
7.1	Contextualizing Key Resources for Community Colleges	116
7.2	Lack of Intentional Design of Physical Space for Student Success	131
7.3	Challenges and Opportunities to Leverage Technological Tools	132
7.4	Leveraging the Institutional Information Systems to Enhance the Student Value Proposition	134
9.1	Tactics for Cost Cutting and Containment	187
9.2	Tactics for Revenue Generation	191

Foreword

Higher education is at a crisis point. We face unprecedented scrutiny politically, economically, and socially. Fundamentally, our business model—carved from decade- and century-old traditions—is outdated.

Thankfully, Christopher Shults dissects the reasons higher education is at risk. He offers clear and practical examples of what a reformation of higher education could and should resemble. As such, community colleges are at the heart of leading the innovation that could save higher education from itself.

With a current financial model based on headcount, Shults certainly articulates why enrollment will not maintain itself over the next decade. Politicians and society seem to see higher education as aloof and disconnected. The political will to fund higher education is at an all-time low. Despite emerging rhetoric of support during a presidential campaign, politicians should not be our hope for a financial solution.

The current enrollment-based business model, employed throughout higher education, will no longer be exempt from population, market, and political shifts. We can either ignore the pending crisis to our peril, or we can do the hard and rewarding work of building a new future.

Shults deftly guides us through the current reality and offers a clear community college business model focused on students and their success. Implementing this model will not be easy. Community colleges will be challenged. Community colleges will be forced to clarify and simplify our mission. Community colleges must confront decades of policy and practice focused on the "replacement" model of enrollment. Yet, community colleges must do it. Shults gives us a roadmap and it starts with defining each institution's "student value proposition."

As we prepare for the next two decades of higher education, community colleges are positioned to transform the entire higher education business model. A skills-based economy gives community colleges a chance to emerge as THE leader of higher education, becoming the first choice for our communities and their students. Shults does not just call us to action based on hypotheses. He offers real examples of community colleges doing this work—and succeeding.

You will find your own college within these pages (good and bad). You will understand why the student value proposition should be where each institution starts its own reform journey. Mostly, you will understand why creating a community college business model is our best hope.

The community college sector is nimble, visionary, and responsive. We are the antidote to the damaging perceptions our country currently holds of higher education as a whole. We can do this.

Russell D. Lowery-Hart
President, Amarillo College

Preface

The "community college" is a uniquely American creation and the embodiment of the massification and democratization principals that expanded higher education's reach. The number of community colleges has grown, as have enrollments, and between 1955 and 1975 nearly one community college a week was established. Currently, nearly half of all undergraduate students attend community colleges. The rise of the community college, primarily out of a need for greater access to higher education in support of a growing and diversifying economy, led to what has historically been the de facto organizational strategy—growth.

This strategy has been expounded upon in numerous publications and with detail in the 2005 publication by Richard Alfred, *Managing the Big Picture in Colleges and Universities: From Tactics to Strategy*. Expanding on the practice and fundamental principle that colleges accumulate all they can and spend all they get, community colleges have largely focused on increasing enrollment to ensure sufficient revenue to cover costs. While historically the norm, this approach was never ideal; has reached unsustainability; and is contradictory to the mission of access, affordability, and success. Inadequate financing of higher education has placed an unfair burden on community college students: students more likely to come from underserved and economically disadvantaged populations. Ongoing reductions in state and local funding along with increasing operational costs increases the real cost of educating students. The result is greater dependence on tuition and new revenue generation. When sufficient new revenue streams are not created, the price of attendance increases. Our student population is extremely price conscious and continued tuition increases is reducing affordability.

Infatuation with student enrollment is problematic for several reasons. First, enrollment fluctuates based on economic trends, and maintaining—let alone growing—enrollment during decreased enrollment cycles is often a fruitless endeavor. Second, enrollment has an upper limit based on space, faculty, and existing facilities. While colleges have sought to increase enrollment through online education, there are significant costs associated with the development and continued operation of well-developed, resourced, and supported online programs. The most substantive issue, however, is that this approach is counter to the true purpose of higher education—to effectively serve current students. Questions community colleges should ask themselves include the following:

- What is the optimal enrollment that ensures effective support for student success?
- Is the enrollment too large to ensure adequate faculty, staff, and physical resources?
- Could the college better support students by prioritizing the success of current students over the recruitment of ever larger incoming classes?

These questions are not hypothetical, but may seem nonsensical given the need to ensure financial resources in a time of public divestment. Therein lies the tension in the infinite growth strategy. Community college can enter a deficit cycle where enrollment increases lead to increased revenues, but also increased costs that must be covered by increased revenues. What community colleges need is to reexamine the de facto business models that focus on growth or depend upon financial and strategic plans and redesign the models for student learning and success as the priority. Community colleges need models that focus on the student value proposition along with the key resources, products, and financing necessary for an exceptional educational experience. What is needed is a reinvented community college business model (CCBM).

Initial reaction to the phrase *community college business model*, from some, will be revulsion, which is understandable given the prevalence of for-profit educational providers that have utilized corporate models to drive profitability rather than enhance student success. Business model research in higher education, however, goes back nearly sixty years and community colleges are in a higher education industry with a responsibility to enhance human development and societal improvement. A business is an organization that is guided by a mission and goals, employs personnel to accomplish objectives, gathers resources to ensure continued operations, and serves customers. The language and these principals are contextualized throughout this publication and it is clear that colleges are social businesses, not corporations and serve students, not customers. A business model encompasses the framework from which an organization designs its operations to ensure achievement of the mission, and community colleges have always maintained these models. The question is are the models intentionally designed for student success?

To be clear, strategy and strategic planning are important. Budgeting, including both resource acquisition and allocation, is important. Mission, vision, outcomes, objectives, and goals are all important. Understanding and seeking ways to better meet student needs, support the faculty and staff who are responsible for establishing and enhancing the teaching and learning environment, and effectively responding to external stakeholder demands are important. Without an overarching, intentionally designed framework that aligns these various elements, however, community colleges render themselves unable to fully leverage the resources, talent, and commitment from faculty and staff needed to increase organizational success. In other words, operating without a comprehensive and intentionally designed business model framework prevents community colleges from designing for student success. This publication seeks to provide guidance in this endeavor by offering the CCBM as the template.

WHAT'S INSIDE?

The first section is titled "Building the Case for a Community College Business Model," and includes three chapters that describe the foundations of the CCBM, the changing dynamics that make the model necessary, and how to manage within a business model framework. The first chapter introduces the concept of the business model and details the four elements of the model. The case is made that organizational success is student success and is enhanced through implementation of a framework designed to understand and address student needs, identify and leverage nonfinancial resources, elevate the educational experience, and generate the financial margins necessary to support the model.

Chapter 2 explores the current and evolving dynamics within today's higher education industry. This chapter emphasizes the significant disruptions to the higher education industry and especially to community colleges. Political, economic, technological, and demographic changes have created unparalleled pressure on existing systems and operational management. The traditional higher education business models were not intentionally designed and are ill-equipped to resolve these tensions. The CCBM takes some of the lessons learned from changing healthcare business models and is built to address the disruptions caused by the pervasiveness of technology, increased compliance requirements, and decreased funding. A philosophical foundation of this chapter is that disruption is unavoidable and must be used as a catalyst for innovation and reimagining the student's educational experience.

Community colleges have spent decades moving toward more effective management, operational, and administrative practices, structures, and processes. As a result of changing funding dynamics and priorities and a continued focus on the growth strategy, however, these institutions often find themselves unable to effectively adapt to changing conditions. Chapter 3 charges that these traditional approaches are insufficient for achieving organizational success within the continually evolving higher education industry. By focusing on strategies that can be utilized to better understand who the college is and is not serving, reconceptualize existing and available resources, more effectively manage operational costs, and address academic programming and student support, the colleges will be in a greater position to achieve organizational success.

The second section of the book, "Creating the Conditions for a New Community College Business Model," examines the institutional environment necessary for developing and implementing the CCBM. Chapter 4 provides a targeted exploration into institutional culture and its impacts on the implementation of organizational change efforts. The chapter provides a conceptual framework of culture in community colleges, examines different culture types, explores the connection between culture type and organizational effectiveness, and details cultural factors that impede or support development of the CCBM. The chapter ends with four hypothetical community colleges, each with a different culture type, that are confronted with the need to redesign their business models.

Chapter 5 explores the issues of administration, governance, and leadership and the role of each in designing and implementing the CCBM. Administration refers to the president and the senior administration; governance refers to the administration, board, and senate bodies; and leadership includes all individuals who are empowered to provide recommendations, lead initiatives, and create change. The section on leadership examines targeted theories, addresses leadership style/college culture fit, and provides information on which styles and clans are most conducive to the development of the CCBM. The hypothetical colleges are included with a focus on how administration, governance, and leadership support model development.

The final section of the book, "Exploring the Community College Business Model," takes the reader through the development of the four foundational elements of a business model. Chapter 6 addresses the most important aspect of the CCBM, which is the student value proposition. The student value proposition is the primary reason why students choose to attend the community college—learning and the attainment of a credential. Put into organizational terms, however, the community college seeks to provide a value proposition that is premised on student learning and success. Since these institutions serve many different student populations, the proposition must focus on the needs and problems unique to each of the subgroups. This is the last chapter utilizing the hypothetical colleges and ends with a real case study from a community college committed to understanding its students and redesigning for their success.

Chapter 7 considers the key resources, including human, physical, and intellectual resources, critical for student success. The most important of these resources are the human resources, which include the faculty and staff who support student success. The chapter explores the actions, attitudes, and behaviors associated with student learning and success as well as keys for supporting, developing, and leveraging the expertise and skill of faculty and staff. Physical resources represent the aspects of the college that students interact with directly—facilities, physical space, and technology. The focus of this section is on the impact these resources have on the educational experience and the ways in which the CCBM can amplify the effects. Intellectual resources refer to the nonphysical resources that play a major role in organizational effectiveness. Within the CCBM, partnerships and tacit knowledge are presented as key resources that help optimize the student value proposition. There are examples of how these resources can be effectively leveraged within each of the three sections.

Chapter 8 is an exploration into the deliverable associated with the student value proposition—the product. In community colleges, the product is the students' educational experience. From preenrollment until completion of a course or credential, students are immersed in an educational experience that must meet their needs, help solve problems, and provide them with support. The product is constructed from three separate, yet intertwined, elements—mechanisms, processes, and structures. Mechanisms refer to the frameworks that students interact with on a daily basis and include academic departments, curriculum, support service units, and administrative supports. Processes are connected to the mechanisms and represent activities including teaching, counseling, advising, and tutoring. Structures are the strategic and operational backbone supports that, within the CCBM, integrate the mechanisms and processes. A real-life case study is presented to demonstrate how an intentionally designed approach to enhancing the student educational experience can have a powerful, positive effect on student success.

Chapter 9 addresses the final element of the business model, which is the profit formula. Maintaining the revenue necessary for enhancing the value proposition requires the establishment of margins, or profit, between costs and revenue. This chapter focuses on better understanding how cost structures, budget approaches, containment of costs, and generation of revenue, impact the business model. The chapter also details approaches for cost constraints that do not sacrifice student success and increase revenue generation without chasing resources. Tactics that have been used by both two- and four-year colleges to constrain costs and generate revenue are provided.

As a community college scholar, practitioner, consultant, and advocate over the past two decades, I understand the importance of organizational culture, strategy, planning, assessment, and evidence-based decision making. I have also come to the realization that these techniques, even when integrated, do not provide the framework necessary to significantly improve student success. The higher education industry has been fundamentally changed and utilizing standard operating practices, which are often unaligned and siloed, simply will not provide us with the structure required to prioritize organizational success. Serving students requires a comprehensive, intentionally designed business model that accounts for our unique environments, population of students, and stakeholders. Our success is determined by only one measure—student success. We cannot continue to operate as we always have because it has not worked. We must acknowledge that the traditional approaches have failed us in our efforts to serve students and that new approaches must be pursued. We need to develop community college business models that position our institutions to recognize and leverage opportunities, proactively address internal and external factors that threaten success, and improve the value we provide to students. By establishing and operating from the CCBM and incorporating these principles into the fabric of our colleges, we better position ourselves to meet the needs of our students, support those who directly impact student learning, and ensure the environment is structured to elevate student success.

Acknowledgments

First, I would like to thank Dr. Richard Alfred for the opportunity to write this publication. Dick has been a mentor, advisor, colleague, and friend for more than fifteen years and I am truly appreciative for his support and guidance. More than just a graduate advisor, he provided me with tremendous opportunities to work with colleges, learn from leaders, and support the work of the Strategic Horizon Network. When he first approached me with the proposition of writing on a redesigned community college business model, I was excited and overwhelmed at the scope of the task. It did not take long for him to convince me that the book was necessary and that with the appropriate guidance and critique, I was up to the challenge. He was correct and I am thankful.

I would also like to thank Dr. Debbie Sydow for her editorial support, patience, and insightful critique of the work. Her sharp insights, broad scope of knowledge, and expertise were brought to bear throughout the process and the book is better as a result. Her kind words and enthusiasm provided me with much needed encouragement and inspiration. While writing comes easy for me at times, this book was a beast to complete. I described the process as trying to wrestle a bull and sometimes getting the horns and she responded with kindness, understanding, and a pep talk. I am thankful that I have gotten to know an amazing community college leader during this process.

Nobody achieves success on their own and I have been blessed with far more mentors than I can possibly name. There are two that I must mention by name—both in honor of their memories and because they were committed to my professional and personal growth. Dr. David Pierce was a giant among giants and one of the wisest, kindest, and most humble people I have had the genuine honor of knowing. Depending on the situation, you could see the former Marine, the CEO of the AACC, or just "an ol' Okie" as he would call himself. Ten minutes after he met me, he called me to the service of the community college student and I continue to serve—in his honor and because it is my great pleasure. I also need to thank Dr. Nathaniel Pugh Jr., who continually challenged me to see what I hear and hear what I see. He would pull me into his office after meetings to quiz me on the interactions, dynamics, and behaviors I had observed. He taught me to never settle, to take risks, and most importantly, to be the man my family, college, and community needs. To both of you I am eternally grateful and will continue to pay your investment forward.

Special thanks go to the faculty, staff, and administrators who I have worked with for the past two decades. I continue to learn more than I teach, to receive more care than I share, and observe more hope than I could possibly offer. Working in the community college is a higher calling and I have had the good fortune of working with so many committed individuals. Lessons that I have learned are reflected in the publication.

I also want to thank the students who we serve. Your strength, determination, and optimism inspire and motivate me each and every semester. You entrust us with your academic futures, seek out resources and support, and depend upon us to help you find your pathway to academic, career, and life success. We must continue to improve our ability to meet your needs and prepare you, whether you are a recent high school graduate, career changer, working adult, or member of the community. This model is designed to optimize the value of your educational experience. You are the primary beneficiary of this approach, and accordingly, it is my hope that you are the primary beneficiary of this publication.

Finally, I want to thank my wonderful family who has supported me throughout this process and in life. My wife of twenty-two years, Keiva, is my best friend, confidant, greatest supporter, and most loving coach. I have benefited from her encouragement, strength, intellect, kindness, and tireless work ethic and I am so grateful to her. I would also like to say thank you to our three children, Niriel, Arianna, and Micah. You constantly remind me what is important in life and show me what love in action looks like.

Section I

BUILDING THE CASE FOR A COMMUNITY COLLEGE BUSINESS MODEL

Tumultuous. Challenging. Uncertain. Precarious. Daunting. These terms appear frequently in articles about the present and future state of colleges and universities. A historical examination of these same publications, however, illustrates that dire concerns about the state of higher education have existed for decades. Community colleges typically ignore these ominous forecasts because these institutions have weathered a lack of adequate funding, increasing scope and scale of competition, and an ever-evolving mission. In the past thirty years, community colleges have been confronted with the following challenges:

- the introduction of online education,
- massive open online courses (MOOCs; which have not created the level of disruption predicted),
- the rise of proprietary education,
- changing economic conditions,
- changing student demographics,
- decreased state and local financial support, and
- greater calls for accountability from myriad external stakeholders.

Despite these difficulties, enrollments have grown and the institutions have largely maintained stability. Until recently, continued operation was a given, political and societal support was strong, and external pressures and conditions, while challenging, were predictable. In recent years, however, the focus on low retention, graduation, and transfer has intensified and scrutiny has grown. Community colleges are being challenged to demonstrate significant improvement regarding their organizational effectiveness.

Community colleges were established as open access institutions, charged with effectively meeting the needs of their respective service area; however, both internal and external forces now demand a greater focus on access *and* success in equal measure. Colleges depending primarily or exclusively on strategic planning, incremental/decremental budgeting, and quantitative inputs to drive resource allocation, are not positioned to significantly improve student success. Community colleges must develop and operate from a framework, a business model, intentionally designed to increase effectiveness. An exploration into the business and organizational management and higher education literature databases offer a limited number of publications on higher education models with many advocating for reinvention, but very few articulating the philosophies, framework, and goals of a higher education, let alone a community college business model.

The objective of this introductory section is to familiarize readers with the concept of a business model—what it is and is not—drawing from the literature on organizations, both inside and outside of higher education. In offering insight into the concept of the CCBM, this section also addresses the conditions that necessitate, as well as the challenges associated with, the development and implementation of this redesigned model.

Chapter One

Introducing the Community College Business Model

The term *higher education business model* has become a more routine discussion point and research topic over recent years. In just the last year, the Chronicle of Higher Education has developed a publication about business models and a recent article provides a pictorial illustration of the exponential growth in higher education business model references.[1] While the phrase has been discussed more frequently, it is not a new concept.[2] Important past higher education publications speak to the importance of a model with the first article referring to a higher education business model dating back to the 1960s.[3]

While more articles, editorials, blog posts, and other publications addressing higher education business models have emerged, the concept has not become any less controversial.[4] Among the more humorous and enlightening takes on how the concept is somtimes viewed in higher education is as follows:

> Reactions to the term "business model" within higher education range from "higher education is not a ^#%$@* business" to "what in the world is a business model?" As a result, those of us in higher education come off as naïve at best and as head-in-the-sand intransigents at worst. To many, we seem to be saying: "Let the rest of the sectors of the economy—whether medicine, construction, manufacturing, publishing, governments (all levels), governmental agencies, professional services, entertainment, libraries, whatever—enjoy being disrupted. Higher education is different."[5]

There are arguments that "colleges are mostly protected from market forces by large government subsidies and a complex regulatory environment . . . [and] although as many as a thousand colleges are at risk of closing or merging in the decade . . . colleges are like cities [and] they evolve as needs change, although many of them will struggle through this next evolution."[6] As will be demonstrated throughout this publication, however, even higher education, which is a unique type of business, is less prepared for and more vulnerable to the negative impacts of changing dynamics than corporations and for-profit educational providers.

THE HIGHER EDUCATION INDUSTRY AND THE BUSINESS OF COMMUNITY COLLEGES

Even if the presumption that colleges risk closure, go through mergers, and struggle to remain open is correct, is institutional survival the *primary* mission of the community college? The more pertinent question is whether engaging in standard change processes position community colleges to offer the greatest educational and life opportunities to our students? Community colleges need to redesign philosophies, structures, and operational management instead of playing at the edge of innovation, continuing marginally effective and siloed operational practices, and pursuing incremental improvements. To realize their higher calling, community colleges must fundamentally redesign for student learning and success.

Before moving on, it is important to answer the question of whether higher education is an industry. While industries can be defined in different ways, the underlining characteristics of an industry include the following:

- Is there a market that they are designed/charged with serving?
- Are competitors offering differentiated products and services?
- Does it impact the economy?
- Is a societal need or want fulfilled?
- Do governmental regulations impact operations?

Community colleges are charged with providing educational opportunities within defined service areas; have experienced increased competition from traditional and on-line proprietary institutions; support, and in some settings drive, local economic development; help develop an educated citizenry and workforce; and are impacted by local, state, and federal regulations. Industries are also identified as a collective of institutions or agencies that establish an independent, isolated economic sector often defined and classified by the primary product or service delivered. The Standard Industrial Classification (SIC) system and North American Industry Classification System (NAICS) both identify educational services as an important industry, so clearly higher education is an industry.

So what about the notion that higher education institutions are businesses? Well, consider the following questions:

- Are the colleges responsible for the servicing of customers/clients?
- Do the colleges produce goods and/or services?
- Are college operations financed through annual budgeting cycles?
- Are tangible resources utilized to meet internal and external stakeholder needs?
- Is there a unifying mission/purpose that organizes workflow and responsibilities?
- Is the college subject to regulatory oversight/control?

Community colleges exist to educate students, meet workforce needs, and provide community outreach. Additionally, students are educated through academic programs and are provided with services and programming to support retention, transfer, and graduation. These support structures require financial resources that are reflected in the institutional budget and deployed through a resource allocation process. While questions about mission drift exist, community colleges have missions that guide daily operations, institutional management, and strategic planning. Finally, the regulatory oversight from governmental entities and accreditation bodies has intensified over the years. While profit is not a motive for the community college, these institutions clearly meet these requirements and are noncorporate businesses.

As businesses within a defined industry, the concept of a community college business model must incorporate relevant organizational behavior, management, and leadership literature, from within and outside of higher education. This publication utilizes appropriate discipline-specific language common to industries and businesses from all sectors, but contextualizes both the terminology and conceptions to the community college mission. The one traditional business term that is not contextualized within the CCBM, however, is the term customer.

Students engage colleges transactionally at times and the college should not ignore research on customer service, satisfaction, or expectations, however, the relationship between the college community and its students is not one of customer and service provider. Students are consumers of the academic products and services provided for their benefit, however, they are not simply consumers. Students are the reason these institutions exist and the community college must understand that its educational business is to strengthen human development and contribute to societal improvement.[7] Conceptualizing the student as a customer must be viewed as antithetical to any community college business model. The CCBM requires that community colleges operate from a distinctly different philosophical foundation than corporations or for-profit entities designed to generate increasingly large profits and beholden to increasing financial return on investment. The goal of this model, which is rooted in the essential mission of the community college, is to provide students with the greatest personal, professional, and financial return on their investment in their education.

Moving beyond the concepts of the higher education industry and the community college as a business, it is important to note that whether a business purposefully, strategically, and intentionally develops a business model, a framework is in place to drive the daily activities and planning of the organization.[8] Specific to the community college, these institutions "make decisions—actively or passively—about how their operations are funded . . . and how they produce their institutional specific mix of outcomes."[9]

A difference is evident, however, between those colleges that make decisions proactively based on an intentional framework and those that make decisions reactively, guided by existing practices and structures. Unfortunately, but understandably, higher education institutions, including community colleges, have too often operated from accidental business models constructed from financial models, compliance systems and processes, and strategic planning. These de facto models, and the strategic and operational practices that guide them, are rooted in outdated perceptions of financial support, societal expectations for higher education, and industry dynamics. The changes within the higher education industry necessitate a more intentional approach to operations and a more innovative and mission-focused business model. This publication seeks to assist colleges in moving away from a siloed, traditional approach to operational management and toward a model built on student success.

What is a Business Model?

It is important to reiterate that all models developed, implemented, and evaluated by community colleges are and must remain fundamentally different than corporate or for-profit models. And as to the questions about whether many of the business models currently being used within higher education are broken, spoiler alert, this book suggests that they are. The one sector of higher education with institutions that have well-designed business models are the for-profit providers.

As institutions designed to maximize financial profit, it is imperative that they drive operations to increase margins and prioritize efficiency over effectiveness. The biggest distinction, philosophically, between the for-profit and non-profit higher education models is that "non-profit higher education [exists for] the education of our citizens, not only for careers, but for civic and community leadership"[10] This statement is reflective of the broader mission and higher calling of the community college—to effectively serve

Table 1.1. Business Model Differences between Community Colleges and For-Profit Colleges

	For-Profit Higher Education	Community Colleges
Motive	Return on shareholder investment and overall profitability	A student's academic, career, and life success
Mission	Delivery of a standardized, replicable educational product	The education of students, workforce development, and economic impact on the service area and community outreach
Institutional Effectiveness	Strategic and operational planning guided by a profit formula designed to maximize efficiencies for cost reductions and greater investment returns	Increasing organizational effectiveness through an enhanced teaching and learning environment, strategic determination of necessary costs, and increased revenue to fund operations
Purpose	Maximization of financial profits	Student learning and success and maximization of social impact

the students and meet the needs of the community. This is in sharp contrast to the traditional understandings of business models, which exist primarily to ensure profit making rather than "creating value."[11] The most important differences between the for-profit higher education business model and the CCBM are illustrated in the accompanying table (see Table 1.1). Future chapters provide structural guidelines to business model development, some of which is shared with the for-profit providers, but the fundamentally different purposes of community colleges negate adoption of a profit-driven model.[12]

In developing an operationalized definition of the intentionally designed business model, it is beneficial to examine some of the definitions throughout the literature. These include the following:

- A business model "describes the resources, processes, and cost assumptions that an organization makes that lead to the delivery of a unique value proposition to a customer."[13]
- "The way that an organization meets people's needs, operates and organizes itself to produce its products or services, and manages its costs and expenses to remain solvent."[14]
- "A model is an organization's blueprint for creating, delivering, and capturing value and for generating the revenue needed to cover costs, reward stakeholders, and reinvest funds in order to remain competitive."[15]

- "The business model describes the balance of resources and processes needed to produce a viable profit formula for the creation of a particular product that has value to some set of consumers."[16]

Although some of the definitions provided above reflect corporate, for-profit terminology, the concepts are instructive in understanding the framing elements of business models. In thinking about how to utilize these concepts within a community college business model, colleges must remember that a primary function of the model is to enable institutions to "analyze how processes, technology, and resources are used to deliver value."[17]

Value delivery is central to business model development and is a consistent theme across the multiple definitions. In considering a business model for community colleges, these four fundamental objectives must be considered:

- identifying and understanding the primary stakeholder for the purpose of meeting needs and delivering exceptional value;
- providing the range and scale of the goods, services, and products necessary to deliver value;
- understanding what resources are required to provide the services and support associated with delivery of the value; and
- ensuring financial solvency through increasing available revenues and decreasing overall costs.

An Intentionally Designed Business Model: The CCBM

Given the value-based mission of the community college, the CCBM has been developed to align with the concept of the social business model. In studying healthcare, a research study examined a large multinational consortia network of more than thirty non-profits with the mission of improving life outcomes.[18] The focus on human development and improvement necessitates the construction of a modified business model, which does not prioritize profit maximization, but still depends upon the generation of substantial financial resources to support labor intensive operations. This social business model possesses the four foundational elements that frame traditional business models (discussed shortly), but emphasizes value creation for patients over profit maximization. Organizations identified as social businesses are those seeking self-sustainability *for the purpose of maximizing social profit*. While the missions of corporate and social businesses are different, in organizational structure, this new form of business is basically the same as profit-maximizing businesses: it is not a charity, but a business in every sense. The managerial mindset must be the same as in a business: when you are running a social business, you think and work differently than if you were running a charity, even though your objective is different from a profit-maximizing company.[19]

The social business model approach is a natural for healthcare because the mission is value based and focused on supporting a healthier population with a greater quality of life. This model also requires healthcare providers to provide optimal care for traditionally underserved populations.[20] Community colleges are charged with serving traditionally underserved populations with the goal of human development and societal improvement. The principles of the social business model and social profit maximization both inform and reinforce the CCBM as the underlying goals, premises, and phraseology perfectly encapsulate the community college mission. It also aids in reimaging community colleges as social businesses that pursue financial viability for the purpose of maximizing social profit through optimized effectiveness.

Community colleges are complex organizations serving a diverse group of stakeholders with numerous, often competing needs and expectations. Effectively serving these stakeholders has become increasingly difficult with expanding compliance and scrutiny, reduced funding, and changing expectations. The CCBM does not represent a march into corporatization, but rather, a pathway to more effectively supporting students. Toward that end, the following operationalized definition of the community college business model is offered:

The community college business model is an intentionally designed operational framework developed to enhance organizational effectiveness (student success), through the provision of an optimized value proposition represented by an exceptional educational experience.

With a definition in place, it is important to detail the four criteria that constitute the business model. Understanding that "academics [may] struggle at the notion of a business model because [of] the language barrier," this publication offers a crosswalk between standard business model concepts and questions contextualized for higher education.[21] The crosswalk table represents a summary of information provided in the article "The Business Model of Higher Education" and is a key reference point within this book (see Table 1.2).

Table 1.2. Translation of Business Model Concepts to Higher Education Questions

Business Model Concept	Question for Higher Education Institutions
Customer Segments	Who do we serve, and what are they trying to do?
Value Propositions	How do we help those we intend to serve do what they are trying to do?
Customer Channels	How do we deliver our services to those we are trying to serve?
Customer Relationships	What is the nature of the relationship we have with those we serve?
Revenue Streams	How do these prior components translate into revenue for our institution?
Key Activities	What are the key activities that create the services we provide?
Key Resources	What are the key resources we need to create the services we provide?
Key Partners	Who are the key partners that help us create the services we provide to those we serve?
Cost Structure	How do the key partners, resources, and activities translate into our institution's cost model?

Source. Deena (2014)

The business model framework offered in this book is designed to help community colleges effectively respond to the questions proposed in Table 1.2. Answering the questions requires the ability and willingness to achieve the following:

- understanding student needs and expectations;
- maintaining, supporting, and growing the human, technological, and physical resources responsible for delivering organizational effectiveness;
- providing academic programs and educational and student support directed at enhancing student learning, support for the learning environment, and student outcomes; and
- ensuring sufficient fiscal resources, through revenue growth and cost containment, to deliver on the value expectations.

These objectives are encompassed within the four constructs undergirding the CCBM. While each receives full treatment in the form of separate chapters, the general concepts, including the standard terminology, descriptions, and shared understandings are introduced below.

The Student Value Proposition

The effectiveness of a business model is dependent upon the ability to address the needs, solve the problems, and meet or exceed the expectations of the primary stakeholder—the student. Effectively serving the primary stakeholder requires that an organization understand exactly who the stakeholder is as well as their unique set of needs, problems, and expectations. All other aspects of the model are rendered irrelevant otherwise. The term used to reflect the needs and expectations of the customer is *customer value proposition*, but within the CCBM, this term is redefined as *student value proposition* (SVP).

An important point, and one considered in great detail in chapter 6, is that community colleges do not serve a homogenous, monolithic student population. Another point is that students consume goods and services during their educational journey and, accordingly, serving students effectively requires a deep understanding of the college's unique mission, vision, and goals. The effective model considers the breadth of student populations currently being served as well as those not being served due to a lack of planning, resources, or outreach.

Given that the value proposition is central to an effectively designed business model, it is reasonable to assert that the best place to start when developing a business model is to "not think about the business model at all."[22] In other words, community colleges should focus on educating and serving students to develop the model. Engaging internal and external stakeholders, and especially the students, in a conversation about the value proposition is a necessary first step. Unpacking the uniqueness of the student populations; mission of the college; and organizational strengths, weaknesses, opportunities, and challenges, position the college to appropriately tailor its business model. This requirement that the CCBM address the specifics of each community college is the main reason this publication proposes one core guideline for the SVP, but not one operational definition. Community colleges must develop their own distinctive understanding of the value proposition.

Managing Key Resources

In order to provide an exceptional value proposition to students, community colleges must provide and leverage the resources necessary to support the educational experience. To ensure greater clarity and understanding regarding the development and implementation of the business model, the distinction between resources and finances must be addressed. Whereas finances reflect the funding formula and, accordingly, the prospect of raising revenues to support operations, key resources represent the combination of human, physical, technological, and relational resources necessary for delivery of the SVP.

Within the CCBM, key resources reflect the assets, capabilities, systems, and mechanisms of support responsible for delivering value to the student. These resources can be classified into a series of elements that must each be understood to effectively develop and implement the model. The most important resources are

- people (primarily the faculty and staff),
- facilities and institutional infrastructure,
- technology (hardware, software, and systems),
- partnerships, and
- tacit knowledge.

Each resource base is essential for supporting student learning and success since this is how students most directly and tangibly experience the college. Understanding, developing, deploying, and leveraging these resources is essential to the successful implementation of a CCBM.[23]

Delivering the Product

Product does not always reflect the creation of a tangible good. The product can reflect a process, a service, or some other form of important, but intangible deliverable. With this broader interpretation of product, the community college most certainly delivers a product to the students and within the conceptualization of the CCBM, it is not a credential. While the credential represents a successful conclusion to the educational journey for many students, the product is the student's educational experience at the college. From preenrollment until the completion of needed coursework, completion of a credential, and/or transfer to another higher education institution, the college delivers an educational experience to the student. This experience includes the mechanisms, processes, and structures that students encounter inside and outside the classroom.

The mechanisms refer to the tangible, experienced aspects of the educational environment that frame the educational experience. Examples include departments, curriculum, educational and student support offices, cocurricular planning, and buildings and grounds. Processes reflect the activities and operations contained within the mechanisms, but must be separated to fully evaluate their impact on the student value proposition. The processes include teaching, advising, tutoring, and counseling, and represent the daily activities of the faculty and staff committed to student learning and success.

Structures are often not directly experienced by the students, but consist of the activities and operations that support the environment for student learning and success. Examples include assessment of student learning, academic and institutional planning, accreditation and compliance, and the major technology systems. These three categories, when considered as foundations for the student's educational experience, provide significant guidance to community colleges committed to developing an intentionally designed business model.

Profit Formula

This concept, when decoupled from the profit motive, offers a solid mechanism for more effectively generating the fiscal resources required to enhance organizational effectiveness. More specifically, the construct, when contextualized for community colleges, considers the cost of delivering the necessary services and support to students while maintaining the financial stability of the college.[24] Without sufficient resources to cover operating costs, community colleges deliver value falling short of expectations. The commonly utilized tactics of growing enrollment, raising tuition, and depending disproportionately on grant dollars, is now unsustainable within the higher education industry. Recent decades have seen the continued erosion of higher education funding even as the economy has recovered. On the cost side of the equation, the finances required to operate community colleges have continued to grow. From deferred maintenance to the increased need for support staff to soaring costs of technology and benefits, community colleges are required to increase financial resources. Unless addressed, this combination of diminishing fiscal resources and increasing costs has and will continue to result in a greater financial burden for students.

The profit formula, which is detailed in chapter 9, pushes community colleges to move beyond budget-directed operations to organizational-effectiveness directed operations. This transition requires that the community college focus on the profit equation not from the position of balancing budgets and securing resources, but rather from the perspective of establishing designed financial practices, policies, and structures that ensure the financial stability and viability required to fulfill the higher calling of the community college.

Refinement of the CCBM from Outside Community Colleges

The key when examining other industries and business sectors is to remember that at its core, the community college business model must remain true to its designation as a framework for organizational effectiveness within the community college. In examining its literature on business models, two sectors offer useful, relevant guidance for the development. These sectors include not-for-profit healthcare and for-profit colleges. Regarding healthcare, these organizations possess numerous similarities that make an examination useful including the following:

- these institutions are in the business of human development and the not-for-profit sector benefits from social business models;
- the value proposition is based on human, not business outcomes;
- a mission, which is based on the overall improvement of the human condition, not the maximization of profit;
- the presence of administrative, professional, and support subcultures with both common and competing values and complex cultural dynamics that make organizational change and shared vision difficult; and
- a heavy dependence on technology and infrastructure that mandates cost containment, utilization of a values-based, not financially driven, profit formula, and the need for participatory management among the various subcultures.

The healthcare industry has experienced changes over that past decades similar to those experienced by community colleges, but the fact that organizational survival is much less of a given for many healthcare providers provided the urgency needed to reevaluate business models. With the many changes imposed by governmental regulations, insurance providers, patient care providers, and patients themselves, healthcare is undergoing a sector-wide transformation from volume or population-based to value-based business models focused on the patient value proposition.[25]

In responding to external pressures, healthcare providers have explored new business models, including social business models. As a result, many providers increased the prioritization of equality of access, equality of patient outcomes, and quality of the healthcare experience.[26] Achieving these lofty ambitions, however, requires an intentionally designed model that reverses decades-long practices that viewed the volume of patients served as the primary success indicator. The practice of moving from volume to value is relevant with community colleges given the historical focus on enrollment growth as the priority and primary revenue-generating tactic.

In examining for-profit colleges' business models, the value proposition, management of resources, and profit formulas are too distinct from the community college mission to provide relevant insight. The other segment of the standard business model structure, delivering the product, however, offers some guidance. While the outcomes are primarily driven by principles of profitability, relevant practices and outcomes are open to exploration. These include the following:

- *Programs*—For-profit education providers have driven innovation into academic programming through the development of new programs, competency based/modularized education, certifications, the use of industry advisory boards, and the expansion of online education that have increased access to education, enhanced course-taking flexibility, and better-aligned education and workforce preparation.
- *Services*—Whether through 24/7 staffing of tutoring, advising, and career assistance offices or the development of comprehensive and extensive modularized academic and educational support, the customer service approach to proactively meeting student needs has led to a greater focus on just-in-time and real-time support for community college students.
- *Processes*—For-profit providers have historically engaged in evidence-based strategic, operational, and long-term planning as well as the integrated planning and institutional effectiveness processes that align planning, assessment, and resource allocation that community colleges are working toward.

Regardless of motive, these institutions have engaged in the delivery of an educational product that is cost effective and takes advantage of scaling for cost containment. In considering the development and implementation of the CCBM, the principles of cost containment and scalability, based on optimizing student learning and success, prove useful.

CONCLUSION

When higher education institutions have attempted to operate from an intentionally designed business model, they have too often attempted to mimic tactics, misinterpret terminology, and inappropriately integrate the various constructs.[27] More often, however, community colleges engage in traditional operational and management practices that include the use of strategic or financial planning as a substitute for a business model. Various processes, functions, and activities need to be decoupled from each other and from the more traditional financial solvency as a business model approach. When these elements are well understood, which is addressed in the third section of this publication, community colleges are positioned to craft unique, relevant, and impactful models geared at enhancing the student experience.

Community colleges have been forced to adapt operations in recent years, so some of the information presented thus far may seem familiar. Many of the concepts provided are especially familiar to community colleges that have engaged in intentional design work, which includes both the Achieving the Dream and Guided Pathways colleges. The new, transformational idea provided within this book, however, is the establishment of an overarching business model designed to reengineer the educational experience for greater student value and success.

Higher education in general and community colleges specifically do not exist within a vacuum. While this chapter has introduced the concept of a business model for community colleges, such a model cannot be constructed without better understanding the changing and fluid dynamics within the higher education industry. The next chapter delves into the changing higher education industry and what these changes mean for business model development.

NOTES

1. Scott Carlson, *Sustaining the Business Model* (Washington, DC: Chronicle of Higher Education, 2018); Keith Hampson, "Business Model Innovation in Higher Education: Part 1," accessed December 15, 2018. http://acrobatiq.com/business-model-innovation-in-higher-education-part-1/.

2. Richard M. Freeland, "Yes Higher Ed is a Business – but it's also a Calling," *Chronicle of Higher Education*, March 18, 2018. https://www.chronicle.com/article/Yes-Higher-Ed-Is-a-Business/242852.

3. George Keller, *Academic Strategy: The Management Revolution in American Higher Education* (Baltimore: Johns Hopkins University Press, 1983); Derek Bok, *Universities in the Marketplace: The Commercialization of Higher Education* (Princeton, NJ: Princeton University Press, 2004); Boyd R. Keenan, "The Need for Closer Conformity to the Business Model," *The Journal of Higher Education* 32(9) (1961): 513–515.

4. Christian Gilde, *Higher Education: Open for Business* (Lanham, MD: Lexington Books, 2007); Juli A. Jones, "Foundation of Corporatization: Lessons from the Community College," *Society for History Education* 41(2) (2008): 213–214; David Schultz, "From the Editor – Public Affairs Education and the Failed Business Model of Higher Education," *Journal of Public Affairs Education* 19(2) (2013): ii; Jeffrey Selingo, *College (Un)bound: The Future of Higher Education and What It Means for Students* (Las Vegas: Amazon Publishing, 2013).

5. Eric Deena, "The Business Model of Higher Education," *Educause Review* (March/April 2014), 62. https://er.educause.edu/articles/2014/3/the-business-model-of-higher-education.

6. Selingo, *College (Un)bound*, xvi.

7. Muhammad Yunus, Bertrand Moingeon, and Laurence Lehmann-Ortega, "Building Social Business Models: Lessons from the Grameen Experience," *Long Range Planning* 43 (2010): 310–314.

8. Christine Flanagan, "Business Model Innovation: A Blueprint for Higher Education," *Educause Review* (November/December 2012). https://er.educause.edu/articles/2012/11/business-model-innovation—a-blueprint-for-higher-education.

9. Louis Soares, Patricia Steele, and Lindsay Wayt, *Evolving Higher Education Business Models: Leading with Data to Deliver Results* (Washington, DC: American Council on Education, 2016), 6. https://www.acenet.edu/news-room/Documents/Evolving-Higher-Education-Business-Models.pdf.

10. David Breneman, "Is the Business Model of Higher Education Broken?" *National Discussion and Debate Series White Paper* (University of Virginia, April 7, 2010), 1. http://web1.millercenter.org/debates/whitepaper/deb_2010_0427_ed_cost.pdf.

11. Thomas W. Malone, Peter Weill, Richard K. Lau, and Victoria T. D'urso, et al., "Do Some Business Models Perform Better than Others?" MIT Sloan Working Paper 4615-06, MIT School of Management, Cambridge, MA, 2006.

12. Clayton M. Christensen, Michael B. Horn, Louis Soares, and Louis Caldera, "Disrupting College: How Disruptive Innovation can Deliver Quality and Affordability to Postsecondary Education." Report, Center for American Progress, Washington, DC, 2011. https://www.americanprogress.org/issues/economy/reports/2011/02/08/9034/disrupting-college/.

13. Alok D. Sharan, Gregory D. Schroeder, Michael E. West, and Alexander R. Vaccaro, "Understanding Business Models in Health Care," *Clinical Spine Surgery* 29(4) (2016): 159.

14. Beth Rubin, "University Business Models and Online Practices: A Third Way," *Online Journal of Distance Learning Administration* 25(1) (2013).

15. Flanagan, "Business Model Innovation," 14.

16. Lloyd Armstrong, "A Business Model View of Changing Times in Higher Education," 2014. https://www.changinghighereducation.com/2014/12/new_business_model_view_of_change_in_higher_education.html.

17. Soares, Steele, and Wayt, *Evolving Higher Education Business Models*, i.

18. Yunus, Moingeon, and Lehmann-Ortega, "Building Social Business Models," 310.

19. Yunus, Moingeon, and Lehmann-Ortega, "Building Social Business Models," 310.

20. Frederica Angeli and Anand Kumar Jaiswal, "Business Model Innovation for Inclusive Health Care Delivery at the Bottom of the Pyramid," *Organization and Environment* 29(4) (2016).

21. Deena, "The Business Model of Higher Education," 62.

22. Mark W. Johnson, Clayton M. Christensen, and Henning Kagermann, "Reinventing your Business Model," *Harvard Business Review* (December 2008), 52.

23. Christopher Shults, "Making the Case for a Positive Approach to Improving Organizational Performance in Higher Education Institutions," *Community College Review* 36(2) (2008); Richard Alfred, Christopher Shults, Ozan Jacquette, and Shirley Strickland, *Community Colleges on the Horizon: Challenge, Choice, or Abundance* (Lanham, MD: Rowman and Littlefield, 2009).

24. Soares, Steele, and Wayt, *Evolving Higher Education Business Models.*

25. Laura S. Kaiser and Thomas H. Lee, "Turning Value-Based Health Care into a Real Business Model," *Harvard Business Review,* October 8, 2015. https://hbr.org/2015/10/ turning-value-based-health-care-into-a-real-business-model; Sharan et al., "Understanding Business Models," 159.

26. Angeli and Jaiswal, "Business Model Innovation."

27. Armstrong, "A Business Model View."

Chapter Two

The Increasingly Dynamic Higher Education Industry

For the majority of higher education's history in the United States, colleges and universities have operated as though immune from external influence on college missions, operations, and philosophies. In addition to being generally respected and well regarded through society, the judicial system has historically shown deference to the academic mission; the federal government has provided only cursory oversight; and states provided consistent, although inequitable, financial support.

Based on these positive factors as well as significant distrust of corporate principles and business practices, higher education lacked the urgency or impetus to create intentionally designed business models. Even community colleges, where workforce development, adult basic education, and continuing education have remained central pillars of the mission, have largely resisted both comprehensive and designed institutional change efforts.[1] Institutional change efforts are typically initiated in reaction to changing governmental structures, external pressures, and the need to maintain financial solvency and viability.[2] This chapter examines the shifting dynamics within the higher education industry that are forcing colleges to adopt more proactive approaches to operational management.

Two decades ago, prompted by a shift in the prioritization of tax dollars, the environment in which community colleges operate began to change. This change was prompted by large scale economic shifts at the national and state level and resulted, even before the Great Recession, in waning financial support. In order to respond to the significant impact on operations, community colleges relied upon traditional change and organizational management tactics such as strategic planning, environmental scanning, and economic impact studies. Change management is difficult even in stable economic conditions, but with financial crises looming for many colleges, institutions struggled with or neglected to introduce innovative business practices.

Greater turbulence within the industry, however, necessitates the development of models built to withstand and respond to unprecedented change and challenge. Additionally, as businesses move through different phases of an industry's lifecycle, environmental changes produce differential impacts and create unique opportunities and challenges that older models are unequipped to address and leverage.[3] Although numerous definitions and classifications exist regarding industry lifecycles, the five standard phases are as follows:

1. Start-up/Introduction—Creation of a new industry based on businesses either providing a new product or service or a reconfigured combination of existing products or services.
2. Growth—As the demand for more businesses providing products or services grows, the number of providers increases, the scope and scale of the mission increases, and the need for focusing on operations, strategy, effectiveness, and efficiency grows.
3. Shakeout—The industry begins to consolidate as businesses evaluate the profitability of continuation with some choosing to expand with new operations or through mergers and acquisitions while others decide to either consolidate or cease operations.
4. Maturity—During maturity, the majority of the businesses are well established with a focus on increasing profitability, enhancing the customer value proposition, and enhancing the strategic, operational, and financial plans, processes, and structures.
5. Decline—The final stage of the lifecycle represents, for several businesses, an intensified shakeout stage where increasing competition, decreasing demand, or external factors create an inhospitable environment for most businesses.

When these phases are modified and reframed for higher education, they offer context for understanding the impact of changing environmental pressures. One adjustment is that since education is a social good, a basic need, and a resource needed to maintain and grow the economy, the concept of decline as a stand-alone phase is not appropriate. Additionally, the concepts of introduction and start-up are most useful when examining the different higher education sectors that have emerged over time. Guided by these features the following is offered as the community college sector lifecycle:

- Founding—Community colleges were established with the founding of Joliet Junior College (JJC) in 1901. The mission was to provide a postgraduate high school program that "academically paralleled the first two years of a four year college or university" and was focused on serving students who

wanted or needed to remain close to home.[4] The college was charged with serving a nontraditional population of students, and the college eventually moved to offer a general education curriculum for the purpose of transfer.
- Growth—The massification movement was fueled by the Truman Commission in 1947, which led to the GI Bill and a focus on providing traditional education and workforce training for returning veterans. As the number of colleges grew—nearly one a week nationally during the 1950s and 1960—so did the scope of these institutions. Dubbed "community colleges," the goal was to provide the academic, workforce, and community outreach programs and services tailored to meet the needs of the service area.
- Maturity—By the mid-1970s and up through the early 2000s, growth slowed and many community colleges started to focus on emerging academic programs and approaches (i.e., bachelor's degrees, applied associate degrees, and synchronous online courses) and business practices (i.e., strategic planning, environmental scanning, and economic impact). Despite reaching maturity, enrollment growth remained the predominant strategy.
- Expansion—Starting in the early 2000s and ending in the mid-2010s, the sector saw a significant increase in the number and types of nontraditional competitors. In addition to for-profit education providers, corporate colleges and other hybrid institutions challenged the traditional business model for community colleges.[5] Emerging competitors approached higher education through a corporate lens and focused on customer satisfaction, adaptability, and profit. These competitors brought significant disruption to the industry and forced community colleges to enhance and expand the use of sound business practices, speed the pace of change, and gain a better understanding of their students. This era in the community college sector lifecycle is when the groundwork was laid for intentional redesign (formalized by the Achieving the Dream and Completion Agenda movements).
- Reinvention—This current stage is typified by significant external impacts to the sector. The student success movement, decreasing financial resources, political and public pressure, and demographic shifts, has led to closures, consolidations, and mergers as institutions seek to maintain financial viability. Community colleges must engage in full-scale redesign to increase organizational effectiveness, ensure financial stability, and meet evolving internal and external demands. The increasing urgency for transformation and redesign has created the need for systematic development of intentionally designed business models.

While community colleges' current place within the sector's lifecycle has similarities with the shakeout and decline stages identified previously for corporate or for-profit businesses, the differences are stark. The shakeout stage is based primarily on business decisions surrounding profitability, whereas shakeout only occurs in the not-for-profit sector during times of financial uncertainty. Tremendous upheaval is currently occurring as indicated by the following:[6]

- The Connecticut State Colleges & Universities Board of Regents is attempting to merge all twelve community colleges in the state. While the initial proposal was rejected by the regional accreditor, state legislators are working to stop the consolidation, and numerous protests have occurred, the board still seeks full consolidation by 2023.
- The state of Georgia has been merging two- and four-year colleges for a number of years, and they continue to pursue this practice.
- The state of Louisiana has announced plans to merge its eight technical and community college campuses.
- The state of Wisconsin has approved a plan to merge some of the community colleges into branch campuses of state four-year universities.

In addition to these statewide efforts, numerous community colleges have sought consolidations and mergers. The reason behind all of these mergers is reduced funding.

Even as concerns have emerged about a higher education bubble (based on the decline of for-profit education) and the higher education industry's long-term financial forecast was downgraded, the industry is intractable given its role in supporting overall economic well-being.[7] Decline, however, is a reality at the individual institutional level and community colleges would be wise to understand their place within the reinvention phase of the sector's lifecycle. The ability to adapt successfully to meet changing needs and respond to challenging conditions is impacted by the college's willingness to accept the reality of the current environment, develop and implement new, effective structures and processes, and increase awareness of the student value proposition (SVP).[8]

Traditional operational management approaches and accidental business models simply are not designed to meet the task of comprehensive evaluation and redesign. Community colleges are now confronted with the need to intentionally design for student success because "nowhere is the imperative for business model innovation more prevalent or more relevant than in higher education, which is under intense scrutiny and facing rising costs and potential disruption from all angles."[9]

Another industry that has undergone intense scrutiny in recent decades and can provide lessons for community colleges in proactively adapting to changing dynamics is healthcare. The healthcare industry has experienced significant disruption from new competitors, regulation, and changing patient expectations. The focus on value-based versus volume-based business models in addition to the invasive and pervasive impact of technology have been among the most important drivers of change.

Competition Impacts within Healthcare

When sudden changes in the industry environment lead to new and differentiated entrants, providers are often left trying to figure out where competitive advantage lies.[10] In healthcare, as in the community college sector, the initial impulse was to compete on price rather than outcomes. Changes in the market, particularly after the Affordable Care Act (ACA), established quality of patient outcomes as the primary success metric and fundamentally altered traditional understandings of barriers to entry.[11]

In looking at the entrance of urgent care clinics and expansion of ambulatory centers (the primary brick and mortar competition for hospitals), it was technology advances and market trends that disrupted the industry by reducing barriers and introducing space for competition.[12] Currently, partnerships are expanding between physician practices and urgent care and ambulatory facilities, which is optimizing care based on a patient-centric value proposition.

Around the same time that the for-profit colleges, through online education, began to impact the higher education industry, telemedicine was introduced into healthcare. The immediate access to personal medical advice instead of requiring referrals, wait times, and face-to-face interactions was a transformative and disruptive innovation.[13] In 2015, more than fifteen million Americans engaged in telemedicine and utilized services that reported on vital signs, monitored chronic conditions, and offered both diagnoses and prescriptions.[14] This entrant into the healthcare industry has provided significant disruption to traditional providers, but results from numerous governmental agencies indicate significant benefits to patients, including reduced healthcare costs, increased convenience and access to specialists, improved patient outcomes, and greater physician engagement.[15] While telemedicine entered the industry as a competitor, these services are now incorporated into many primary care practices and allow physicians to treat more patients and more easily consult with other physicians.

One of the changes occurring across the county as a result of changes to the law is the creation of new and innovative partnerships between insurance providers and healthcare systems. The partnerships appear to be reducing readmissions, and a statewide study indicates that new approaches to care are likely the reason for better health outcomes.[16]

Regulation Impacts within Healthcare

Medicare and Medicaid reimbursement rules were significantly impacted by the ACA with a focus on a value-based approach to care versus the more traditional volume or population-based approach. The regulations shifted the focus to quality of patient outcomes, and hospitals and healthcare centers now find themselves financially liable when patients return to the hospital within thirty days for the same medical issues.[17]

Given that hospitals and healthcare centers must remain financially viable, the ability to control costs without sacrificing care is essential. Healthcare providers must evaluate the effectiveness of services provided across all units and divisions to understand where greater integration can improve care, increase efficiency, and reduce costs. In a recent study, researchers found that hospitals are experimenting with vertical integration into subacute care services to reduce the financial and transactional costs associated with patient movement through the system as well as readmissions.[18] These changes, when aligning awareness of patient needs, operational management, strategic direction and prioritization, and environment, provide long-term benefits to the patients and the healthcare facilities.

Changing Expectations within Healthcare

Studies from around the world document that the demand for expensive emergency medicine increases yearly both for emergency rooms and urgent care clinics.[19] The authors note that an aging population and an increase in chronic conditions are fueling the increase, but that behavioral changes regarding healthcare expectations, greater information, convenience, and individual expectations continue to expand healthcare usage. As patient price burdens increase however, they pursue more affordable options like urgent care clinics and ambulatory facilities that are convenient, offer greater engagement, and deliver positive health outcomes.[20]

The expansion of technology into the healthcare industry, which has increased access to medical information and triage services, has created a more engaged patient. This increasing awareness has contributed to the expansion of individualized (personalized) medicine, which also includes a more acute focus on preventative medicine.[21] Basically, access to information and services has fundamentally altered patient needs and expectations. The patient value proposition has been adjusted due to disruptions in the industry. Hospitals and health systems must not only react swiftly, but act proactively. They are being required to innovate and adapt their business models to ensure organizational viability with a primary focus on patient health and well-being.

Community colleges can gain some valuable insight into dealing with industry disruptions by examining the adaptation and evolution of healthcare business models. As with the community college sector, healthcare providers were forced to reevaluate operations, processes, and strategies as a result of invasive competition. The expanding impact of technology has provided the opportunity and expectation to better serve demanding and educated patients.

Community colleges have greater access to technological tools and student expectations have been elevated as a result. The concept of personalized medicine, just like personalized education, represents a fundamental shift to historical institutional practices. Healthcare providers have modified their organizational and operational approaches and developed more robust business models to effectively respond to changing conditions. Community colleges are now being required to innovate and adapt their business models to ensure organizational viability with a primary focus on student learning and success.

Disruption to the Community College Sector

In the past, institutional survival was hyperbolic, but the threat of closure through mergers is now a reality. Outside of state systems, many community colleges have consolidated operations with other two-year or even four-year institutions. The inability to provide a significant value proposition to students, contain costs, and secure resources is creating unprecedented challenges within the higher education industry. The turbulence has been created externally, but the community college must work to proactively align resources and operations, engage in strategic decision making and financing, and provide a unique and powerful educational experience for students.[22] Engaging in this proactive process necessitates understanding and embracing the concept of disruption.

Changes to the higher education industry can be described appropriately as disruptive because they have infiltrated its very foundations.[23] These disruptive forces have incented the revision of historical assumptions about higher education as community colleges endeavor to make sense of the changing environments. Making sense of disruption starts with focusing on the three forms of innovation available to address its impacts, these include sustaining innovations, hybrid innovations, and disruptive innovations. Sustaining innovations are powerful because they

> push organizations forward along their current trajectory. Sustaining innovations tend to be well accepted by organizations with healthy business models. They generally involve changes to an organization's deployment of resources or, occasionally, to the development of new processes that complement or

enhance existing ones. Disruptive innovations, on the other hand, spark improvement along an entirely new dimension. Disruptive innovations require a shift in the organization's priorities and thus are at great risk of being rejected by a strong business model.[24]

Sustaining innovations preserve and enhance an existing business model, however, these innovations do not always reflect minor, insignificant improvements. Colleges and universities engage in sustaining innovation to enhance operations or effectiveness when they reduce the ratios for advisors, increase funding for tuition waivers, or expand the availability of tutoring. Academically, sustaining innovation is the norm as faculty regularly change syllabi, review and adopt new pedagogical models, and adjust courses based on the use of assessment data.

Sustaining innovations can also generate marked improvements in the student experience. For example, increasing the percentage of full-time faculty, reducing student–faculty ratios, and implementing mentoring and academic coaching initiatives to improve retention among typically underserved college students, all represent sustaining innovations. Sustaining innovations in higher education can and often do improve or expand offerings for students, and their beneficial impacts should not be understated. The question is, however, will sustaining innovations work as the primary or sole strategy for positioning community colleges to thrive in an increasingly volatile industry?

Alternatively, embracing disruption as a force for innovation is an admission that current approaches, operations, and strategies are ineffective and require modification. Regardless of the disagreements about the fate of higher education, there is no doubt that the scale and scope of change thrust upon the industry has rendered traditional approaches to operational management ineffective for optimizing the SVP. Inarguably, community colleges have been permanently and irreversibly impacted by the innovations brought into higher education by industry disruptions of technology and competition.

By engaging in the disruptive process of implementing the CCBM, the community college positions itself to more adeptly focus on teaching and learning, support the learning environment, and utilize operational philosophies and management necessary to enhance student success. Disruption, however, requires significant changes to current approaches. Some examples of embracing disruptive innovation for the purpose of increasing organizational effectiveness include the following:

- redefining who the community college serves by reaching out to current nonstudents—both those attending other institutions and the educationally unserved;

- utilizing technological solutions and predictive analytics to better understand student needs and obstacles to success and to provide proactive academic and student support;
- fundamentally altering the organizational architecture through administrative reorganization, academic program restructuring, and designed integration of complementary educational and student support functions;
- pursuing partnerships with similarly missioned entities from organizations outside the higher education industry
- incorporating nontraditional academic experiences and course models into mainstream educational opportunities for students; and/or
- eliminating operations that do not directly contribute to enhancing the value proposition.

What is clear is that external forces have ushered disruption into the higher education industry.[25] The remainder of the publication addresses engagement in fundamentally disruptive innovation—designing and implementing a business model centered on organizational effectiveness for the purpose of delivering an enhanced value proposition to students.

Hybrid innovations represent a bridge between the more familiar sustaining innovations and the disruptive innovations that challenge sensemaking and cultural understandings. They enable organizations to build the capabilities required for disruptive strategies in the future while adjusting, rather than redesigning, the current business model. Hybrid innovations allow for a balance between the risk and attraction of disruption without fully abandoning existing business models. When appropriately deployed, this approach to innovation mediates disruptive risks in the short term; enhances capabilities, operations, and the value proposition on an exponential curve (slow, but progressively increasing in speed); and builds institutional tolerance for disruption. These innovations can provide a powerful signal to students, alumni, and trustees that the institution is paying attention to innovation and investing in the future. However, they cannot tackle affordability challenges at scale. Hybrid innovations are "ultimately sustaining—they do not fundamentally upend the behemoth cost structure undergirding traditional higher education institutions."[26] As is the case with both sustaining and disruptive innovations, certain situations warrant the use of hybrid innovations, and this is discussed in the chapters on culture and business model implementation.

Demography as a Disruptive Force

Demography is cyclical in nature with the more critical aspects including birth rates, the number of recent high school graduates, and the socioeconomic status, racial and ethnic makeup, and the greying of populations. Historically, the waxing and waning of the traditional-aged college student has been the primary driver for higher education demand, although community colleges, with an explicit workforce mission, also experience inverse relationships between enrollment and economic strength. Community colleges have generally been more effective than other non-profit higher education sectors in reacting to changing conditions; however, the coming changes demand greater proactivity and forethought.

While demography is best understood regionally and at the local level, significant changes are impacting the industry as a whole. The first is that "the United States is running out of teenagers."[27] Although college enrollment has boomed for decades, one of the factors which made the higher education industry more attractive for new entrants has been the enrollment of millennials. Given that the oldest within this generation are now in their late thirties however, the number of traditional-aged students in the pipeline is shrinking. The immediate impact of the shrinking pipeline will be minimal, however, since higher education enrollment is projected to increase 3 percent, to 20.5 million; enrollment of students who are fourteen to twenty-four is projected to increase 5 percent; and enrollment of students who are twenty-five to thirty-four is projected to decrease by 1 percent between 2016 and 2027. The increase in enrollment is outpaced by projected associate degree attainment rates as degrees are projected to increase 5 percent between 2015–2016 and 2027–2028, with females experiencing a 6 percent increase while males are expected to increase by 5 percent.[28]

Although the overall high school graduation rates and college-going rates are currently increasing, birth rates are declining and many colleges and universities have already experienced significant enrollment declines. While the overall increase in high school graduates is projected at 3 percent, up to 3.6 million for 2026–2027, significant decreases are anticipated afterward.[29] It is important to note that these apparent discrepancies are due to the unevenness of the regional shifts predicted between 2012–2013 and 2027–2028. Overall high school graduation rates broken out by region indicate a[30]

- 7 percent decrease for the Northeast,
- 2 percent decrease for the Midwest,
- 17 percent increase for the South, and
- 4 percent increase for the West.

In considering the impact of demography for community colleges, an important consideration is the breakdown of high school graduates by race/ethnicity. Community colleges are among the most racially diverse institutions within higher education, so disaggregating these trends is essential for future planning. Although the overall number of graduates is expected to increase between 2012–2013 and 2027–2028, tremendous differences are present by race and ethnicity:[31]

- White high school graduates are projected to *decrease* by 14 percent to 1,541,000,
- Black high school graduates are projected to *decrease* by 1 percent to 458,000,
- Hispanic high school graduates are projected to *increase* by 52 percent to 975,000, and
- Asian/Pacific Islander high school graduates are projected to *increase by* 25 percent to 223,000.

Providing perhaps the most extensive dive into the impacts of demography on higher education demand, a recent article offers a robust analysis into the substantial and unequal impacts of demography by sector.[32] Through an examination of longitudinal data, community colleges are predicted to be more significantly and negatively impacted by changing demographics than four-year colleges. The rationale is that the student populations most likely to attend community colleges are those with the lowest college-going rates.

The analytics used to calculate these projections reflect the differential likelihood of attending college based on sex, race/ethnicity, parental education, geography, family income, family composition, and nativity. Previous analyses of longitudinal higher education datasets have long since identified that community college students fit many of the demographic "risk factors" associated with lower college-going rates, increased stop-out, and attrition.[33] In considering how to proactively address the impending demographic shifts, community colleges must consider the needs of the students coming through the door, now and into the future, in order to provide an enhanced value proposition.

Funding Shifts as Disruptive Force

Given the dependency on state finances, the extreme reduction in state funding that occurred during and after the Great Recession has devastated college budgets. Consider that nearly all states reduced higher education funding during and in the aftermath of the 2008 economic recession and that as of 2014–2015, forty-seven of the fifty states were spending less per student than in 2008.[34] In fact, state spending on higher education was 20 percent less per student when compared to 2008 levels. When taking inflation into account, students, on average, are paying 29 percent more for tuition, and in some states, students are paying as much as 65 percent more.

The scale and scope of higher education budget cuts represent a significant public disinvestment. The higher education industry of today is significantly different than even a decade ago, and external impacts are sharper and cut deeper than at any point in the history of community colleges. All signs, unfortunately, point to these reduced levels of state support as the new baseline, not a downward adjustment to be reversed. At this point in history,

> government tax revenues now exceed pre-recession levels and spending in almost every budget category has grown since 2008 [but] higher education is not following the same pattern. America's public colleges and universities enjoy the dubious distinction of being the only major budget category in which states are cutting back.[35]

A major reason for this divestment is that while "state revenues have improved significantly since the depths of the recession . . . many states are now experiencing new budget pressures [with] two-thirds of the states [facing or addressing] revenue shortfalls."[36] Impacted by these shortfalls, state funding has been lower and when adjusted for inflation include

- higher education spending by states fell by $1,448 per student (16 percent),
- state funding per student increased in only five states,
- Arizona reduced state funding per student by more than 50 percent, and
- eighteen states reduced funding by 20 percent per student and eight reduced funding by more than 30 percent.

The most significant competition for state revenues comes from healthcare, law enforcement and corrections, and human services, all of which have resource requests that have increased by more than 10 percent. Most notably, higher education finds itself competing with federal programs and pension systems for limited public dollars. Medicaid, for example, constitutes a significant portion of state budgets, and while federal dollars are available, state cuts to the program result in matching cuts from the federal government. Few states are in the position to reduce federal support for their healthcare systems. Second, many states have large pension responsibilities with constitutional protections limiting the reduction of funding. Finally, powerful interest groups are fighting to preserve funding within their sectors, which typically results in a zero-sum gain. Higher education often loses out on funding because "it's the largest line item that states can cut without facing significant legal and political barriers."[37]

Additionally, community colleges continue to receive less financial support because many states believe the colleges can increase quality and efficiency without substantial investment. States want the community colleges to use "their low-cost business model [consisting of] adjunct faculty, no faculty research overhead and affordability to absorb much of the growth in higher education in the state."[38] This position is problematic as it reinforces the infinite enrollment growth strategy, which has been proven to negatively impact student success. This is a financial argument, not one focused on the mission of the community college and these de facto "business models are cracking under enormous pressure as state appropriations decline and net tuition growth wanes. Business as usual simply can't continue."[39]

The financial picture for community colleges is, at best, murky and complicated.[40] What needs to be remembered, however, is that the mission of the community college is not to remain open and solvent, but rather to meet the needs and expectations of those within its service area. The increase in tuition necessitated by decreasing state funding threatens this mission as an affordability crisis has emerged.

College Affordability as a Disruptive Force

Tuition within public colleges has increased by more than 60 percent over the past decades and, subsequently, student debt has increased to over one trillion dollars.[41] One, students from families with fewer financial resources are saddled with increasingly higher debt loads, and two, many potential students no longer view college as accessible for them.[42] Commitment to access is a historical value imbued within the mission and must remain so as institutions consider new business models and value propositions. Rather than simply asking if students are being priced out, the community college must ask *which students* are being priced out. Is the college able to confidently assert that students who would benefit most from access to a high-quality education are not being priced out? When tuition is adjusted upward to generate sufficient revenue, who are the students most likely to be negatively impacted?

Over the past three decades, the price of attendance at public colleges has increased by 400 percent while overall wage growth has remained flat.[43] The double blow of low wages and increasing tuition impacts most American families, but especially those most likely to attend and benefit from a community college education. "As the affordability crisis has worsened, deep disparities continue to persist in higher education along race and class lines, which is leaving critical [education and training] opportunities out of reach for a growing population."[44] Since the one constant revenue source is tuition, community colleges must ask at what point does an education, especially for the traditionally underserved student, become unattainable?

Accountability as a Disruptive Force

Increasingly onerous regulations and compliance standards have often stifled innovation and creativity. The standard response to these changes has been to act conservatively and manage innovation at the margins. Competing priorities from critical stakeholders requires greater collaboration inside and outside of the college, direct evidence of student learning and success, and documentation of the return on investment (ROI). Meeting these challenging and more pervasive requirements necessitates an intentionally designed, college-specific business model.

To fully understand the intensifying accountability requirements, colleges must consider the three primary regulatory bodies that impact higher education—the federal government, state governments, and regional accrediting bodies. Whereas higher education has traditionally been spared from intensified accountability, changing economic conditions along with inequitable outcomes and increased debt levels from for-profit colleges intensified attention. With more than one hundred fifty billion dollars going to colleges and universities in the form of federal aid, the focus is now on the ROI of public dollars. Tax dollars are finite and funding requirements have increased across all public sectors.

For context, student loan debt nationally now exceeds that of credit card and auto loan debt. While student loan debt reflects an investment in people and future economic health, increasing levels has introduced greater scrutiny.[45] Default rates have decreased in recent years, but perceptions regarding the value of higher education and public investment were altered by the higher debt levels generated within for-profit colleges throughout the late twentieth and early twenty-first century.[46] Numerous publications provide insight into the negative impact of the disproportionately poor student and employment outcomes within for-profit education.[47] Enrollment in for-profit colleges has diminished in recent years and while no causal assumption is being made, student loan default rates have declined substantially during this time. The intensifying scrutiny from the federal government regarding student loan policies, student loan debt, and default rates, however, is not likely to dissipate given that debt and college affordability have become public flashpoints.

The most notable accountability change impacting community colleges is the push for performance-based funding, which has been adopted by more than thirty states. As of today, these efforts have not produced the expected outcomes of demonstrable gains in student performance, reduced cost per graduate, or greater employment and wage gains.[48] In fact the lack of additional supports has actually created greater difficulties for colleges to meet their mission. Despite these results, states continue to demand greater accountability.

The final accountability agents disrupting higher education are the regional accreditors. The federal government has significant impact over the role of accreditation, both through the mandates and regulations embedded within the Higher Education Act (HEA). In the last three years, two separate bills have come from the Senate seeking to transform higher education accreditation within the United States, and congressional committees have increased the number of hearings with accreditation commission presidents.[49]

As a result of the increased scrutiny, community colleges across all six regions are responding to revised and more robust accreditation criteria. Specifically, regional accrediting bodies have focused more on documentation of compliance with federal standards; assessment and evaluation of student learning; and efforts to improve retention, transfer, and graduation. The intensifying expectations regarding the documentation of student learning and support for the student learning environment, however, do not align with the overall reduction in state financial support.[50] To summarize the focus of the various agents, expected results, and impact on community colleges, a compliance table has been provided (see Table 2.1).

Table 2.1. Impact of Changing Compliance Expectations on Community Colleges

	Accountability Focus	Expected Results	Impact on Community Colleges
Federal Government	Federal financial aid	Decreased default rates Increasing wages for graduates More adults with credentials	Pressure to review academic programs Increasing burdens on student support staff Increasing pressure to recruit students
State Government	Effective use of state resources	Improving graduation rates Increasing wages for graduates Increasing enrollments	Greater focus on academic and educational support Greater pressure to partner with business and industry Additional hiring of faculty, staff, and administrators
Regional Accreditors	Federal regulations student outcomes	Compliance with changing standards Improved assessment and evaluation Evidence of student learning and success	Increasing resources for accreditation events Increasing resources for assessment Additional hiring of faculty, staff, and administrators

Technology as a Disruptive Force

The final category of disruptive forces necessitating the utilization of the CCBM is technology. While competition has existed in the form of corporate universities, vocational high schools, middle colleges, other community colleges, and four-year colleges, open competition for students historically has been relatively limited.[51] The disruptive change that increased competition was the rise of the for-profit provider as a significant player in the higher education industry. In 2000, 37 percent of students attending Title IV (financial aid eligible) degree-granting institutions were in community colleges, but that percentage dropped to 33 percent by 2012. Over this same time frame, for-profit enrollments increased from 3 percent to 9 percent, and based on numerous studies, these institutions were competing for many of the same students.[52] Neither enrollments nor degree completions declined for community colleges when a new for-profit institution opened within the same market but rather, overall higher education enrollments within the service area increased.

In fact, the number of community college certificates awarded increased with the new entrant. The presence of the for-profit colleges forced community colleges to enhance their workforce development missions. Although enrollments in for-profit colleges dropped precipitously between 2010 and 2015 (around 40 percent) the boom period continues to impact the community college sector even today through the incorporation of stronger marketing, innovative academic programing, online education, and consumer-inspired support services.[53]

In considering the disruptive influence of technology on community colleges, it is clear that this force has provided the greatest threat to the accidental business model.[54] Internet-based platforms, online education, broadband access expansion, and the rise of mobile computing and communication have fundamentally altered student expectations. Anticipated advancements and modifications to academic programming, support services, and facilities has forced community colleges to evaluate and redesign approaches to teaching and learning, student support, and the environment for student success. Exploring and better understanding the disruptive effects of technology better positions the institution to develop an effective CCBM that enables the delivery of an enhanced student value proposition.

Several examples of how colleges and universities have utilized technology to fundamentally enhance their business models include the following:[55]

- Southern New Hampshire University was a traditional college until 1995 when it started an online program. The college now maintains an online enrollment of around eighty thousand students. In keeping with its mission, the institution still provides an on-campus program to around five thousand students. Recently the college has developed its Advantage Program, which offers an AA degree and is a direct competitor with community colleges.

- Arizona State University has partnered with Starbucks and developed the Starbucks College Achievement Plan. This program ensures that any employee of Starbucks, regardless of location, is provided with an opportunity to earn a college degree.
- Purdue purchased Kaplan University, which reflects co-option as a strategy for addressing competition. The merger of a public research university and a for-profit has been designated as a non-profit entity called Purdue Global. The new venture is branded as an institution with academic tradition and the flexibility demanded by working adults.

These examples illustrate how higher education institutions are transforming their business models to take advantage of technology and, in some cases, co-opting competition through mergers and acquisitions. These examples are not without controversy and this publication is not promoting any of these models as exemplars. Rather, they are being presented because they utilized technological disruption to modify their business models. In later chapters, examples from within the community college sector with more context and descriptions of alignment with the mission are provided. For the purpose of this chapter, however, it is imperative to document methods and techniques used within the higher education industry to proactively address the disruptive impacts of technology and competition.

Thus far, this book has sought to identify what a business model is and establish a rationale for why a CCBM is necessary. Chapter 3 marks a transition point; a transition from making the case for this modified approach to discussing the mechanics for designing and implementing the model. This portion of the book delves into the operational management aspects of the CCBM to differentiate intentional design versus accidental framing. In short, it progresses the conversation from understanding and conceptualization to engagement and implementation.

NOTES

1. George B. Vaughan, *The Community College Story* (Washington, DC: Community College Press, 2006).

2. Mark W. Johnson, Clayton M. Christensen, and Henning Kagermann, "Reinventing Your Business Model," *Harvard Business Review* (December 2008), 51–52.

3. Robert Sheets, Stephen Crawford, and Luis Soares, *Rethinking Higher Education Business Models: Steps Toward a Disruptive Innovation Approach to Understanding and Improving Higher Education Outcomes* (Washington, DC: Center for American Progress, 2012), 1–2. https://www.americanprogress.org/issues/education-postsecondary/reports/2012/03/28/11250/rethinking-higher-education-business-models/; Michael Cusumano, Steve Kahl, and Fernando F. Suarez, "Produce, Process, and Service:

A New Industry Lifecycle Model." Center for eBusiness@MIT, Paper 228, Massachusetts Institute of Technology, Cambridge, June 2006, 1–2. http://digital.mit.edu/research/papers/2006.06_Cusumano_Kahl_Suarez_Product%20Process%20and%20Service_228.pdf.

4. Joliet Junior College, "History." Accessed July 23, 2019. https://www.jjc.edu/about-jjc/history.

5. Richard Alfred and Associates, *Managing the Big Picture in Colleges and Universities: From Tactics to Strategy* (Westport, CT: American Council on Education/Praeger, 2006).

6. James Patterson. "Connecticut Community Colleges to Merge in Two Stages," *EducationDive* (June 20, 2018). https://www.educationdive.com/news/connecticut-community-colleges-to-merge-in-two-stages/526111/.

7. Derek Thompson, "This is the Way the College 'Bubble' Ends: Not with a Pop, but a Hiss," *The Atlantic* (July 26, 2017). https://www.theatlantic.com/business/archive/2017/07/college-bubble-ends/534915/; Paul Fain, "Moody's Downgrades Higher Education Outlook," *Inside Higher Ed* (December 6, 2017). https://www.insidehighered.com/quicktakes/2017/12/06/moodys-downgrades-higher-educations-outlook.

8. Andrija Sabol, Matej Sander, and Durdica Fuckan, "The Concept of Industry Life Cycle and Development of Business Strategies." Paper presented at the Management, Knowledge, and Learning International Conference, Zadar, Croatia, June 2013, 641–642.

9. Christine Flanagan, "Business Model Innovation: A Blueprint for Higher Education," *Educause Review* (November/December 2012), 12. https://er.educause.edu/articles/2012/11/business-model-innovation—a-blueprint-for-higher-education.

10. Danny Miller, "Configurations Revisited," *Strategic Management Journal* 17(7) (1996): 510.

11. Michael E. Porter, "How Competitive Forces Shape Strategy," *Harvard Business Review* (October 1979). https://hbr.org/1979/03/how-competitive-forces-shape-strategy.

12. Leemore S. Dafny and Thomas H. Lee, "Health Care Needs Real Competition," *Harvard Business Review* (December 2016). https://hbr.org/2016/12/health-care-needs-real-competition.

13. Rainer Kretschmer and Michael Nerlich, "Assessing the Impact of Telemedicine on Health Care Management," *The Impact of Telemedicine on Health Care Management*, Michael Nerlich and Rainer Kretschmer, eds. (Amsterdam: IOS Press, 1999), 46–51.

14. Melinda Beck, "How Telemedicine is Transforming Health Care," *The Wall Street Journal* (June 26, 2016). https://www.wsj.com/articles/how-telemedicine-is-transforming-health-care-1466993402.

15. Beck, "How Telemedicine is Transforming Health Care."

16. Jennifer Mellor, Michael Daly, and Molly Smith, "Does it Pay to Penalize Hospitals for Excess Readmissions? Intended and Unintended Consequences of Medicare's Hospital Readmissions Reductions Program," *Health Economics* 26(8) (2017): 1048–1050.

17. Paul E. Larrat, Rita M. Marcoux, and F. Randy Vogenberg, "Impact of Federal and State Legal Trends on Health Care Services," *Pharmacy and Therapeutics* 37(4) (2012): 224–225.

18. Tory H. Hogan, Christy Harris Lemak, Nataliya Ivankova, Larry R. Herald, et al., "Hospital Vertical Integration into Subacute Care as a Strategic Response to Value-Based Payment Incentives, Market Factors, and Organizational Factors: A Multiple-Case Study," *Inquiry* 55 (2018). https://www.ncbi.nlm.nih.gov/pmc/articles/PMC6047235/.

19. Joanne E. Coster, Janette K. Turner, Daniel Bradbury, and Anna Cantrell, "Why do People Choose Emergency and Urgent Care Services? A Rapid Review Utilizing a Systematic Literature Search and Narrative Synthesis," *Academic Emergency Medicine* 24(9) (2017): 1140–1145.

20. Dafny and Lee, "Health Care Needs Real Competition."

21. Larrat, Marcoux, and Vogenberg, "Impact of Federal and State Legal Trends," 218–219.

22. Lloyd Armstrong, "A Business Model View of Changing Times in Higher Education," 2014. https://www.changinghighereducation.com/2014/12/new_business_model_view_of_change_in_higher_education.html.

23. Clayton M. Christensen, Michael B. Horn, Louis Soares, and Louis Caldera, "Disrupting College: How Disruptive Innovation Can Deliver Quality and Affordability to Postsecondary Education." Report, Center for American Progress, February 8, 2011. https://www.americanprogress.org/issues/economy/reports/2011/02/08/9034/disrupting-college/.

24. Alana Dunagan, "College Transformed: Five Institutions Leading the Charge in Innovation." Report, Christensen Institute, February 2017, 7. https://files.eric.ed.gov/fulltext/ED586366.pdf.

25. Christensen, Horn, Soares, and Caldera, "Disrupting College."

26. Dunagan, "College Transformed," 16

27. Thompson, "This is the Way the College 'Bubble' Ends."

28. William J. Hussar and Tabitha M. Bailey, *Projections of Education Statistics to 2027: Forty-Sixth Edition* (Washington, DC: National Center for Education Statistics, 2019), 23–32.

29. Peace Bransberger and Demaree K. Michelau, *Knocking at the College Door: Projections of High School Graduates, 9th Edition* (Boulder, CO: Western Interstate Commission for Higher Education, 2016), 11.

30. Hussar and Bailey, *Projections of Education Statistics*, 16.

31. Hussar and Bailey, *Projections of Education Statistics*, 17.

32. Nathan D. Grawe, *Demographics and the Demand for Higher Education* (Baltimore, MD: Johns Hopkins University Press, 2018).

33. Cliff Adelman, *Answers in the ToolBox: Academic Intensity, Attendance Patterns, and Bachelor's Degree Attainment* (Washington, DC: Department of Education, 1999). https://www2.ed.gov/pubs/Toolbox/index.html; Joann Horton, "Identifying At-Risk Factors that Affect College Student Success," *International Journal of Process Education* 7(1) (June 2015): 86.

34. David Swanger, "Innovation in Higher Education: Can Colleges Really Change?" White Paper, Fulton-Montgomery Community College, New York, June 2016, 6. https://www.fmcc.edu/about/files/2016/06/Innovation-in-Higher-Education.pdf.

35. Daniel DiSalvo and Jeffrey Kucik, "Pensions are Killing Higher Education: States are Opting to Fund Pensions and other Obligations over Education," *U.S. News and World Report* (June 2, 2017). https://www.usnews.com/opinion/articles/2017-06-02/public-pensions-are-killing-higher-education.

36. Michael Mitchell, Michael Leachman, and Kathleen Masterson, "Funding Down, Tuition Up: State Cuts to Higher Education Threaten Quality and Affordability at Public Colleges." Report, Center on Budget and Policy Priorities, Washington, DC, August 15, 2016. https://www.cbpp.org/research/state-budget-and-tax/funding-down-tuition-up.

37. DiSalvo and Kucik, "Pensions are Killing Higher Education."

38. Christensen, Horn, Soares, and Caldera, "Disrupting College."

39. Dunagan, "College Transformed," 3.

40. Mark Toner, "The Highly Endangered Business Model (and How to Fix it)." June 12, 2015. https://www.acenet.edu/the-presidency/columns-and-features/Pages/The-Highly-Endangered-Higher-Education-Business-Model.aspx.

41. Lucie Lapovsky, "The Higher Education Business Model: Innovation and Financial Sustainability." Accessed November 17, 2018. https://www.tiaa.org/public/pdf/higher-education-business-model.pdf; Lucie Lapovsky, "The Changing Business Model for Colleges and Universities." *Forbes* (February 2018). https://www.forbes.com/sites/lucielapovsky/2018/02/06/the-changing-business-model-for-colleges-and-universities/#bc299495ed59; Thompson, "This is the Way the College 'Bubble' Ends."

42. Mark Toner, "The Highly Endangered Business Model."

43. Thompson, "This is the Way the College 'Bubble' Ends."

44. Dunagan, "College Transformed," 4.

45. Armstrong, "A Business Model View of Changing Times."

46. John Ebersole, "The Unexamined Factors behind the Student Debt 'Crisis.'" *Forbes* (September 15, 2016). https://www.forbes.com/sites/johnebersole/2015/09/15/the-unexamined-factors-behind-the-student-debt-crisis/#5123ac334b89.

47. Yuen Ting Liu and Clive Belfield, "Evaluating For-Profit Higher Education: Evidence from the Educational Longitudinal Student." CAPSEE Working Paper, Center for Analysis of Postsecondary Education and Employment, New York, 2014, 7–16; Tressie McMillan Cottom, *Lower Ed: The Troubling Rise of For-Profit Colleges in the New Economy* (New York: The New Press, 2017); Adela Soliz, "College Completion: The Effects of the Expansion of for-Profit Colleges on Student Enrollments and Outcomes at Public Colleges." Ed.D Thesis, Harvard University, Cambridge, MA, 2016.

48. MacGregor Obergfell, "Performance Based Funding is Here to Stay," *New America* (June 21, 2018). https://www.newamerica.org/education-policy/edcentral/performance-based-funding-here-stay/.

49. Lydia Emmanouilidou, "Sen. Warren Introduces Legislation to Fix 'Broken' Accreditation System," *Washington Monthly* (September 23, 2016). https://washingtonmonthly.com/2016/09/23/sen-warren-introduces-legislation-to-fix-broken-accreditation-system/; Paul Fain, "Rubio Reintroduces Accreditation Bill," *Inside Higher Ed* (March 15, 2017). https://www.insidehighered.com/quicktakes/2017/03/15/rubio-reintroduces-accreditation-bill.

50. Gary King and Maya Sen, "The Troubled Future of Colleges and Universities," *Political Science and Politics* 46(1) (2013): 84; Beth Rubin, "University Business Models and Online Practices: A Third Way," *Online Journal of Distance Learning Administration* 25(1) (2013).

51. Alfred and Associates, *Managing the Big Picture*, xiii–xiv.

52. Soliz, "College Completion," iv.

53. Soliz, "College Completion," iv.

54. King and Sen, "The Troubled Future of Colleges and Universities."

55. Lapovsky, "The Higher Education business model"; Lapovsky, "The Changing Business Model."

Chapter Three

Operational Management in a Community College Business Model

Developing and implementing the community college business model (CCBM) requires some working knowledge of organizational behavior, management, and operations and each are addressed throughout this publication. As an intentional change process designed to reposition the community college for greater effectiveness, this is a heavy lift and demands commitment from the college community.

Engaging the community in these discussions must start, however, with a reiteration that model development is "far from emulating for-profit colleges or business enterprises [as] the new community college business [model] is guided—as always—by a fierce commitment to a singular mission and set of values."[1] There are understandable concerns about the phraseology given lowered budgets, increasing part-time faculty ratios, greater oversight and compliance, and the proposition that colleges should focus on students as customers.[2] The common thread among these and other critiques of "the business model" within higher education, however, is not the concept itself. Rather, apprehension emanates from worries about commercialism and corporate values driving colleges. The purpose of the CCBM is to optimize the student value proposition and is focused on human development and societal improvement through education. Truly, the CCBM is the anti-corporate business model built for community colleges committed to enhancing the student educational experience.

The remainder of this book is intended to help community colleges develop a framework unique to their unique culture and established through formal, inclusive, and fully participatory efforts. While this publication utilizes the disciplinary language of business and management language to provide a starting point for development and implementation, it also advocates for community colleges to develop their own unique vocabulary during model development. Concerns about language are to be expected and must be taken seriously even though the concept, while more pronounced, is not new.[3] What makes the term so divisive at this point in time is precisely the reason that community colleges need to engage in development—dynamic industry changes that challenge the ability to deliver upon the mission. Community colleges must move from sustaining and hybrid innovation approaches to one that welcomes, and is established by, disruption.

The traditional, reactive community college business models have been premised on "low tuition, little or no private funding, and slow curriculum development within program and discipline silos."[4] While community colleges have applied sustaining business practices, focused on financial management, and pursued strategies and tactics to improve operations, these activities have remained segregated. The issue, historically, is that accidental higher education business models have utilized "financial management functions [whereas] the impact of the new model is much deeper" and includes a "business dimension" (product development, curriculum, educational and student support services, continuing education, workforce development, etc.) and a "finance dimension" that addresses "the management and development of human, financial, physical, technological, and information resources."[5] The purposefully designed integration of all aspects of operational management is central to the four pillars of the CCBM discussed in subsequent chapters.

DIFFERENTIATING THE CCBM FOR OPERATIONAL MANAGEMENT TECHNIQUES

For the better part of two decades, community colleges have engaged in prototypical operating practices augmented by strategic planning and effectiveness modeling. The problem underlying these efforts, however, is the disconnected nature of planning and evaluative processes and lack of actionable information and comprehensive, foundational structures. And while community colleges maintain missions, institutional goals, strategic objectives, and institutional values, these often remain unconnected to the patchwork of framing structures designed to guide decision making and direction setting.

From an organizational management perspective, the distinction between the cohesive and comprehensive structure of the CCBM and the vast array of management, operational, and planning tools used by community colleges is vital. The inventory of tools, which are provided in Table 3.1, remain both important and useful, and need to be incorporated in the model. They must be utilized to ensure that (a) faculty, staff, student, and administrator activities and initiatives are aligned with the mission; (b) student learning, support for the student learning environment, and student outcomes are prioritized; (c) the

Table 3.1. Limitations of Standard Management Techniques in Driving Organizational Effectiveness

	Purpose	Connection to Organizational Effectiveness	Limitation in Driving Organizational Effectiveness
Strategic Planning	To establish college priorities that align with college mission	Identifying strategic objectives with performance indicators and targets for tracking progress	Not all activities will align with the strategic plan and the plan is not for operational management
Operational Planning	Provide departments/ units a structure for alignment	Information from plans document goal and objective achievement	Provides a reporting and planning structure limited to departments/units
Financial Planning	Provide structured process for allocating funds	Resource allocation to achieve key objectives	Finances support the mission but cannot drive operations
Integrated Planning	Align assessment, planning, and resource allocation	Aligns operational management techniques central to effectiveness	Process is about alignment and reacting and is not proactive
Institutional Effectiveness	Align management process with mission achievement	Aligns management techniques to track progress and modify operations through evaluation	Framework for alignment of management techniques, but not a structure for assessment of value

needs of internal and external stakeholders are addressed; and (d) resources are available to finance college operations. They are necessary, but insufficient for driving increased organizational effectiveness.

Strategy represents "a systematic way of positioning an institution with stakeholders in its environment to create value that differentiates it for competitors and leads to a sustainable advantage."[6] The purpose of strategy is to establish institutional value, while the business model is designed to deliver an exceptional value proposition to students. Strategy details actions, philosophies, plans, and methodologies for decision making and direction setting while the CCBM is a comprehensive framework that integrates all aspects of the college toward student success. Strategy is important for the prioritization of actions that occur, but is not a substitute for a business model. Associated with the overall strategy are the tactics used for its implementation. These tactics, especially if developed through consensus-building and across departments, divisions, and units, can unify efforts to accomplish institutional priorities.

A more practical, robust, and action-oriented tool is institutional planning. Arguably, the three most important forms of institutional planning impacting effectiveness are strategic planning, operational planning, and financial planning. They influence college operations through reaffirmation and revision of the mission, goals, and objectives; establishment of institutional priorities; provision of frameworks for strategic plan operationalization; and the evaluation of resource allocation. Each process offers a framework for action, but all are limited in scope. None offer an integrated structure designed to guide the college in establishing an exceptional educational experience.

While a business model is designed to enhance organizational effectiveness, it is not itself a measure of institutional effectiveness. Institutional effectiveness reflects the degree to which an organization has successfully achieved its mission. It is best understood as the result of an integrated planning approach that aligns assessment, planning, and resource allocation. Even when elevated to an integrated institutional effectiveness (IIE) model, it remains a well-developed tool, not an operational framework.[7] When effectively designed, implemented, and evaluated, however, IIE models enhance the impact of the CCBM.

Underlying each of these mechanisms are two basic and essential tools—assessment and evaluation. These activities provide information for continuous improvement and evidence of the extent to which outcomes and objectives are being met. These are the primary tools for gathering and reporting progress and achievement as well as for detailing the impact of institutional decision making. Developing and implementing a community college business model does not eliminate the need for these mechanisms and tools. Instead, it elevates and amplifies their importance by aligning them within a framework and establishing them as key structures for enhancing the student value proposition.

Managing a community college based on a comprehensive, intentionally designed, and mission-focused business model represents a disruptive approach to operational innovation. The philosophy underlying the model is not just about enhanced value proposition, but also determining where the college is and is not achieving organizational effectiveness. It is designed to guide in visualizing the desired educational experience for students and designing/redesigning all operational aspects to work together to deliver an optimal value to students.

Intentional Design as a Theoretical Underpinning of the CCBM

Two national efforts have focused on challenging community colleges to redesign their operations around increased student success: Achieving the Dream (ATD) and the American Association of Community College's

(AACC) Pathways Project. ATD has engaged hundreds of community colleges in the process of redesign under the philosophy that "the future of our country requires that we strengthen our communities by relentlessly addressing systemic inequities within higher education to increase social and economic mobility for all students and families [and focusing on] leading America's largest network of community colleges working to become strong engines of student and community growth."[8] AACC's initiative is also grounded in design thinking and highlights the need to bring interventions to scale through "substantial redesign of students' educational experience."[9] Pathways requires colleges to focus on improving early student outcomes through comprehensive planning, implementation, and evaluation efforts. While the CCBM is not based on the work of these initiatives, commonality exists regarding the principles, strategies, and desired outcomes.

Design thinking allows the community college to move beyond traditional operational management approaches. The shift, which is intentionally disruptive, is premised on better understanding and meeting the needs of the student. It is a reengineering process that focuses on solutions through a continuous team-based problem-solving approach designed to diagnose the causes of complex operational problems and devise verifiable solutions.[10]

Without fully understanding the problems that exist (value proposition), what resources must be provided (key resources), necessary services and support (delivery of the product), and how to ensure adequate financial support (profit formula), community colleges, quite unintentionally, underserve and under support students. Operating without an intentionally and purposefully designed operational framework no longer effectively supports student success, nor the environment supporting their journey. Put simply, maintaining the current trajectory prevents community colleges from realizing optimized performance and organizational effectiveness.[11]

Even with the inclusion of design thinking, moving into business model development will likely prove challenging. This approach to organizational management and redesign consists of five standard design thinking stages and has been used by higher education institutions to successfully implement comprehensive reforms.[12] The stages include the following:

- Empathize—Understanding the needs of the group being served by observing, working with the impacted stakeholders, and intentional, but organic two way-communication.
- Define—Analyzing the gap existing between the desired outcomes and the current situation for the impacted stakeholder.

- Ideate—Engaging in a participatory and collaborative brainstorming process designed to come up with a potential list of solutions for remedying the gaps between the current and desired situation.
- Prototype—Moving away from piloting since this stage is about modeling initial solutions for each problem that needs to be addressed.
- Test—Scaling up and fully developing and testing prototypes by the individuals most directly associated with the solutions to determine the appropriateness and effectiveness of the intervention.

These stages are essential and are incorporated indirectly throughout the publication. The one stage central to the CCBM, however, is empathizing. Enhancing the student value proposition is impossible without deeply understanding student needs and problems. The value proposition requires the development of effective solutions, but these solutions remain undiscoverable if students are not actively involved.[13] To adequately prepare the college for engagement in a solutions development process, the following strategies should be considered:

- Operate from a solutions-focused and strengths-based organizational mindset rather than one limited by a problem-centric and deficit-grounded organizational mindset;
- Commitment to a continuous improvement process that does not presuppose solutions, is not hampered by anecdote and conjecture, and is engineered for adaptation as new information becomes available and relevant; and
- Integrated and participatory recommendation structures that distribute authority, builds responsibility, grows engagement, and requires extensive involvement from the students, faculty, and staff.

These strategies assist with the development and implementation of the CCBM, but effectively managing within the model requires an institutional commitment to solutions-focused rather than problem-identification thinking. The CCBM is a solutions-oriented framework and contrasts the financial models and infinite growth tactics that have served as de facto models.

The financial model is premised on financial solvency as the institutional priority. Guided by denominator management and characterized by across-the-board cuts, this approach is aimed at fixing financial problems. The infinite growth approach is also ineffectual because it seeks to solve financial revenue problems with increased enrollment. It has created systemic management and operations issues that the financial model has sought to address. With increases to enrollment, the need for everything else increases—space, faculty, staff, programs, and so forth. This strategy requires more and more finances, which in turn requires increasing enrollment as a financing strategy, which in turn leads to the need for more enrollment. The more that the financing cycle determines operational priorities, the greater the likelihood that the college operates within a student success deficit cycle.

Strategies for Managing within the CCBM

Managing within this model requires that the community college engage in some disruptive tactics that transform the effectiveness of existing operations. Using situational examples, this section demonstrates how different methods of management set the stage for enhancing the students' educational experience. While chapters 6 through 9 provide an extensive examination of the four central constructs within the model, this chapter provides insight into how the value proposition, key resources, and delivery of the product are transformed by engaging in the disruptive practices central to the CCBM.

The student value proposition is the primary focus of the CCBM and, as noted earlier, is the driver of organizational effectiveness. Student success has become increasingly important over the last decade, but to what degree is student success integrated into all aspects of college operations? Perhaps a better question is whether the current business model is hindering or enhancing student learning and success? Even with significant tweaks to existing operations (the hybrid approach to innovation), failing to alter the business model precludes significant improvement in the student experience. Table

Table 3.2. Student Value Proposition in a Traditional Business Model and CCBM

	Traditional Business Model	Community College Business Model (CCBM)
Gathering Student Input	College depends on satisfaction and engagement surveys	College uses surveys, creates student forums, and incorporates student voice in decision making
Understanding the Student	Utilize the student information system (SIS), surveys, and assessment data	Use SIS data, survey data, and assessment data in predictive analytics as well as student forums and reporting from departments and units
Recruiting Non-attending Students	Gather demographic data to determine enrollment gaps and build marketing/recruitment plan	Engage in outreach to non-attendees and non-completers to identify institutional barriers to attendance and analyze service area data to identify unserved populations
Increasing College Affordability	Pursue additional revenue streams to keep tuition rates stable	Pursue mission-aligned new revenue streams while strategically reducing non-priority costs, increasing campus work opportunities, and reducing time to graduation and transfer

3.2 provides a comparison of how traditional and redesigned business models approach the student value proposition.

While many community colleges likely identify with statements in both columns, the lack of a comprehensive intentionally designed business model limits the effectiveness of the value proposition. The community college must also be honest about the degree to which student success is, indeed, a fundamental goal that is driving college operations. Community colleges often possess pockets of innovation; however, the degree to which these concepts are integrated into the foundation of operational management represents a deeper understanding and sense of commitment.

The concept of the key resource is not specific to the CCBM and is likely well understood within all community colleges. What differs, however, is the definition of resources as well as which resources are identified as key. For example, the redesigned business model framework identifies nonfinancial resources as key resources, including faculty and staff tasked with directly or indirectly supporting student learning and outcomes, the technological and physical infrastructure central to the delivery of a positive educational experience, and the partnerships that amplify and enhance operational management. An important reason for placing each of these constructs under the classification of key resource is to strengthen the statement that resources exist to support the value proposition rather than any of these resources being the value proposition. Table 3.3 explores how fundamental questions that involve key resources are answered differently based on the model being utilized.

Three primary elements must each be evaluated and enhanced to deliver an exceptional product—the mechanisms, processes, and structures that encapsulate the experience. These elements are described and explored individually (and in depth in Chapter 8); because each directly impacts the student experience, however, they are also interconnected. Processes, for example, are contained within mechanisms (i.e., curriculum within academic programs), structures are key in improving processes (i.e., assessment and evaluation impact teaching), and structures are revised based on mechanisms (i.e., academic departments significantly impact the academic planning process). The intentional connection between the elements is a central feature of the CCBM. Contrary to a standard business model, enhancement to the educational experience (product) is not always reflected in greater efficiency, lowered cost, or increased productivity. The sole success metric regarding the product is whether it was enhanced as evidenced by greater student success. Table 3.4 provides a comparison of product delivery within an inadvertent college business model and the CCBM.

Managing within the CCBM requires significant adjustments and modifications to the standard operational and managerial practices in community

Table 3.3. Key Resources in a Traditional Business Model and CCBM

	Traditional Business Model	Community College Business Model (CCBM)
How is leadership operationalized?	The governance structure ensures input from faculty, staff, and students in major organizational decision-making and direction-setting efforts.	Governance is used, but the college provides intentional, regular opportunities for input into major organizational decision-making and direction-setting efforts.
What role does technology play?	Technology is designed to solve systemic issues, serve students, and inventory important data.	Technology is integrated and driven by technology plans that assess the impact on the student value proposition.
What role does space management play?	Space utilization and student FTE (full-time equivalent) to FT^2 (facilities square footage) ratios are gathered to determine efficient use of space.	Space utilization is assessed against student needs and problems to identify priorities and allocate academic, educational, and student support space.
What role do partners play?	Partnerships are established to reduce costs, increase revenues, and provide learning, internship, support, and career opportunities.	Partners are connected as part of the college's partner network to amplify the impact of the college to the community, create consortia, strengthen relationships, and provide exceptional value to students.

colleges. Disruptive change is abnormal within higher education, so working to design, implement, and manage a framework that reconceptualizes institutional priorities may prove difficult. Additionally, colleges contain multiple subcultures that often possess different expectations and values—some of which are in conflict—so one well-understood mission, set of values, or expectations for higher education is highly unlikely.

Despite these differences and points of contention, clearly the community college must move toward a designed business model that focuses operational management on delivering an enhanced value proposition to students. The next section of this publication offers some guidance on creating the conditions necessary for the development of a redesigned community college business model by considering the role of culture as well as the roles of, and distinctions between, administration, leadership, and governance.

Table 3.4. Product Delivery in a Traditional Business Model and CCBM

	Traditional Business Model	Community College Business Model (CCBM)
How are academic programs enhanced to support student success?	The academic program review (APR) gathers curriculum and student data to plan for program improvements.	The APR is used along with regular review of dashboards, reports, and analytics to identify gatekeeper courses, equity gaps, and areas for program improvement.
How are career services utilized to support student success?	Students are provided with access to wage data, career counseling, job listings, planning tools, workshops, and internships.	Academic departments and career services partner to provide planning tools, mentorship, career exploration, and internships.
How is operational planning utilized to support student success	Annual planning and reporting provides updates on progress made in the strategic plan and within departments and units.	Institution, division, department, and unit activities are evaluated through benchmarking, analytics, and data mining to chart progress and uncover systemic issues.
How are retention outcomes used to support student success?	Retention rates are tracked by the program- and college-wide, and best practices are integrated into academic and support programs to improve the rates.	Retention rates are disaggregated and tracked by the program and college-wide with predictive analytics used to understand the factors associated with attrition, information is shared with retention committees, and scorecards are used to document progress.

NOTES

1. Gundar Myran, "The New Community College Business and Finance Model," *New Directions for Community Colleges* 162 (Summer 2013): 103.

2. Christian Gilde, *Higher Education: Open for Business* (Lanham, MD: Lexington Books, 2007), 1; Keith Kroll, "Teaching in the Commercialized Community College," *The Radical Teacher* 93 (Spring 2012): 13–14; William J. Lowe, "Can Business Learn from Higher Education?" *Change* 32(2) (2000): 4; Juli A. Jones, "Foundation of Corporatization: Lessons from the Community College," *Society for History Education* 41(2) (2008): 213–215; Charles A. Zappia, "Academic Profes-

sionalism and the Business Model in Education: Reflection of a Community College Historian," *The History Teacher* 33(1) (1999): 58–59.

3. Boyd R. Keenan, "The Need for Closer Conformity to the Business Model," *The Journal of Higher Education* 32(9) (1961): 513–515. https://www.jstor.org/stable/1979688.

4. Myran, "The New Community College Business and Finance Model," 94.

5. Myran, "The New Community College Business and Finance Model," 94.

6. Richard Alfred and Associates, *Managing the Big Picture in Colleges and Universities: From Tactics to Strategy* (Westport, CT: American Council on Education/Praeger, 2006), 6.

7. Association for Higher Education Effectiveness, "About AHEE." Accessed August 10, 2019. https://ahee.org/about/.

8. Achieving the Dream, "About Us." Accessed August 10, 2019. https://www.achievingthedream.org/about-us.

9. American Association of Community Colleges, "AACC Pathways Project." Accessed August 10, 2019. https://www.aacc.nche.edu/programs/aacc-pathways-project/.

10. Tim Brown and Barry Katz, "Change by Design," *The Journal of Product Innovation Management* 28(3) (2011): 381–383.

11. Beth Rubin, "University Business Models and Online Practices: A Third Way," *Online Journal of Distance Learning Administration* 25(1) (2013).

12. Aaron Apel, Phil Hull, Scott Owczarek, and Wren Singer, "Transforming the Enrollment Experience Using Design Thinking," *College and University* 93(1) (2018): 46.

13. Brown and Katz, "Change by Design," 381–383.

Section II

CREATING THE CONDITIONS FOR A NEW COMMUNITY COLLEGE BUSINESS MODEL

This section provides a bridge between describing and making the case for the CCBM and model development. Development and implementation of a new business model amounts to an exercise in organizational change and institutions ill-prepared or resistant to change are unlikely to implement a comprehensive business model. This section examines culture and leadership—both critical factors that impact change management.

Organizational culture is a construct that impacts the entire college whether understood or not. It influences the daily routines, decisions, and direction setting at the college. Chapter 4 is designed to aid the reader in contextualizing organization and culture within community colleges, exploring different culture types, and documenting cultural factors that support or hinder organizational change.

While Chapter 4 explores what culture is and how it impacts change (the what), Chapter 5 works through the how of business model development by considering the impact of governance, management, and leadership practices, processes, and structures. This chapter addresses internal subgroups within the college—faculty, staff, administration, and students—and their role in pursuing organizational change initiatives. While formal mechanisms that involve governance and management are central to successful change efforts, the informal mechanisms play a more powerful role in sustaining these changes. Chapter 5 focuses extensively on informal mechanisms for direction setting and decision making, which are reflective of a participatory leadership approach aimed at increasing investment and commitment, not buy-in. These two chapters, when considered together, provide readers with the practical insight necessary to move into the business model development process.

Chapter Four

Organizational Culture, Organizational Change, and the Business Model

Organizations are often understood as a collection of buildings, facilities, and inorganic material. In reality, however, they are congregations of people with specific roles, responsibilities, and a shared purpose. They exist so individuals with various knowledge, skills, and abilities can work together for the accomplishment of a mission. As a result of this shared purpose and common goals, individuals are provided with a deeper sense of meaning that allows for better, more effective, and more impactful experiences within their work environment.[1]

Individuals rely not only on the experiences, perceptions, and knowledge they bring into the workplace, but also the prevailing values, structures, and relationships. Given the continual need for sensemaking, large scale change can complicate the process and lead to dissonance. The design and implementation of the CCBM is disruptive to the existing state and requires awareness and preparation. Four key properties that offer insight into how organizations respond to major change initiatives include the following:[2]

- Organizations are complex—Convening individuals with different values, perspectives, and experiences and then creating smaller subgroups with unique values and beliefs results in an environment where behaviors and actions can be difficult to anticipate.
- Organizations are surprising—Uncertainty is assured since even with substantial information, representative input, evidence, and trend analyses, impacts from decisions, initiatives, and actions may net unexpected (positive, neutral, or negative) results.
- Organizations are deceptive—At times, actions and behaviors are illogical and can include portraying negative findings as biased, downplaying the impact of external pressures, or redirecting attention from undesirable findings.

- Organizations are ambiguous—"The sum of complexity, unpredictability, and deception is rampant ambiguity."[3]

The conclusion to be drawn from these properties is that responses to organizational change efforts cannot be fully predicted. It is imperative to understand the structure of community colleges and subculture impact on culture, culture types, and the factors that impact change.

Organizationally, the community college is referred to as a professional bureaucracy.[4] Despite myriad changes to the higher education industry, including disruption through new competitors, community colleges have maintained essentially the same organizational architecture for decades. A professional bureaucracy is paradoxical because it is designed to provide decentralization, where possible, and standardization, where necessary. This structure was intentionally designed to create three operational subgroups within the college—faculty, staff, and administration—to manage the day-to-day activities without strict oversight (decentralization). Respect, autonomy, and trust are central principles and effectiveness is dependent upon the professional expertise that exists within each of the subgroups.

Overall responsibility for the institutional mission, strategies, and operations (standardization) largely falls to the administration. This bifurcation reduces the ability to move quickly in response to change because "professionals are insulated from formal interference, freeing them to use their expertise" with the result that "individual professionals may be at the forefront of their specialty, while the institution as a whole changes at a glacial pace."[5]

A related concept requiring understanding and attention is coupling.[6] It reflects the degree of cohesion existing within subgroups and community colleges and, based on their purpose and mission, community colleges are loosely coupled. These institutions are structured to contain multiple subgroups that maintain values, goals, and expectations specific to their individual group in addition to the values, goals, and expectations at the institutional level.

These subgroups exist in different worlds and engage in different routines, interact in very different ways with students, and experience external pressures differently. Moving from loose (emphasizing subculture) to tight coupling (emphasizing institutional culture) requires that commitment to a shared understanding of, and investment in, the mission. Community colleges must increase "the extent to which subsystems have common variables between them and the extent to which the shared variables are important to the subsystem . . . , the subsystems are likely to be relatively tightly coupled, and changes in one should produce clear changes in the other."[7]

With the natural order leaning toward loose coupling, colleges often experience tension between institutional and subculture values. The successful design and implementation of the CCBM not only requires greater cohesion between the subcultures, but when fully developed, it enables greater cohesion through a commitment to enhance the student value proposition.

Organizational Culture

Culture is ubiquitous throughout both the business and higher education literature. Organizational management scholars have provided definitions through the years and the common elements include the deeply held and shared beliefs about the mission; a set of rules, norms, and mores that guide behavior; and the use of rituals, stories, symbols, myths, and sagas to enculturate new organizational members.[8] In considering many of these and other definitions of organizational culture, the following definition for community colleges is offered:

> The community college institutional culture consists of the connected and integrated values, attitudes, and philosophies that are both shaped by and help shape the understandings of the faculty, staff, students, and administrators and which, in turn, guide behaviors, develop in and out groups, and determine norms and mores.

An instructive question in understanding the impact of culture is as follows: Do organizations *have* cultures or *are* organizations cultures?[9] Organization and culture are constructs created for the purposes of sensemaking, creating goals that unify work routines, better understanding and predicting human behavior, and establishing shared purpose and responsibilities. It reflects the degree of cohesion existing in and between subgroups and the college. As a result of their purpose and mission, community colleges are necessarily loosely coupled. They are intentionally designed to maintain subgroups with specific values, goals, and expectations that occasionally conflict with those at the institutional level.

As noted, college subgroups each possess their own cultures. The characteristics embedded within the organizational culture (values, norms, beliefs, etc.) also exist within each of the subcultures and the process of culture change is impacted by these interactions. To add to the complexity, both the institutional culture as well as the subcultures are impacted by societal, higher education, and community college sector cultures.

During times of great disruption, either internal or external, the college and subgroups are provided with the opportunity to address, question, and potentially revise the deeply held beliefs and values that guide daily activities. Development of the CCBM not only represents a disruptive practice, but

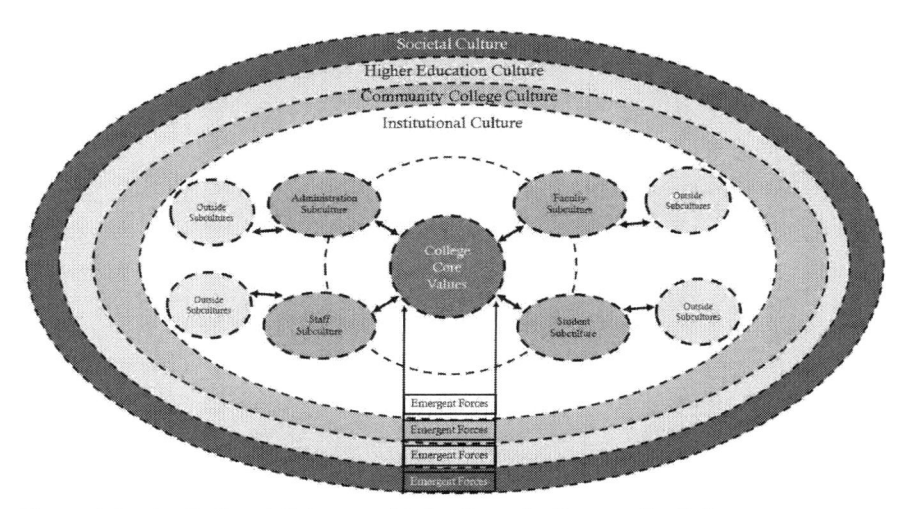

Figure 4.1. Institutional Culture and Subcultures in Community Colleges

also an institutional response to industry disruptions. By understanding the uniqueness of the community college and the interaction of the subcultures, the college is better equipped to establish its business model. Figure 4.1 offers a conceptual framework that demonstrates the complexity of culture change in the community college.

This figure was intentional in the use of both dotted and solid lines. The dotted lines reflect the continual influence between the subgroups. Starting with the societal culture and moving inward, changes in values, norms, and expectations in the outermost rings impact the college and subgroup cultures. Within the institutional culture, continued subgroup interactions with cultures inside and outside of the college lead to regular, incremental evolution of values, behaviors, and understandings. The solid lines identified as emergent forces represent major disruptions that, for a time, force the college and individuals to consciously consider, question, evaluate, and potentially revise the values that often lie dormant within the institutional subconscious.

While major disruptions provide opportunities to evaluate the appropriateness of operations, effectiveness of strategies, and the degree to which the mission is being achieved, the natural order is typically to resist change and retreat to subculture values.[10] Although change in the higher education industry is more pervasive than ever, change to the values and philosophies still reflect punctuated equilibrium. This term reflects the desire from individuals to address disruptive forces as necessary and then return to standard operations.[11] It is a dissonant experience to consciously consider, question, evaluate, and potentially revise the values that routinely lay unquestioned and unconsidered. Examples of disruptions that have forced colleges to examine the values that drive operations include the following:

- Societal culture—Mass shootings in educational settings are profoundly sad, shocking, and tragic. As a result, community colleges reevaluated policies, practices, and relationships with law enforcement; extended emotional and mental health services; and examined their commitment to ensure safe and supportive educational environments.
- Higher education culture—The expansion of technology in the 1990s led to a proliferation of for-profit educational providers. This expansion, fueled by online programs, provided a watershed mark for traditional higher education. Community colleges initially struggled with questions of mission, tradition, pedagogy, and the impact of technology in the classroom. Some community colleges still struggle with the place and role of distance education, but few refuse to offer online courses at this point.
- Community college culture—When the Achieving the Dream (ATD) program started, design thinking was new to higher education. ATD challenged community colleges to examine their missions, reengineer operations, and intentionally design for student success. The concept of intentional design is now mainstream and many colleges are participants in ATD, American Association of Community College's Guided Pathways, or other design efforts.
- College culture—Major organizational change efforts like addressing changing accreditation standards, strategic planning, and a new president present an opportunity for institutional review and renewal. The development and implementation of a business model provides the same opportunity. It is intentionally disruptive and brings issues and concerns, along with questions about the mission and goals, to the surface for discussion, consideration, and potential conflict.

The exploration into the interactions of each of the cultures connected with, essentially, both the organization and culture, are premised on relationships and values. The CCBM is designed around the shared belief that student success is organizational effectiveness and the goal of enhancing the student educational experience. Focusing on these two concepts not only makes implementation of the model more likely, but also increases its relevance.

Culture Archetypes

Culture is a complex concept; however, it is important to note that is not a monolithic one. As a result of different factors and inputs, colleges possess a unique set of values, norms, expectations, beliefs, and philosophies.

Table 4.1. Culture Type by Decision-Making Category and Institutional Orientation

	Description	Decision Making	Institutional Orientation
Clan	A culture that reflects a strong culture focused on consensus, relationship building, tradition, and loyalty. Meeting the needs and expectations of students, caring for all college community members, and participatory practices are highly valued.	Flexible	Internal
Adhocracy	A culture that possesses an environment of creativity, innovation, and risk-taking in pursuit of mission accomplishment. Institutional structures, processes, and practices are regularly evaluated to ensure proactivity and adaptability. Diffused decision making and direction setting are highly valued.	Flexible	External
Hierarchy	A culture that values formality, structure, adherence to rules, standardization, and efficiency. These cultures pursue operations, decision making, direction setting, and strategies that ensure stability and a sense of order.	Control	Internal
Market	A culture that is focused on evidence of success through the achievement of tangible results. Uncompromising dedication to achieving goals, outperforming competing institutions on tangible metrics, and adapting to proactively address external challenges are all institutional values.	Control	External

Although cultures are specific, typologies have been established to classify elements common across colleges. Four higher education culture types have emerged and been validated as frameworks for understanding organizational effectiveness, readiness for change, and institutional values and priorities.[12] These types, along with the dimensions of decision making and institutional orientation are provided in Table 4.1.

To examine how culture types impact organizational effectiveness within the community college, a framework with nine dimensions was created.[13] Each dimension aligns with one of the four elements of the CCBM, which provides insight into the culture types most conducive to model development and acceptance. Overall, colleges with adhocracy cultures are best equipped to design, implement, and utilize the business model approach. The clan culture was also highly rated and the commonality between the two is the preference for flexible decision making, which reflects comfort with innovation and continuous change.[14] The hierarchy culture type was least well positioned and ranked last in seven of the dimensions. Controlled decision making reduces the ability to respond to changing conditions and engage in innovative practices.

The CCBM is designed to optimize the student value proposition through regular evaluation of key resources, product delivery, and the profit formula. Within the culture type/organizational effectiveness framework, cultures guided by flexible thinking and decision making scored highest on eight of the nine dimensions of effectiveness. Adhocracy was clearly the best aligned with the CCBM, not only because of the flexible decision making, but also because of the external focus.

Colleges designed to address external pressures and leverage opportunities, engage stakeholders as resources, and pursue revenue generation that align with the mission are better equipped to improve the educational experience. Community colleges identified as possessing a clan culture are also well equipped to engage in the process, based on the decision-making process, however, the internal focus could be a limiting factor. These colleges must work to more effectively engage external stakeholders to ensure the institution is aware of opportunities, innovations, and possibilities that enhance the student value proposition.

Cultural Factors that Impact Organizational Change Efforts

Institutional history is the most important cultural factor impacting the willingness to engage in major change efforts. Members of the college community utilize myths, stories, sagas, and other cultural artifacts to shape perceptions as they discuss the successes or failures of past change efforts. Another important element of history is the sharing of subculture values and norms that may contradict institutional culture. American higher education has historically been allowed to operate without substantive oversight. As a result, discussions about business models, value propositions, key resources, and profit formulas may cause resistance. Some members of the college refuse to accept that changing conditions warrant major change efforts and question why higher education institutions are even considering business models and practices.[15]

Academic culture values deliberation and resists adapting operations and activities based on external pressures and demands.[16] Rather than viewing these assumptions and cultural values as barriers to innovation and the development of a model, the community college should view designing a business model as an opportunity to effectively and comprehensively answer questions, address concerns, and establish commitment to development and implementation.

A recent publication provides insight into some tactics that can help facilitate change. Based on an analysis of organizational change theories though a historical lens, "variations in how we conceptualize change are underpinned by different assumptions about history and its relationship to our capacity for change."[17] To better understand how organizations react to change based on conceptualizations of institutional history, four models are provided (see Table 4.2). In preparing to engage in the development of the CCBM, colleges should consider the ways in which institutional history is utilized to influence organizational change.

Cultural facilitators and barriers will impact the successful design and implementation of an intentionally designed business model. Institutional history is often the most prevalent and most visible, but community colleges must be aware of the many additional factors that impact change initiatives. Table 4.3 provides a summary of additional factors for consideration.

Culture Types and the CCBM: Four Hypothetical Community Colleges

To provide context regarding openness to business model development across different culture types, four hypothetical case studies representing the four different idealized culture types are offered. While reading, consider the culture type descriptions and impact of various cultural factors on organizational change efforts. While few community colleges perfectly align with any culture type, they often resemble one primary type. After reading the examples provided, consider answering the questions to gain a greater awareness of how cultural factors and types directly impact the ability for the colleges to engage in the development of the CCBM.

Clan Culture (Flexible, Internal) —
Commonwealth Community College (CCC)

CCC is a rural community college with an enrollment of six thousand five hundred students. Located centrally in Jackson County, the institution is the primary feeder for two smaller colleges (one public and one private) and the agricultural campus of Midwestern State University (MSU). Although chartered as a community college, more than 85 percent of the students are enrolled in associate of arts programs, the only two associate of science degrees are in agriculture-related programs (students transfer to MSU), and the only certificate program is a one-year general education certificate designed for transfer.

Table 4.2. Methods in Which Institutional History is Used to Impact Organizational Change

	Description	Challenges to Major Organizational Change Initiatives	Facilitators for Change
History as Fact	In this approach, history exists as a barrier to change based on reverence to the college's founding purposes and activities.	Values have been solidified over time, which makes questioning difficult. The passage of time has created expectations and beliefs that have been integrated into structures, policies, and practices.	Since the institution is bound to historical approaches, external pressure or a mandate is often necessary to force the college to change course.
History as Power	Organizational change is impacted by the use of historically important power structures and coalitions to either support or block change.	Power structures are complex with past failures and long periods of stability creating strong resistance to disruptive change	Existing or newly established coalitions must be empowered and engaged to question and modify values, roles, routines, and structures
History as Sensemaking	History acts as a conscious mechanism for communicating values at the individual and subgroup level.	Shared understandings drive how individuals experience their environments and make sense of actions, so dissonance creates resistance.	Change efforts must communicate and demonstrate how they build on shared interpretations and align with college and subculture values
History as Rhetoric	This approach views history as highly subjective and open to interpretation. It will encourage or discourage change based on the agenda of the person using it.	Time is a malleable concept and those attempting to resist change can memorialize certain events or work to create institutional forgetting of key moments.	Change efforts must be viewed as authentic to college values, which will allow for the use of rhetorical language to frame change as appropriate and necessary.

Table 4.3. Inventory of Cultural Factors that Impact Organizational Change Efforts

	Description
Strength of Relationships	Degree to which the ties between subcultures are weak or strong
Quality of Relationships	Degree to which interpretations of cultural values are shared across multiple subcultures
Values and Beliefs	Degree to which the college initiative challenges deep values and beliefs
Cultural Ethnocentrism	Degree to which the change initiative creates an us versus them dynamic
Personalization	Perception that the change initiative is an indictment on the status quo
Cultural Compatibility	Degree to which the change initiative is in direct conflict with norms
Sensemaking	Degree to which the change initiative aligns with how community members experience the culture
Strength of Traditions (Stories, Myths, and Sagas)	Narratives passed along through enculturation that reinforce a cultural value
Comfort with External Inputs	Degree to which the culture accepts guidance from sources external to the college
Decision Approaches	Degree to which participatory decision making is a cultural norm
Risk Comfort	Degree to which the culture embraces uncertainty
Openness to Innovation	Degree to which the culture seeks new solutions and approaches

Source. Zaltman and Duncan (1977), Weick (2000), Clark (1972), Chandler (2013), and Smart and Hamm (1993a).

President James Thompson has led the college for almost thirty years and during his tenure, three primary foci guide the college—improving the student experience, maintaining a culture of care, and operating as a center of learning for the community. During his time, the college has added dorms, established a men's and women's college (cohort programs), significantly grown leadership and professional development programs, flattened the college's administrative structure, grown the dual enrollment program, and established a community scholars' program to welcome the community onto the campus.

The enrollment has remained relatively steady, and as the primary feeder for the four-year colleges in the county, the transfer program is highly valued. The college is regularly recognized as one of the top places to work in the state, and as a result, faculty and staff retention is very high with very few new hires. Despite regular concerns regarding finances, infighting and contentious meetings are rare. The health and welfare of the faculty, staff, and students is the primary concern at CCC. Accordingly, little time has been spent understanding the role of the college in the workforce development and economic well-being of the county.

To fill the gap, two brick and mortar proprietary colleges, one focused on healthcare and technology and the other on business management and hospitality, have moved into the county. In spite of national trends and the fact that the tuition and fees are more than double that of CCC, these institutions continue to grow their enrollments. Clearly the private colleges are meeting economic needs, but at what cost to the residents who are taking on a significant financial burden? Based on the information provided and the culture type, consider the following:

- What factors make the design and implementation of the CCBM at the college *necessary*?
- What factors *facilitate* the design and implementation of the CCBM at the college?
- What factors *inhibit* the design and implementation of the CCBM at the college?

Adhocracy Culture (Flexible, External) – Vicissitude College (VC)

Located in a middle class county thirty miles outside a major metropolis, VC serves more than forty thousand credit and noncredit students on two campuses and operates more than one dozen off-site centers. Under the leadership of Dr. Themba Yonda for the past fifteen years, VC operates under and holds itself accountable to the motto "Serving the Top 100 percent of our students," a motto she shares regularly with internal and external stakeholders.

To ensure that the college continually focuses on student success, the institution has built a robust governance and leadership program to stimulate relevant participation in major decision making; partners with all high schools in the county to expand college preparation and dual enrollment; establishes formal partnerships with local business and industry to grow experiential learning, paid internships, and workforce development programming; utilizes a home-grown data analytics system to strengthen academic and student support; and operates from a three-year strategic plan to prevent "stagnant thinking."

The college joined a state-sponsored partnership between three regional high schools and the flagship university to offer coursework from the junior year in high school up through a limited number of masters programs in one location. Faculty and staff satisfaction surveys, historically, have shown high levels of satisfaction with the college; however, some of the ratings (i.e., commitment to professional development, understanding the mission, care for faculty and staff) have slipped over the past five years. During this time, the number of academic programs, student enrollment, and staff (student support and information technology) have increased while the percentage of full-time faculty dropped below 45 percent. Based on the information provided and the culture type, consider the following:

- What factors make the design and implementation of the CCBM at the college *necessary*?
- What factors *facilitate* the design and implementation of the CCBM at the college?
- What factors *inhibit* the design and implementation of the CCBM at the college?

Hierarchy Culture (Control, Internal) — Officialdom Community College (OCC)

Officialdom Community College (OCC) maintains an enrollment of around ten thousand students and is located in a county that is equal parts working and professional class. While not an official tagline, the college operates with the slogan "process over progress." The institution is guided by conservative approaches to finance, role adherence through formalized structures, and the belief that faculty and staff can solve any problems that arise.

Dr. Thaddeus Harris, who has been president for five years, has worked to maintain the values of respect, structure, and formality that have defined the college for decades. The most important guiding document at the college is the governance plan, which provides an extensive description of the philosophies, processes, and structures that position shared governance as an institutional priority.

In addition to the regular Faculty Senate, Staff Senate, and Student Government Association meetings, which are attended by executive team members as invited, the president meets with the presidents of these bodies once a month. These bodies are also expected to gather input from their constituencies and offer suggestions through formal channels. The most utilized process for input gathering is the convening of ad hoc task forces, which are problem specific, must offer a recommendation, and can be convened by any member of the college community with vice-presidential approval.

The president walks the campus frequently and is cordial, but formal with his interactions. He attends many events held on campus and expects his cabinet to do the same. The college maintains a robust array of academic programs, each with formalized articulation agreements with local four-year colleges and universities while on the noncredit side, the Office of Continuing Education oversees all noncredit programming as well as a limited number of workforce contracts. Perhaps because contention and challenge are rare at the college, innovation tends to occur only within institutional bubbles. Based on the information provided and the culture type, consider the following:

- What factors make the design and implementation of the CCBM at the college *necessary*?
- What factors *facilitate* the design and implementation of the CCBM at the college?
- What factors *inhibit* the design and implementation of the CCBM at the college?

Market Culture (Control, External) —
Exchange Community and Technical College (ECTC)

ECTC is a large, urban community and technical college with the mission of providing transfer and terminal degree programs in career-oriented fields and workforce development training. Under the guidance of Dr. Jennifer Peterson, the college has grown to an enrollment of more than twelve thousand students with eighty degrees and certificates offered through six departments: business, media, and information systems; nursing and allied health; culinary arts and hospitality; corrections and law enforcement; education and social services; and general studies. With the exception of the associates of art in general studies, all programs leading to the associates of applied science, associates of science, and associates of applied arts structured to ensure stackable credentials aligned with the numerous apprenticeships and short-term, one-year and two-year certificate programs.

ECTC has recently added a general education certificate, which is 100 percent online, to support the small population of students pursuing the one general education program at the college (associates of arts in general studies). Dr. Peterson spends almost all of her time in the community and as a result, the college maintains more than fifty workforce development contracts with many of the companies supplying members to the mandatory department-based industry advisory boards. The college maintains two-, three-, and four-year graduation rates and transfer rates that are higher than the state average. All programs eligible for specialized accreditation are accredited in good standing, licensure pass rates are all above 90 percent, and job placement statistics are among the best in the state.

Academic and educational support is a priority at the college with professional advisors and tutors, robust adult and continuing education programming, a cohesive and interconnected career service center, and partnerships with local mental health clinics to provide mental and emotional support to students. Given the extensive menu of traditional academic programs and certificates, the college depends heavily on competency-based education, prior learning assessments, and adjunct faculty (around 80 percent) to meet the demand for academic programs. The college is visited regularly by politicians, consistently receives awards from the Workforce Investment Board, and is touted as a model for the career benefits of higher education.

Based on the information provided and the culture type, consider the following:

- What factors make the design and implementation of the CCBM at the college *necessary*?
- What factors *facilitate* the design and implementation of the CCBM at the college?
- What factors *inhibit* the design and implementation of the CCBM at the college?

CONCLUSION

Empirical evidence has shown the power of culture in mediating the effects of external factors given that culture type impacts decision-making approaches, mission and priority alignment, and institutional commitment.[18] Community colleges can facilitate proactive approaches to changing conditions with internal cohesion around values, a culture that embraces opportunities for innovation, and the maintenance of intentionally designed processes and structures focused on effectiveness. The community college business model is designed to push colleges toward organizational effectiveness, and college culture is either a driver towards or impediment to successful change efforts.

Organizational cultures can create a paradox for community colleges seeking to respond to changing needs. The culture types that are internally focused and/or characterized by controlled decision making inhibit the ability to respond to changing needs and demands. Institutions are being forced to adapt and not all community colleges would classify themselves as an adhocracy or a clan. Often in spite of their cultures, community colleges have evolved incrementally. This quote accurately reflects the reality of change for community colleges:

> Those who claim that [higher education is] incapable of change are clearly wrong in light of the reforms that have taken place [as] the demands placed on [colleges] to accommodate larger numbers of students and expand their func-

tions and orientations to meet the needs of the global knowledge economy has resulted in significant change and reform over the past half-century.[19]

The issue is not that cultures have prevented community colleges from changing, but rather that culture types and factors have made change difficult and created barriers to innovation. What community colleges need is to intentionally design for adaptability in order to provide exceptional value to students. So while, yes, community colleges have adapted to meet changing regulations and compliance standards, many of the underlying structures, processes, understandings, and values have not evolved sufficiently. This, put simply, is the challenge that culture presents to colleges seeking to move proactively.

A reasonable argument can be made that culture never changes, but instead evolves and is modified over time. As shown, the power of history to enculturate new college community members, as demonstrated through the rituals, stories, symbols, myths, legends and other cultural artifacts is real. The challenge for colleges working to engage in the design and implementation of an intentionally designed community college business model is how to harness the positive, student-centric aspects of the culture and leverage them for optimal organizational performance. While this chapter was designed to illuminate and communicate the challenge, the next chapter examines how the campus community can and must work collaboratively to move the institution forward.

NOTES

1. Karl E. Weick, *Making Sense of the Organization* (Hoboken, NJ: Wiley-Blackwell, 2000); Karl E. Weick, *Sensemaking in Organizations* (Los Angeles: Sage Publications, 1995).

2. Lee G. Bolman and Terrence E. Deal, *Reframing Organizations (3rd Edition)* (San Francisco: Jossey-Bass, 2003).

3. Bolman and Deal, *Reframing Organizations*, 20.

4. Henry Mintzberg, *The Structuring of Organizations* (Englewood Cliffs, NJ: Prentice Hall, 1979).

5. Bolman and Deal, *Reframing Organizations*, 77.

6. Karl E. Weick, "Educational Organizations as Loosely Coupled Systems," *Administrative Science Quarterly* 21(1) (1976): 1–19.

7. Robert Birnbaum, *How Colleges Work: The Cybernetics of Academic Organization and Leadership* (San Francisco: Jossey-Bass, 1988), 39.

8. Clifford Geertz, *The Interpretation of Cultures* (New York: Basic Books, 1973); William G. Tierney, "Organizational Culture in Higher Education: Defining the Essentials," *The Journal of Higher Education* 59(1) (1988): 8; Terrence E. Deal and

Allan A. Kennedy, "Culture: A New Look Through Old Lenses," *Journal of Applied Behavioral Science* 19 (1983): 501–503; Edgar Schein, *Organizational Culture and Leadership* (San Francisco: Jossey-Bass, 1992).

9. Bolman and Deal, *Reframing Organizations*.

10. Nick Chandler, "Braced for Turbulence: Understanding and Managing Resistance to Change in the Higher Education Sector," *Management* 3(5) (2013): 244.

11. Chandler, "Braced for Turbulence," 244.

12. Kim S. Cameron and Deborah R. Ettington, "The Conceptual Foundations of Organizational Culture," *Higher Education: Handbook of Theory and Research, Volume V*, John C. Smart, ed. (New York: Agathon, 1988), 356–396; Robert Quinn and John Rohrbaugh, "A Spatial Model of Effectiveness Criteria: Toward a Competing Values Approach to Organizational Analysis," *Management Science* 29 (1983): 367–374.

13. Kim S. Cameron, "Effectiveness as Paradox: Conflict and Consensus in Conceptions of Organizational Effectiveness," *Management Science*, 32 (1986); 550–552; Kim S. Cameron, "Measuring Organizational Effectiveness in Institutions of Higher Education," *Administrative Science Quarterly* 23 (1978): 627–630; John C. Smart and Russell E. Hamm, "Organizational Effectiveness and Mission Orientations of Two-Year Colleges," *Research in Higher Education* 34(4) (1993a): 495–499.

14. Min Z. Carter, Achilles A. Armenakis, Hubert S. Field, and Kevin W. Mossholder, "Transformational Leadership, Relationship Quality, and Employee Performance During Continuous Incremental Organizational Change," *Journal of Organizational Behavior* 34(7) (2013): 953.

15. Ronald G. Ehrenberg, "American Higher Education in Transition," *The Journal of Economic Perspectives* 26(1) (2012): 195; David Swanger, "Innovation in Higher Education: Can Colleges Really Change?" White Paper, Fulton-Montgomery Community College, New York, June 2016, 4–7. https://www.fmcc.edu/about/files/2016/06/Innovation-in-Higher-Education.pdf.

16. William J. Lowe, "Can Business Learn from Higher Education," *Change* 32(2) (2000): 4.

17. Roy Suddaby and William M. Foster, "History and Organizational Change," *The Journal of Management* 43(1) (2017): 20.

18. Cameron, "Effectiveness as Paradox," 550–552; John C. Smart, George D. Kuh, and William G. Tierney, "The Roles of Institutional Cultures and Decision Approaches in Promoting Organizational Effectiveness in Two-Year Colleges," *The Journal of Higher Education* 69(3) (1997): 261–264; John C. Smart and Russell E. Hamm, "Organizational Culture and Effectiveness in Two-Year Colleges," *Research in Higher Education* 34(1) (1993b): 101–105.

19. Philip G. Altbach, "Patterns of Higher Education Development," *American Higher Education in the 21st Century: Social, Political, and Economic Changes 4th Ed*, Michael N Bastedo, Philip G. Altbach, and Patricia J. Gumport, eds. (Baltimore: Johns Hopkins Press, 2016), 199.

Chapter Five

Administration, Governance, and Leadership

Major organizational change efforts will not succeed if misaligned with cultural values, but success also requires institutional collaboration during discussion, design, and implementation. Perusing change through an integrated approach rather than an administratively or externally driven process greatly enhances the chances of success. Since the terms *administration*, *governance*, and *leadership* are often used incorrectly or synonymously, they are operationalized within this publication as follows:

- Administration—The executive team tasked with accountability over departments, divisions, and units at the college. The major responsibilities for this group include budgeting, personnel, planning and operations, and general institutional oversight.
- Governance—Formal, codified recommending and/or decision-making entities in and outside of the college. The external body is the lay board (i.e., Board of Trustees, Board of Regents) while internal governance bodies include college councils, academic senates, staff senates, student government associations, and in some cases faculty and staff unions.
- Leadership—Individuals involved in direction setting and decision making without consideration for title or formal, codified structures and processes. The more flexible the decision-making structure at the college (i.e., clan and adhocracy culture types), the more individuals within the college who are recognized, acknowledged, and empowered as leaders are encouraged and expected to provide leadership.

Administration

The role of administration is critical in the design and implementation of the CCBM. Academic institutions, as indicated in the previous chapter, are

Centralization of Decision Making

⟵————————●————————⟶

Administratively　　　　　　　　　　　　　　　　　　　　Shared
Driven　　　　　　　　　　　　　　　　　　　　　　　　　Governance

Standardization of Behaviors

⟵————————●————————⟶

Shared Norms　　　　　　　　　　　　　　　　　　　　　Individualism
and Mores

Formalization of Policies

⟵————————●————————⟶

Official Policies　　　　　　　　　　　　　　　　　　　　Codified
　　　　　　　　　　　　　　　　　　　　　　　　　　　Practices

Specialization of Decision Making

⟵————————●————————⟶

Central　　　　　　　　　　　　　　　　　　　　　Interdepartmental/
Governance　　　　　　　　　　　　　　　　　　　Interdivisional

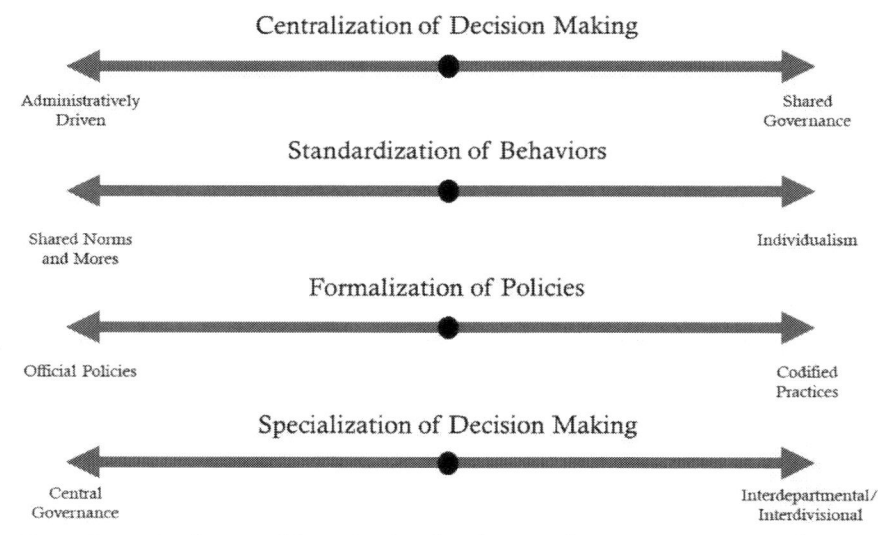

Figure 5.1. Continuum of Organizational Business and Management Approaches

not monolithic entities however, and it is imperative that the college administration understands the institution's unique cultural dynamics. To ensure that the change management process is successful, senior leaders must understand the various operational vectors that guide how colleges experience and expect change.[1] These vectors indicate college-wide expectations regarding decision making, organizational behaviors, and the formalization of policies. Figure 5.1 provides a representation of the vector continuum that helps bridge culture and management.

Centralization refers to the degree to which decisions are made by senior administrators. The degree of commitment to innovation, belief in the vision of the college, and willingness to engage in change processes are impacted by cultural expectations and alignment of administrative behaviors with the culture. Standardization reflects the degree to which shared norms or individual beliefs shape behavior. Administrative practice must utilize an approach that identifies and addresses concerns from both individual and group perspectives.

Formalization represents the degree to which formal policies guide daily operations. Administration must be aware as to whether formal policies or codified practices primarily govern activities at the college, division, departmental, and unit level. Specialization reflects the degree to which the decision-making structures are integrated. College culture dictates expectations as to whether decision making lives primarily in the formal governance structure or through interdepartmental and interdivisional interactions.

While each of the subcultures within the community college impact, and are impacted by, the overall college culture, the senior administration is held responsible and accountable for the state of the institutional culture. This team must embrace the responsibility of making the case for, and maintaining, the momentum of the development of the community college business model. This group, more than any other, must possess an understanding of cultural values, but also a deep awareness of the campus climate.

Even if the change process is initiated in a manner congruent with overall expectations and understood values, failing to account for the institutional temperature and readiness for change hinders success. This team cannot abdicate the responsibility to assess and enhance the morale and climate of the college. Whereas faculty and staff are on the frontlines of student learning and supporting the learning environment, senior managers are tasked with consistently evaluating college direction, performance, and organizational health.

Given this responsibility, it is the duty of this group to introduce strategic and operational principles into their divisions and units. By doing so, individuals throughout the college gain the opportunity to understand how their positions directly impact the delivery of an exceptional educational student experience. It is important to remember that "senior leaders must be cognizant of connecting change efforts to leaders at all levels in the organization."[2]

In leading change, the first tactic is to determine the scale of change. The scale of change determines the scale of the representation required. If the change impacts the overall college community, as when designing and implementing the CCBM, then the entire college must be represented in the process. In alignment with underlying cultural values and expectations, the "length, frequency, and intensity of punctuations" must be carefully planned for with the need to maintain "a healthy balance between periods of punctuated change and productive equilibrium."[3]

Another useful tactic is to determine the pace of change. Administration must understand not only the feasibility of the scale, but also the pace at which each subculture can realistically adapt. While not linear, this team must understand the culture and align the effort with the mission and values; forge a solutions-based strategy; identify and empower the champions (discussed later both in governance and leadership); support innovative ideas and behaviors; and communicate progress with recognition, appreciation, and celebration.

The administrative team should also utilize an abundance approach when engaging the college in change efforts.[4] This refers to resourcing change through the use of strengths-based philosophies and actions that encourage creativity in establishing needed change resources. Financial resources have become increasingly scarce; however, a college can work "to nurture an organizational mind-set of growth and abundance—an approach centered on what is working well and a belief that the necessary resources can be acquired through collaboration, creativity, and focused effort."[5]

While there is no substitute for additional funding, community colleges have demonstrated the ability to leverage through stretch, strategic reprioritization, and mission-based resource allocation. The ability to inspire, model, and grow this mindset is key in finding the resources necessary to implement the CCBM. The administration must work to build investment in a process designed to improve the overall educational experience of the student, not to secure buy-in for administrative planning and restructuring of priorities.

GOVERNANCE

Although the unique governance structures within community colleges differ, three primary groups responsible for ensuring that the professional bureaucracy is functional and effective exist. The degree to which these groups engage as partners in the governance process determines the degree to which governance is experienced as a shared practice. Governance that is shared in action, not simply in title, leads to more effective discussion, design, development, and implementation. These essential groups are as follows:

- Board of Trustees—Charged as "the steward of public trust responsible for ensuring that the assets (financial, reputational, and physical) are safeguarded," this body is the final decision-making entity for policy matters at the college. They can be appointed or elected and represent institutions, systems, or all higher education entities within states. Their primary responsibilities are financial stewardship and presidential review, but using subcommittees and connections with the college, they can contribute to the overall effectiveness of the college as members of the greater college community.[6]
- College Executive—Charged with the day-to-day running of the institution, the chief executive officer (i.e., president, chancellor, provost, etc.) is ultimately responsible for the effectiveness of all operational and strategic actions at the college. This individual relies heavily on the senior managers charged with the direct leadership and day-to-day operations of the divisions, department, and units under their purview.
- Faculty Senate—Charged with leadership over academics at the college, this body is often the primary recommending body in regards to academic policies, teaching and learning, curriculum, instruction, academic freedom,

and matters directly impacting departments and faculty. Depending on the structure and the formal governance policies, this body may act in conjunction with college-wide staff and student governance bodies on nonacademic issues that impact the environment for student success.

When considering the development of the CCBM, the board must be involved, but must not drive the process. The board must support the work and be offered opportunities to provide input and review results, but perceptions of board control decreases the likelihood of success. This process cannot be successful and effective if construed as a top-down endeavor.

Working with the board is a key responsibility of the president and appropriate senior leadership. To provide guidance on how governing boards can work to support continuous improvement, the Association of Community College Trustees (ACCT) offers a list of essential principles, many of which are central to development of a community college business model.[7] These include acting as a unit, representing the common good, monitoring performance, creating a positive college climate, supporting and advocating the interest of the institution, and leading as a thoughtful informed team. The board is an essential part of major organizational change, but only when trust and shared vision are present. When this relationship is functioning properly, it creates a partnership that elicits solutions. When the relationship is ineffectual, the board may be viewed as another external interloper seeking to manage college affairs.

To better understand the potential impact of boards in leading change efforts, consider the following five instrumental roles:[8]

- setting the mission and strategy,
- monitoring organizational performance,
- selecting and evaluating the president,
- developing and safeguarding the institution's financial and physical resources, and
- serving as a conduit between the institution and its environment as an advocate.

Crafting and implementing an intentionally designed business model focused on student learning and success provides an opportunity for the board to engage proactively and meaningfully in each of these roles. For example, when the college goes through the next strategic planning process, the review of the institutional mission, goals, and objectives can include an assessment of alignment with the student value proposition. The CCBM can also drive the development of performance metrics (organizational performance), establish annual progress targets (presidential review process), determine the effectiveness of resource allocations (safeguarding resources), and provide data and talking points about institutional priorities and achievements (advocacy).

As a governing function, the college executive refers to the president and their cabinet of administrators. This body is ultimately responsible for approving and evaluating the CCBM, which is designed to align college operations for the purpose of enhancing the value proposition. As the senior managers tasked with oversight over operations and strategic directions, they must adhere to the principles of the model. While the board is responsible for overall financial stewardship, this team is responsible for fully leveraging resources; evaluating and improving the educational experience; and improving the profit formula through cost containment, increased efficiencies, and the acquisition of additional fiscal resources.

The final branch of the standard governance structure is the Faculty Senate. This body maintains direct responsibility over the academic matters of the college as well as indirect involvement over the policies, practices, and mechanisms that impact enrollment, retention, and student support. As a body tasked with representing the faculty and ensuring a venue for vigorous debate from discipline specialists and academic professionals, this group must be directly involved with the development of the CCBM. It is imperative that the senate play a foundational role in the discussion about business models, participate in the various committees or workgroups charged with building the model, support college-wide communication, and assist in the evaluation and revision efforts. Faculty are directly responsible for student success, and, accordingly, they must be a valued, respected partner in the process.

While governance provides a structure for ensuring formal participation in decision making and direction setting from non-managers, the process of engaging in shared governance is important for college-wide investment in the CCBM. Without a formal decision-making structure in place, the college simply could not operate within today's environment. What is different, however, is that "unlike more traditional hierarchical organizations, where authority is correlated with one's administrative position, colleges and universities are defined by their dual sources of authority—bureaucratic (or administrative) and professional (or academic)."[9]

Moving toward shared governance reflects adherence to a philosophy that the college is most effective when those most directly responsible for student success hold a meaningful role in enhancing student outcomes. The spirit of shared governance reflects this philosophy, and although it formally establishes a bifurcated authority structure, the expectation is that major institutional processes require engagement and collaboration from both the professional and administrative subcultures.

Ensuring an exceptional value proposition requires investment from the administrative and professional subcultures. Central to this shared investment is trust in the motives of the other groups. Trust and respect between the groups is essential for working through the difficult process of evaluating the college's strengths and weaknesses, areas where resources are effectively and ineffectively leveraged, necessary and unnecessary costs, and the programs and services vital to improving student success.

Shared governance does not ensure that business model development will be successful, but is an important factor in ensuring commitment to engaging in a potential organizational changing moment. Many of the core activities and the foundational pillars of the business model approach are already built into the governance documents and processes. By tying all aspects of the development process into existing structures and leveraging the recommending bodies, existing procedures, and opportunities for communication, the relevancy of the process is better understood and greater opportunities for college-wide discussion emerge.

Shared governance is a process that provides a formalized participatory structure for holding the college accountable to involving all subcultures in direction-setting and decision-making processes. Operating from the shared governance approach positions the college to pursue shared responsibility for student success. Shared governance requires participatory management and celebrates the college culture. Colleges must do more than simply comply with the documented, codified procedures to engender the commitment and establish the momentum required to design and implement the CCBM. The institution must recognize, engage, and empower faculty and staff through the adoption of comprehensive, participatory leadership.

LEADERSHIP

Leadership Style and Clan Type

Whereas governance and administration include formal roles, responsibilities, and authority structures, leadership has no such limitations. Governance and administration are positional while leadership is action oriented. Without going into an extensive review of the literature on leadership, the following definitions are provided to offer some additional context:

- "Leadership . . . revolves around vision, ideas, direction, and has more to do with inspiring people . . . than with day-to-day implementation [and] must be capable of inspiring other people to do things without actually sitting on top of them with a checklist."[10]

- "Leadership is a process whereby an individual influences a group of individuals to achieve a common goal."[11]
- "Leadership is the art of influencing others to their maximum performance to accomplish any task, objective, or project."[12]

Each definition incorporates the concepts of knowledge, philosophy, and influence for the purpose of leveraging skills, talents, and commitment toward a common goal. Accordingly, leadership styles have been detailed, researched, and evaluated to provide guidance on encouraging the pursuit of a shared mission.[13] Table 5.1 provides a helpful typology on the various leadership styles along with an indication of which culture types are congruent and incongruent with the development of a CCBM.

Two approaches to leadership are congruent with the two clan types (clan and adhocracy) best aligned with the principles of the CCBM. The democratic/participative approach is based on allowing subgroups to both maintain independence and participate meaningfully in the overall direction of the organization. This approach requires structure and formal authority, but allows for creativity, innovation, and ownership of processes at the subgroup level.

The laissez faire approach also seeks to empower individuals within subgroups to actively participate in direction setting, but lacks the formality and structure of the democratic approach. The CCBM is an operational framework designed to provide a structure for enhancing the student value proposition, so there is a degree of misalignment between this approach and the CCBM. Situational leadership is an amorphous concept, but individuals well versed in the cultural values, expectations, and factors that both enhance and impede organizational change can utilize this approach to bring individuals into the design and implementation process.

Congruence aside, none of these styles are inherently good or bad since leadership is a value neutral construct. It is also important to remember that management and leadership are different. The styles referenced in the table reflect approaches to influencing individuals and subgroups and are bound by formal organizational architecture and governance structures. Although one style was well aligned with the CCBM (democratic/participatory), not all college cultures are primarily adhocracies or clans. Consequently, colleges must determine appropriate influencing approaches based on the unique characteristics of the institution.

In looking at leadership styles and culture types, an example of leadership style/culture alignment is autocratic leadership and hierarchy culture. Community colleges with hierarchy as their primary culture type value structure, formality, and a sense of order. These institutions are not characterized by shared decision making and authority outside of representative governance

Table 5.1. Leadership Styles and Culture Type Alignment

	Description	Strengths	Weaknesses	Congruent Cultures	Incongruent Cultures
Autocratic/ Authoritarian	The lead manager maintains power, exerts influence, and accomplishes goals through talent, personality, knowledge, and reward/punishment.	Compliance Security Efficiency Discipline	Lack of trust Fear Rivalry Suppression	Hierarchy Market	Adhocracy Clan
Democratic/ Participatory	Formal and informal leaders are empowered to participate in decision making and direction setting.	Commitment Innovation Tacit knowledge Strong relationships	Inefficiencies Analysis paralysis Lack of urgency	Clan Adhocracy	Hierarchy Market
Laissez-Faire/ Delegative	Formal subgroup leaders provide direction setting and decision making while the senior manager removes barriers and encourages innovation and creativity.	Independence Freedom Creativity Ownership	No minority voice No accountability Abuse of power	Clan	Hierarchy Market
Bureaucratic	Rules and regulations must be followed and shared decision making and direction setting can occur if built into the structures.	Understanding Awareness Efficiency Stability	No innovation No questioning Statusquoism	Hierarchy Market	Adhocracy Clan

bodies. If formal leaders (managers and governance heads) were to situate informal leaders as official leaders in the discussion, design, and implementation of the CCBM, the result would be confusion and dissonance. A leadership style change would certainly reflect an emergent change that brings the value structure of the college into question.

Conversely, if the primary culture type within the community college is adhocracy, then empowering formal and informal leaders would mirror college expectations. This type of college would anticipate facilitated leadership that provides significant, intentional, and numerous opportunities for input. Here, the dissonance created by introducing an intentionally designed business model would be minimized as a result of the college community's comfort with change, questioning of roles, and external influence. In summary, individuals viewed as leaders must work within the expectations of the culture to effectively craft an appropriate CCBM. Understanding the culture type and the expectations for leadership is important for engaging in this potentially disruptive practice.

Distributed Leadership and the CCBM

Significant empirical evidence has emerged in recent decades demonstrating that distributed leadership is more effective for developing thriving organizations.[14] These shared approaches have many names such as collective leadership, collaborative leadership, and networked leadership, but the common thread is awareness that leadership resides in, and represents, the lived experience of organizational members, and belongs to all who engage in its practice.[15] This approach recognizes the importance of structures and roles while equally valuing agency, tacit knowledge, and collaborative decision making.[16] As professional bureaucracies that value subculture freedom *and* maintain structured decision-making architectures, this approach is ideal for community colleges looking to develop and implement an intentionally designed model.

The development of the CCBM, from discussion through evaluation and revision, represents an opportunity to engage in distributed leadership. In fact, the successful implementation of the CCBM is difficult without borrowing from these distributed leadership principles. This approach requires understanding actions and behaviors as impacting the network of leaders from all subcultures who are intentionally empowered to facilitate change and decision-making and direction-setting processes.[17] The CCBM requires that structures, processes, initiatives, activities, and policies be evaluated against the value proposition and in doing so, requires that faculty, staff, and administrators most directly connected to operations, take the lead. Effective practices associated with the distributed leadership approach include

- empowering individuals by giving them a chance and charge to lead,
- engaging faculty and staff in all aspects of the process so they live out their leadership,
- encouraging individuals to own their leadership practices by developing, supporting, and recognizing efforts, and
- expecting the community to take the responsibility of providing model stewardship.

Distributed leadership was also found to directly impact the effectiveness of community colleges during the development of the community college abundance model (CCAM). This model examined institutional effectiveness based on the integration of positive psychology, positive organizational scholarship, and positive organizational behavior. The central finding was that the community college performance is comparable to human health. The college categories of challenge, choice, and abundance mirror the human vitality categories of illness, health, and wellness. What was clear was that distributed leadership practices were central to success, were required for achieving abundance, and "leadership in abundant organizations begins and ends with people" rather than plans, processes, or structures.[18]

An examination of community colleges demonstrated that effective leadership within abundant colleges reflected understanding and building on strengths over correcting deficiencies and valuing people over process and deliverables. Congruent with a systems approach, managers emphasized networks and collaboration over hierarchal decision making and siloed operations while recognizing leadership outside of formal titles. Formal leaders in the abundant community college

- look at the college as a human community,
- remain committed to developing strategic capabilities,
- reinforce and build on shared understandings that transcend and unite subcultures,
- appreciate and reinforce the importance of accepting unique subculture values,
- act and communicate consistently that people are more than their position,
- encourage and assist members of the college in understanding the importance of the college and its work, and
- believe the primary outcome of education is enhanced societal value.

Another study explored the relationship between the president, senior managers, and faculty and staff to better understand the impact of perceptions of leadership on overall performance.[19] As a result of examining abundance practices, the following were found to move community colleges toward abundance:

- consciously and consistently engaging in positivity and optimism,
- treating the development of human potential as an organizational priority,
- working to ensure congruence between the college and external environment, and
- embracing the opportunity to act as organizational anchor and sensemaker.

Based on the prevalent themes within the distributed leadership and abundance literature, five leadership practices should be utilized by colleges seeking to develop the CCBM. These practices, which are included in Table 5.2, are enhanced by the addition of behaviors, actions, and philosophies associated with the distributed leadership approach.

As noted in the last two chapters, certain culture types and leadership approaches are better aligned with successful organizational change efforts. In summary, the adhocracy culture type has been empirically shown to result in more successful organizational change efforts due to the prioritization of flexibility over central control and greater comfort with external influences. The clan culture, based on the ability to introduce external influences, can also result in more successful change efforts. Implementing the community college business model is a very disruptive process for many colleges and requires greater flexibility in regard to organizational control. Therefore, the leadership type most congruent with this approach is the democratic or distributed approach.

Both the adhocracy and clan culture types are equipped to embrace this style of leadership. Table 5.2 inventories the behaviors, actions, and philosophies associated with successful change based on the distributed approach to leadership. This publication does not take the view that other culture types and leadership styles prevent the development of a community college business model, but rather that greater focus, engagement, and energy will be required. Regardless of culture type and leadership approach, this information is provided as a guide to engaging the college community in the development of the CCBM.

Administration, Governance, Leadership, and the CCBM: Four Hypothetical Community Colleges

Chapter 4 introduced four hypothetical community colleges to assist the reader in understanding the factors leading to the need for the CCBM. Carrying these colleges forward, the reader is now asked to consider the roles of

Table 5.2. Leadership Principles and Practices Central to Distributed Leadership

	Behaviors	Actions	Philosophies
Make People the Priority	Seek investment and commitment, not buy-in	Recognize and reward hard work and effort Verbalize appreciation	The college is a community of people, not a collection of subgroups People are the most important resource
Recognize the Role of the Community College in Society	Understand the importance of external influences	Enhance alignment between internal and external stakeholder values	Community colleges exist to improve society
Value Shared Purpose	Prioritize shared values Prioritize meaningful collaboration	Lead sensemaking efforts Verbalize the importance of the value proposition	All subcultures are equally valued Formal and informal leaders share responsibility for shaping culture
Belief in the College's Capacity for Success	Prioritize human development	Model optimism and positivity Empower informal leaders	The college community has the capability to optimize the SVP
Value Continuous Improvement	Understand that adaptability is central to student success	Prototype changes and scale to amplify student success	Designed change is central to thriving Dissonance is a necessary condition for innovation

administration, governance, and leadership in introducing the CCBM to the college community. The narrative is consistent, but has been shortened with new, targeted questions designed to challenge the reader in determining how each body can, and should, provide leadership over initiation of the process.

Clan Culture (Flexible, Internal) —
Commonwealth Community College (CCC)

CCC is a rural community college with an enrollment of six thousand five hundred students. Located centrally in Jackson County, the institution is the primary feeder for three colleges and the majority of students are enrolled in traditional transfer programming. The president, who has led the college for three decades has utilized a distributed leadership approach to allow more voices in the direction-setting and decision-making processes at the institution. The primary areas of focus during his tenure have been improving the student experience, maintaining a culture of care, and operating as a center of learning for the community.

The enrollment has remained relatively steady, the transfer program is highly valued, and the college is recognized as one of the top places to work in the state. The lack of crises have created an environment where the majority of faculty and staff are long-tenured, cultural values are extremely well established, and the lack of urgency or new voices has created a complacent environment. Although the community is welcome on campus, the college is insular in its thinking, planning, and operations and rarely considers the impact of the external environment.

As a result of the lack of connection to the community and awareness of external changes, two proprietary colleges have opened in the county. These institutions are career focused and are charging a much higher tuition rate. While the college has yet to experience major enrollment declines as a result of the new institutions, some faculty, staff, and administrators are beginning to voice concerns about the presence of these institutions. Questions are beginning to emerge about whether the college should attempt to compete within the same academic space. As a result, meetings at the college are becoming more spirited since the terms *competitor*, *workforce*, and *economic development* are being discussed for the first time.

Based on the information provided and the culture type, consider the following:

- What actions should the college administration take to initiate the process of developing the CCBM?

- What actions should the Board of Trustees and the Faculty Senate take to initiate the process of developing the CCBM?
- What factors *facilitate* the involvement of the college community, who are not part of the administration or governance leadership?
- What factors *inhibit* the involvement of the college community, who are not part of the administration or governance leadership?

Adhocracy Culture (Flexible, External) — Vicissitude College (VC)

Located in a middle class county situated thirty miles outside a major commercial center, VC serves more than forty thousand credit and noncredit students on multiple campuses and in centers across the county. Under the leadership of Dr. Yonda, the college has engaged in democratic leadership principles highlighted by an extensive shared governance process that not only requires representative participation, but has codified significant opportunities for college-wide input on major change efforts. At the center of these changes is the philosophy that student learning and success are institutional priorities and that all students must be provided with an exceptional education.

The college is a vital partnership hub within the community as it works with and has connected K–12, other higher education providers, and the business community. Accordingly, VC has to not only provides greater opportunities for students, but has also positively impacted the economic well-being of the county. As a result of the institution's comfort in interacting with the external environment, the college engages in continual assessment and evaluation process and maintains shortened planning timeframes to enhance flexibility.

Recent reporting, however, indicates that the hard-charging nature of the college may be having some unintended consequences. First, there are concerns that the college is creating an environment where certain student groups are realizing greater success than others. Second, faculty and staff are questioning whether or not the college is drifting away from its mission and does not fully understand the purpose of all the partnerships. Based on the information provided and the culture type, consider the following:

- What actions should the college administration take to initiate the process of developing the CCBM?
- What actions should the Board of Trustees and the Faculty Senate take to initiate the process of developing the CCBM?
- What factors *facilitate* the involvement of the college community, who are not part of the administration or governance leadership?
- What factors *inhibit* the involvement of the college community, who are not part of the administration or governance leadership?

Hierarchy Culture (Control, Internal) — Officialdom Community College (OCC)

Officialdom Community College (OCC) maintains an enrollment of around ten thousand students and is located in a county that is equal parts working and professional class. The president has been at the college for five years and has instituted a more bureaucratic form of management to ensure greater sensemaking and a sense of purpose within the college. Expanding on the historical expectations for strong administrative influence, Dr. Harris has worked with the governance bodies to establish a strong governance process highlighted by a manual that explicitly lays out roles, responsibilities, and expectations. An important element of the plan and process is that formal teams can be convened to recommend solutions for problems that impact operations or the teaching and learning environment.

While the college maintains a rigid administrative hierarchy, the environment is typified by strong relationships and collegiality. Contention is rare since expectations are clear and codified and the president regularly meets with formal bodies and interacts with the college community. An unintended consequence of the internal focus and tight coupling, however, is that the college fails to engage in innovative practices, question the effectiveness of operations, or focus on strengths-building and solution approaches. Based on the information provided and the culture type, consider the following:

- What actions should the college administration take to initiate the process of developing the CCBM?
- What actions should the Board of Trustees and the Faculty Senate take to initiate the process of developing the CCBM?
- What factors *facilitate* the involvement of the college community, who are not part of the administration or governance leadership?
- What factors *inhibit* the involvement of the college community, who are not part of the administration or governance leadership?

Market Culture (Control, External) — Exchange Community and Technical College (ECTC)

ECTC is a large, urban community and technical college with the mission of providing transfer and terminal degree programs in career-oriented fields and workforce development training. Under the direction of Dr. Peterson for the last decade, the enrollment of the college has grown by more than 50% with the addition of numerous academic programs, credentials, and workforce contracts. Dr. Peterson is a fixture in the community and, accordingly she has established a hierarchal management structure where the vice presidents run the daily operations and report to the executive vice president for operations. The president meets with her cabinet to receive insights, but rarely spends more than one or two days a week on campus.

The focus of the college is to ensure that the service area continually maintains an educated and well-prepared workforce to ensure economic growth and stability. The college has been structured to meet these needs with academic programming that is career, rather than transfer, focused; a heavy dependence on adjunct faculty members active in the fields they teach; powerful industry advisory panels; and requirements for cabinet members to sit on local boards. While the majority of students do not transfer directly into four-year colleges, those earning AA degrees do transfer at high rates and non-transferring students graduate, obtain credentials, and obtain career-aligned jobs at very high rates. Despite these successes, some unintended consequences of Dr. Peterson's approach are that the college community does not know who she really is, there is low morale and a disjointed campus climate, and questions are emerging about student success beyond the first job they obtain after leaving ETCC. Based on the information provided and the culture type, consider the following:

- What actions should the college administration take to initiate the process of developing the CCBM?
- What actions should the Board of Trustees and the Faculty Senate take to initiate the process of developing the CCBM?
- What factors *facilitate* the involvement of the college community, who are not part of the administration or governance leadership?
- What factors *inhibit* the involvement of the college community, who are not part of the administration or governance leadership?

CONCLUSION

Administration, governance, and leadership each play a significant role in leading community colleges. While roles and responsibilities are different, each have a duty to enhance the educational experience of the students. The CCBM provides a framework for aligning all aspects of the college toward this goal. It is up to the administration and governance bodies to provide an environment where individuals outside of formal positions of influence or authority can utilize their informal influence and participate meaningfully in decision making and direction setting.

At this point in the publication, the concept of the CCBM has been introduced, the challenges of the higher education industry have been provided, the difficulties of managing organizational change efforts have been discussed, and the role of culture and leadership in change have been explored. The final section of the book provides an examination of the four pillars of the CCBM—the student value proposition, key resources, delivery of the product, and profit formula. With this introductory material provided and substantial context offered, the reader is now asked to delve into the development of an intentionally designed business model.

NOTES

1. Beth Rubin, "University Business Models and Online Practices: A Third Way," *Online Journal of Distance Learning Administration* 25(1) (2013).

2. Randall VanWagoner, *Competing on Culture: Driving Change in Community Colleges* (Lanham, MD: Rowman and Littlefield, 2018), 70.

3. VanWagoner, *Competing on Culture*, 71–72.

4. Christopher Shults, "The Impact of Presidential Behaviors on Institutional Movement toward Greater Abundance in Community Colleges: An Exploratory Study." PhD dissertation, University of Michigan, 2009; Christopher Shults, "Making the Case for a Positive Approach to Improving Organizational Performance in Higher Education Institutions," *Community College Review* 36(2) (2008); Richard Alfred, Christopher Shults, Ozan Jacquette, and Shirley Strickland, *Community Colleges on the Horizon: Challenge, Choice, or Abundance* (Lanham, MD: Rowman and Littlefield, 2009).

5. VanWagoner, *Competing on Culture*, 75.

6. Peter D. Eckel and Adrianna Kezar, "The Intersecting Authority of Boards, Presidents, and Faculty: Toward Shared Leadership," *American Higher Education in the 21st Century: Social, Political, and Economic Changes*, 4th ed., Michael N. Bastedo, Philip G. Altbach, and Patricia J. Gumport, eds. (Baltimore: Johns Hopkins Press, 2016), 156.

7. Association of Community College Trustees, "A Guide to the Election and Appointment of Community College Trustees." Accessed June 24, 2019. https://www.acct.org/article/guide-election-and-appointment-community-college-trustees.

8. Richard P. Chait, William P. Ryan, and Barbara E. Taylor, *Governance as Leadership: Reframing the Work of Nonprofit Boards* (Hoboken, NJ: Wiley, 2004), 14.

9. Eckel and Kezar, "The Intersecting Authority," 170.

10. Warren G. Bennis, *On Becoming a Leader* (New York: The Perseus Book Group, 1989), 139.

11. Peter G. Northhouse, *Leadership: Theory and Practice* (Thousand Oaks, CA: Sage, 2007). 3.

12. William A. Cohen, *The Art of the Leader* (Englewood Cliffs, NJ: Prentice Hall, 1990), 9.

13. Muhammad Saqib Khan, Irfanullah Khan, Qamar Afaq Qureshi, and Hafiz Muhammad Ismail, et al., "The Styles of Leadership," *Public Policy and Administration Research* 5(3) (2015): 87–91.

14. Northouse, *Leadership*, 241–268; James P. Spillane, *Distributed Leadership* (San Francisco: Jossey-Bass, 2006).

15. Richard Bolden, "Distributed Leadership in Organizations: A Review of Theory and Research," *International Journal of Management Reviews* 13(3) (2011): 251–269; Peter Gronn, "Distributed Leadership as a Unit of Analysis," *The Leadership Quarterly* 13(4) (2002): 423–451.

16. James P. Spillane and John B. Diamond, "Taking a Distributed Perspective," *Distributed Leadership in Practice*, James P. Spillane, John B. Diamond, and Joseph F. Murphy, eds. (New York: Teachers College Press, 2007), 189–213.

17. Louis Soares, Patricia Steele, and Lindsay Wayt, "Evolving Higher Education Business Models: Leading with Data to Deliver Results." Report, American Council on Education, Center for Policy Research and Strategy, and TIAA Institute, Washington, DC, 2016. https://www.acenet.edu/news-room/Documents/Evolving-Higher-Education-Business-Models.pdf.

18. Alfred et al., *Community Colleges on the Horizon*, 263.

19. Shults, "The Impact of Presidential Behaviors," 453–477.

Section III

EXPLORING THE COMMUNITY COLLEGE BUSINESS MODEL

This section of the book describes, in detail, the four elements that constitute the intentionally designed community college business model. This publication is not providing nor advocating for a singular CCBM, but rather an approach to effective model development. The purpose is to assist community colleges with the development of a model that addresses and responds to their unique conditions and the elements of culture that drive operations, management, and mission accomplishment.

Chapter 6 builds on the information provided in previous chapters and presents the central query of the community college business model development—what is the student value proposition (SVP)? As indicated earlier, the value proposition for the community college is student learning and success and is reflected by an optimized educational experience. This chapter explores how the community college defines its SVP based on its mission, with consideration given to changing conditions, culture, leadership approaches, and involvement from invested stakeholders. The primary goal is to lead community colleges into deeper analyses of student needs and what the value proposition means for the different student populations served.

Chapter 7 addresses the key resources required to deliver an exceptional educational experience to students, which include human, physical, and intellectual resources. Human resources refer to the faculty and staff who engage students inside and outside the classroom as well as those who either directly or indirectly support the environment for student learning. Physical resources are the tangible elements of the college that directly impact the student experience and include facilities, grounds, physical space, and technology. Finally, intellectual resources include tacit knowledge and the partnerships that exist to support the student value proposition.

All businesses deliver a product and the community college is no different. The product delivered by the community college is the students' educational experience and Chapter 8 examines the three components that constitute the experience: mechanisms, processes, and structures. *Mechanisms* are perceptible aspects of the student experience and include academic departments, majors, facilities, and student support offices. *Processes* represent the actions and activities that occur within the mechanisms such as teaching, tutoring, counseling, and career service support. Finally, *structures* support the functioning of the units and departments at the college and include assessment and evaluation, planning, and computing systems. Each area influences, directly or indirectly, the student educational experience and the CCBM provides an integrative framework with the goal of optimizing the experience.

Chapter 9 addresses the issue of financial resources, which includes both costs and revenue, through an examination of the profit formula. Profit, within social businesses, reflects the margins or fiscal slack necessary to deploy financial resources into the areas of the business most connected with the value proposition and the product. This formula incorporates lessons from Baumol's cost disease to understand the need for cost control and containment, and the strategic redeployment of fiscal assets, and creative and innovative revenue generation. The other side of the equation, *resource generation*, is also addressed and the chapter offers caution in continuing to count solely on traditional revenue streams for financing. Community colleges must find new and differentiated revenue sources because delivering an exceptional educational experience requires capital and necessary funding will not come solely from decreasing expenditures.

Chapter Six

The Student Value Proposition

Business model development begins with understanding the customer. This entails understanding who they are, their needs, and how to effectively meet expectations. For-profit organizations have thrived, survived, or failed based on value provided to customers and, accordingly, have spent tremendous effort in gathering information and adjusting operations to meet customer demand. When considering the development of a community college business model, however, colleges do not serve customers. While students at times interact transactionally with the college and expect service that mirrors their experiences outside the colleges, colleges do not exist to sell students a good, service, or product. Students do pay for services at the college, but it is as a consumer of the educational experience, not as a customer. While transactions occur, the relationship between the college community of faculty, staff, and administrators is not transactional.

A major aspect of the student educational experience is the degree to which commitment to teaching and service, investment in their well-being, and genuine care are operationalized. Delivering an exceptional product requires colleges to truly understand their students, especially their needs, expectations, and the degree to which these expectations are met. The development and implementation of an effective business model is premised on delivering optimal value through an exceptional educational experience that leads to enhanced student success.

While the business model "describes the rationale of how an organization creates, delivers, and captures value," it is helpful to think of it as "a blueprint for a strategy to be implemented through organizational structures, processes, and systems."[1] The intentionally designed community college business model is a framework that focuses on understanding, developing, and evaluating the human, physical, and technological resources; processes, systems, and support; and financial viability and health required to optimize the value offered to students. In considering the business and higher education literature on the subject, the following information is offered for the community college student value proposition (SVP):

> The SVP represents the value provided to students as a result of their engagement in the educational opportunities provided by the college. While each college needs to come up with a unique definition, the definition should be a culturally relevant statement about student learning and the achievement of positive student outcomes. *For this publication, the SVP is defined as enhanced student learning and student success.*

This chapter begins the process of developing a model based on a deeper understanding of students, their needs, and the problems they encounter.

When working to understand who the business is serving, two questions should start the conversation: For whom are we creating value? and who are our most important customers? In operationalizing these questions for the community college, they can be reworded and conceptualized as follows:[2]

- Based on our mission, which student populations are we focused on creating value for?
- Which student populations are the community college focused on serving?

This second question may seem inappropriate to some given that the traditionally understood role of the community college is to be all things to all people. This chapter is not suggesting that some student groups should be served and others should not. On the contrary, the philosophy underpinning this question is that not all students can be effectively served by taking a singular approach.

In developing and implementing a business model, the community college must move beyond the concept of "student" as a monolithic group and, instead, understand that students are individuals and members of different segments with different needs. Students are not homogenous, so the value proposition cannot be either. The needs of the community college student are as varied as the demographics within the groups.

When considering students participating in a traditional academic program at a community college—whether through concurrent enrollment; developmental education; or coursework for a certificate, degree, or transfer—the primary beneficiary of the value provided is the student, and the secondary beneficiary is the college. When considering coursework provided for the purposes of contract training, continuing education, or workforce development, the primary beneficiary of the value provided is the student, but important secondary beneficiaries besides the college include the various affiliated external stakeholders (companies, community-based organizations, governmental bodies). When considering the community outreach mission, the access to college expertise, programming, facilities, and learning opportunities provided to members of the community make them the primary beneficiary of the value; however, both the college and the community reap tangible and intangible benefits through the programming, networking, and increased good will.

To address the question about which student populations the community college is focused on serving, it is important to subset student population so that the student value proposition can also be subset. Customer segmentation, which is referred to as "student segmentation" in the CCBM, is a construct that helps businesses classify the various customers (students) into groups that maintain and display "common needs, common behaviors, and other attributes."[3]

In examining the classification of segmentation approaches, the one that fits the higher education industry best is segmentation as opposed to mass market, niche, diversified, or multisided approaches. The segmented classification is appropriate when attempting to "distinguish between . . . segments with slightly different needs and problems."[4] While similarities exist between the different student segments, the specific inputs, needs, desires, and expectations of each group reflect nuanced populations. Table 6.1 offers a comparison of different students with different occupations, interactions with the college, and expectations to address this point.

The decision to identify each of the individuals as a community college student was intentional. While community colleges recognize that they serve multiple populations, often the greater, if not sole focus, is on students who are matriculating within academic programs. While understandable from a historical perspective, building out a relevant and effective CCBM requires consideration of the educational experience of all students. With the presentation of fictionalized students from different student populations offered, along with their expectations, the focus shifts to addressing what value looks like for each student group.

To effectively answer this question, community colleges need to consider a series of other questions that address the overarching value propositions. In contextualizing value for the community college student, the following four questions are provided:

- What benefits do we deliver to our students?
- Which of our students' problems are we helping to solve?
- Which student needs are we meeting?
- What services are we offering to each student segment?

Table 6.1. College Expectations by Different Student Populations

	Descriptors	Occupation	Interaction	Expectations
Mary	Seventeen-year-old honors high school student	Community college and high school student	Taking concurrent college courses to earn college credit	Complete at least twenty credits while in high school before attending a four-year college
James	Eighteen-year-old recent high school graduate	Student with two part-time jobs	In his second semester, took two developmental courses and has a 2.0 GPA	Complete associates in criminal justice in two years and transfer to a four-year college
Anna	Twenty-three-year-old second generation American	Student with one part-time job	In her fourth semester and changed majors; has a 3.2 GPA and forty-five credits	Obtain a paid internship, finish her degree next semester, and transfer to a four-year college
Charles	Thirty-seven-year-old with a BS in radiology	Student and full-time radiology technician	Enrolled in nursing night program and in his second semester earning college credit	Academic support, caring faculty, and immediate employment
Sally	Sixty-two-year-old daycare owner without a degree	Student and full-time daycare owner	Attends academic talks and sends staff for certifications	Gain new knowledge and use training opportunities
Frank	Fifty-year-old computer programmer with a BS in CIS	Student and full-time programmer in a large IT company	Taking computer courses in continuing education	Obtain Apple Swift certification and complete the Apple Python boot camp
Monica	Forty-three-year-old manager at the local credit union	Student and full-time bank manager	One of fifteen students from local non-profits taking a customer service course	Enhance her knowledge about customer service and improve her managerial skills

Table 6.2. Benefits, Student Problems, and Student Needs by Mission Type

	Benefits Delivered	Problems to Be Solved	Needs Being Met
Academic Programming	Exceptional educational experience	Lack of college readiness	Access to higher education
	Affordable education	Food/housing insecurity	Basic needs
	Degree/credential	Lack of credentials	Career preparation
	Financial stability	Lack of exposure to diversity	
Workforce Development	Exceptional educational experience	Local workforce skills gap	Development of new skills
	Credential/certification	Underemployment	Access to educational content
	Just-in-time skills training	Loss of employment	Professional development
	Greater employability	Lack of requisite skills	Local workforce development
Community Outreach	Exceptional educational experience	Lack of community meeting space	Access to knowledge
	Improved quality of life	Lack of access to education	Educational programming
	Connections and networking	Affordable skills training	Meeting space
	Access to content and expertise	Health and wellness issues	Community building

The remainder of this chapter offers guidance on how to address the first three questions while Chapters 7 and 8 delve into the services and product delivery offered. Table 6.2 introduces these concepts by student subset.

Table 6.2 is presented to demonstrate some of the information that community colleges must consider when developing the student value proposition. While a formal definition of student value proposition has been provided, an operationalized definition could read as follows:

> While the student value proposition is student learning and success, an *exceptional* value proposition reflects the community colleges' ability to provide optimal solutions that address students' problems and meet their needs through appropriate and targeted educational programs and services.

What is the optimal response that should be provided to the student? Answering this question requires understanding the depth and scope of the need.[5] To effectively serve and support its students, the community college must know why they are attending, who they are, and what they expect.[6]

This information is essential in determining the degree to which current operations enhance or detract from the ability to deliver value.

In addition to ensuring that the value proposition is contextualized by student segment, the unique mission of the community college must frame the process. While the specific needs of the service area will influence the community college in prioritizing which sub-mission is most visible, colleges typically maintain a mix of academic, continuing education and workforce development, and community outreach. Community colleges are at times asked to be all things to all people; however, that statement is both unattainable and a platitude. Resources are finite, so the community college must effectively deploy resources to deliver an effective proposition.

To develop an appropriate value proposition, however, the college needs to consider both the direct and indirect beneficiaries.[7] The direct beneficiaries are those groups for whom the value proposition is directed. Students are always a direct beneficiary, although not always the only one, and the indirect beneficiaries represent groups who receive benefits based on the students' educational experience. Accordingly, each of the internal and external stakeholders who receive benefits should have some impact on the understanding of the value proposition for each student segment. Consider the following and their role regarding the development of the student value proposition:

Direct beneficiaries

- Students—Students are the most important stakeholder when developing the student value proposition. Understanding the benefits expected is important, but where the student voice is most helpful is in identifying needs to be met and problems to be solved. Students should be provided with significant opportunities to provide direct input about their needs as well as indirect input through surveys and the collection of other data.
- Faculty—Given the unique relationship between professors and students, faculty are in the best position to understand the impact of student needs and concerns relative to organizational effectiveness. Faculty should be integral in developing the value proposition by providing input and feedback and engaging in an evaluation of the effectiveness of the academic program in delivering benefits, mediating problems (i.e., academic unpreparedness), and meeting needs.
- Staff—Community college staff directly impact the ability to deliver an exceptional value proposition. Given that many of the problems and student needs require solutions outside of the classroom, these individuals, like the faculty, should be heavily involved with the development of the value proposition. In addition to providing input, they are content

experts equipped to evaluate the effectiveness of the support mechanism in offering the solutions required for students to receive the benefits of their college experience.
- Business and industry—Workforce partners are direct beneficiaries of the realization of the value proposition through their employees who attend the college. Whether through direct intervention in programming as a result of contracted training or as a result of course taking for obtaining knowledge, developing skills, or earning certifications, the employers reap the benefits of access to a high-quality educational experience.
- State and local government—Economic impact studies show that governments receive incredible returns on investment for every dollar allocated to community colleges. They are a direct beneficiary based on increased disposable income, improved health outcomes, decreasing dependence on social services, and greater tax revenues.

Indirect beneficiaries

- State and local government—Given compliance requirements and regulations, these agencies play an indirect role in determining the value proposition by tracking and requiring improvements regarding retention, graduation, transfer rates, and earnings.
- Local community—The connection between the college and the local community through the provision of programming, access to services, and utilization of facilities increases community quality of life. Additionally, as the college increasingly becomes a partnership hub, it develops the ability to create networks of for-profit, not-for-profit, and governmental agencies that can provide economic benefits throughout the service area.
- Transfer institutions—Transfer institutions play an indirect role in determining the value proposition through joint programming and articulation agreements that impact the academic programming at the community college and decrease barriers for student transfer. Students who obtain associate degrees before transferring perform as well as or better than native four-year college students, so these institutions are often eager to accept transfers given the overall improvements made to their own value proposition.

The community college must consider the expectations of new students, transfer students, employers, faculty, staff, and the public in the development of their model and value propositions. Each group plays an important role, but the community college must never forget that the proposition must remain focused on meeting student needs and expectations and mediating problems.

THE STUDENT VALUE PROPOSITION AND INFORMATION

Establishing the student value proposition and evaluating the degree to which it has been optimized requires the collection, analysis, and utilization of data and information. Community colleges should employ a comprehensive strategy that integrates newer approaches (i.e., predictive analytics, student needs data) and effectively leverages existing resources (student information systems, student engagement data, satisfaction surveys, etc.) to better profile and understand how to effectively serve and support students. Organizational effectiveness requires an optimized value proposition, and the pathway to success begins with reviewing the data.

Data collection and analysis in support of operationalizing the student value proposition beings with an exploration into the metrics of student success.[8] In addition to the standard student outcomes (GPA, retention, graduation), the community colleges should examine a variety of progress-based data points including student opinions and experiences and relevant external data. To ensure broad understanding of the proposition for each of the subgroups, colleges should rely on information from multiple sources as well as both quantitative and qualitative data. The metrics used should also incorporate faculty and staff and appropriate external stakeholders. While Table 6.3 provides information that can be gathered from multiple sources, developing the appropriate student value proposition requires the ability to effectively integrate the information across topics, sources, and data points.

The Student Value Proposition and College Affordability

The price of attendance is increasing at nearly eight times the rate of wages; college costs increased by 260 percent versus 120 percent for all consumer goods from 1980 to 2014, and rose by 213 percent from 1988 to 2018.[9] As noted previously, public funding for higher education has been decimated and resulted in steep increases in tuition, which has become increasingly problematic for colleges and students. "For most of the 20th century, increasing tuition was a reliable [method for raising] revenue because family incomes were rising. When family incomes stopped rising . . . federal and state government [support] intensified by providing basic grants and assistance . . . however, tuition is outstripping that assistance."[10] Standard financing approaches will not allow community colleges to withstand substantial decreases to state revenues *and* remain affordable.

The traditionally underserved student populations are especially hard hit by soaring tuition. "Increasing numbers of students are receiving some sort of financial aid [and] although this action has changed the population of

Table 6.3. Data Usage and Evaluation of the Student Value Proposition

	Data Source	Data Points	Insight from Information
Student Outcomes	IPEDS	Retention rates	Positive results document progress made and negative results provide guidance and urgency on how to enhance the value proposition.
	VFA	Graduation rates	
	NSC	Licensure/ certification rates	
	NCCBP	Job placement	
Student Surveys	Noel-Levitz	Program satisfaction	Information about how students experience the college is useful for determining if needs are being met. Perceptions about the college impact student success
	CCSSE	Student support satisfaction	
	Campus climate	Sense of belonging	
	Opinion surveys	Satisfaction with facilities	
Predictive Analytics	Analytics software	Course sequence impacts	Prior data is used to build a model that allows for the use of proactive measures to increase student success and evaluate the impacts of policy, practices, and processes.
	SIS	Academic momentum	
	LMS	Risk indicators	
	Business intelligence	Utilization of support services	
Student Outreach	#RealCollege Survey	Basic needs insecurities	Data about nonacademic and noncognitive factors that enhance or inhibit student success provide a deeper understanding about student needs and perceptions.
	Focus groups/ forums	Equity and inclusion	
	College forums	Department/ unit cultures	
	Academic/ AES reviews	Culture of care indicators	

students who can feasibly attend, it hasn't . . . made it possible for educationally disadvantaged students to attend."[11] The continued increase of tuition is pricing students out of attendance, thereby precluding from attending the very student populations that community colleges were established to serve.

Traditional thinking about student financing of higher education is that if tuition and fees are covered or community colleges become tuition free, students have no financial need.[12] Many already view community college as free due to "'technical jargon used in the financial aid system today [where] tuition and fees are called 'direct educational expenses' while everything else, including food, rent, gas money, and books, is called 'indirect' or 'noneducational.'"[13] This language miscommunicates the true cost of college and the impact on students and "despite its good intentions, our current financial aid system is failing today's students."[14] Given the students served by the community college, "the current financial model increasingly [is] at odds with much of the population meant to be served."[15] Continuing to increase tuition limits access to higher education for students from the lowest socioeconomic classifications, so where is the value proposition for the students priced out of attendance? If affordability is compromised for the institutions founded on access, community colleges *are not* providing a viable student value proposition and the business model has failed.

Another problem that must be addressed involves basic needs insecurity. "Paying tuition allows students to go to class, but they will fail if they have no books, no pencils, no gas money to get school, and no food in their stomachs."[16] Basic needs insecurity is an insidious barrier to success and an optimized student value proposition enables the college to more effectively address these needs. The SVP is focused on student learning and success, but empirical evidence documents the linkages between academic performance and basic needs insecurity.[17]

Community colleges have long supported the mission of serving traditionally underserved student populations, however, the scale and scope of basic needs has only recently been realized. The Hope Center for College, Community, and Justice conducts a national study to gather information on food and housing insecurity and the latest report—which includes data from eighty-six thousand students—offers the following for community colleges:[18]

- 53 percent of students have high or marginal food insecurity,
- 60 percent of students experienced housing insecurity, and
- 18 percent of students experienced homelessness.

These numbers are not only troubling, but overwhelming. While the report and the center's website provide significant amounts of data as well as potential solutions for addressing student needs, the sheer scope of basic needs insecurity is daunting. Nevertheless, the better we understand our students, the more equipped we are to develop an exceptional student experience that addresses their needs and helps mediate their problems. Playing at the margins and using traditional approaches does not equip community colleges to adequately address these issues. Solutions require a framework intentionally designed to improve student learning and success. It takes a CCBM.

When developing the student value proposition, it is important to remember that each group must have a uniquely understood proposition, but that colleges need not develop a different definition for each subset. One definition can include all students served and the college can detail the needs and problems specific to each student population. By choosing one statement and then ensuring that all student groups' needs are met and problems served, the college is ensuring that the business model is relevant and meaningful. Three of the four hypothetical colleges are provided below to illustrate this point. Note how the value proposition definitions for each college include all student groups, but the needs and problems identified are specific to each subset.

Student Subset Focus—Traditional Academic Programs

Vicissitude College (VC) — Adhocracy Culture,
Distributed Leadership Approach

Located in a middle class county situated thirty miles outside a major commercial center, VC serves more than forty thousand credit and noncredit students a year on two campuses and more than one dozen off-site centers. While the college states that it is focused on serving the top 100 percent of students and avoiding stagnant thinking, student outcomes are not meeting the expectations of the local politicians, transfer colleges, the public, or the college community. Additionally, recent surveys indicate that the rapid growth has left faculty and staff confused about the vision and direction of VC.

The president, with significant input from the faculty and staff senates as well as college forums, has decided to move toward the development of an intentionally designed business model. Labeled as the VC student success model, the college is currently working to develop the student value proposition for students enrolled in the traditional academic program. VC has inventoried the significant amount of available information on student outcomes and student experiences; utilized predictive modeling to better understand pathways for success; and increased outreach through focus groups, college forums, and participation in the national #RealCollege survey.

Student value proposition definition:
VC students receive a high-quality educational experience that leads to increased knowledge and results in enhanced success outcomes.

Primary problems that need solutions (proposition for students in academic programs):

- More than 70 percent of students are placed into developmental courses, but the analytics indicate that students taking one or more developmental

courses have a 48 percent one-year retention rate compared to 78 percent for students taking no developmental courses.
- Around 50 percent of students are first generation, but a recent survey indicates that these students are significantly less sure about their choice of programs, more likely to report feelings of isolation, and less likely to report feeling like they belong at VC.
- Graduation rates have increased by 30 percent over the last five years, but retention rates have declined over the same period. Further study indicates that probation is the best predictor of attrition, which is particularly alarming since 25 percent of the first-time, full-time freshmen entered probation in their second semester.
- Students in cohort-based programs have an 82 percent first-year retention rate as compared to 68 percent for the general student population; however, less than 10 percent of students are currently in cohort programs.

Primary needs that must be addressed (proposition for students in academic programs):

- The median family income for VC students is $42,000 a year compared to the county's median income of $70,000 for a family of four. While the college has been growing the number of paid internships, only around two hundred fifty have been established and the work study program has not been fully leveraged.
- According to data gathered on basic needs, nearly half of the students report housing insecurity, and around 40 percent report food insecurity.
- Students, on average, are working 1.7 jobs, so creating schedules that provide needed flexibility is difficult. VC, however, has maintained a traditional approach to course scheduling and has relatively few online programs and no night or weekend programs.
- Based on the college application and entering student surveys, more than 90 percent of students want to graduate, 80 percent want to transfer, and 75 percent are looking to enroll in academic programs with a clear path to a career.

Student Subset Focus—Workforce and Continuing Education Programs

Commonwealth Community College (CCC)—Clan, Distributed Leadership Approach

CCC is a rural community college with an enrollment of six thousand five hundred students and is the primary feeder for three colleges. Most academic programs are transfer oriented, and the lack of career-oriented programs and workforce development opportunities opened the door for two for-profit colleges to enter the service area. Around a year ago, the president was asked to join the county's workforce and education board, which includes small business owners, representatives from the agricultural and finance sectors, members of the Chamber of Commerce and Workforce Investment Board, both K–12 and four-year college administrators, and local politicians.

The president has been confronted with the lack of workforce development opportunities and the financial burden placed on residents of Jackson County who choose to attend one of the for-profit colleges. He has taken the concerns back to CCC for discussion and after a semester of meetings, the college has decided to begin moving cautiously toward workforce development with a limited number of certificate programs. The college currently has AA degrees in both social work and education and will be developing certificates designed to provide immediate job opportunities as well as transfer of coursework to the associate degrees.

Additionally, CCC has AA degrees in agriculture, outdoor education and leadership, hospitality management, and marketing, all of which can offer certificates applicable to the hospitality, forestry and wildlife, and burgeoning agritourism industries. The college is in the beginning stages of developing a business model to assist with the intensifying focus on career, continuing education, and workforce development.

Student value proposition:
In an environment of care, CCC students access exceptional academic and career-focused educational opportunities that lead to personal growth and development, further education, credentials, and a better quality of life.

Primary problems that need solutions (proposition for continuing education students):

- In reviewing the county's latest economic impact study, more than one thousand residents commute to the next county for employment opportunities that do not currently exist at scale within Jackson County.
- The impact study also indicated that the current return on investment for CCC was $2.25 for every dollar spent, but the workforce and education board would like to see the return on investment (ROI) grow to $3 for every dollar invested.
- Based on reviews of multiple Department of Labor reports, the fastest growing industries within the service area are education, social assistance, agriculture, forestry and gaming, and hospitality and tourism, with most of the estimated growth at the "some college, no degree and postsecondary non-degree" award levels.

- Industry surveys have indicated that hospitality management and tourism companies are interested in relocating some operations into Jackson County given the abundance of opportunities for hunting, fishing, wildlife tourism, and agritourism, however, the workforce does not exist to support expansion at this time.

Primary needs that must be addressed (proposition for continuing education students):

- The college does not offer many career-focused academic programs and lacks a robust career development office, internship and externship partners, and a dedicated workforce/ continuing education function.
- The lack of broadband access across the county has created a digital divide where many students do not possess the requisite technological skills to compete in the marketplace.
- The majority of county residents have never traveled more than two hundred fifty miles, so students have not been exposed to diverse ideas, people, or potential career paths.
- Given the high levels of poverty and underemployment, many of the college students need access to, and support from, social assistance agencies.

Student Subset Focus—Community Outreach

Officialdom Community College (OCC) — Hierarchical, Formal Leadership

Officialdom Community College (OCC) maintains an enrollment of around ten thousand students and is located in a county that is equal parts working and professional class. The college focuses on process over progress and has maintained relatively steady institutional and student outcomes. Formality, tradition, and structure are highly valued and while innovation is not stifled, risk-taking is neither encouraged nor common. The college is generally well respected within the county and has historically been well-supported financially by the community; however, OCC has remained relatively disconnected from the K–12 community as well as business and industry. The college, in many ways, is more like a junior college than a community college.

Three years ago, however, tremendous changes in the political and social climates in the county occurred. As the financial recovery continued to move extremely slowly, residents of the state and county decided to vote in candidates focused on job growth, dealing with increasing health issues, and addressing the lack of educational attainment. Members of the state and county legislatures along with the city council have placed pressure on OCC to better integrate with the community to move the county forward. The college increased outreach to the business community through contract training and working with individuals engaged in career transfer.

What did not happen, however, is outreach to the high schools, adults without high school diplomas, the growing immigrant community, or social agencies to address health concerns. OCC has now been pressured to develop a college preparation program, start a high school equivalency (HSE) program, offer English as a second language (ESL) courses, and provide facilities and programming designed to improve health outcomes throughout the county. While a substantial number of faculty, staff, and administrators are balking at the requests, they are nevertheless considering how to meet these external demands. No discussions about a business model and only rudimentary efforts to develop a value proposition have occurred thus far.

Student value proposition:
OCC students are provided with opportunities to pursue an education that prepares them for college, transfer, career, and life.

Primary problems that need solutions (proposition for students in the community):

- The college does not have strong relationships with the twelve public high schools or charter schools, so the only students in the county with access to college preparation programs are from the private high schools (academies).
- The college has few faculty members with reading, literacy, or ESL backgrounds or credentials.
- Focus groups held throughout the community revealed that county residents are intimidated and uncomfortable with the thought of taking classes at OCC.
- The college has the facilities to engage the community in discussions about health and wellness, but does not have the requisite partnerships to bring programming to campus.

Primary needs that must be addressed (proposition for students in the community):

- In reviewing the county's latest reports, the most recent high school graduation rate was 81.5 percent, which is below the 87 percent state average.
- According to Census Bureau reports, only 84.3 percent of adults twenty-five and over in the county have a high school diploma.
- Census reporting also indicates that the county's population has increased by 4 percent in the last ten years due primarily to immigration.

Nearly 20 percent of the households in the county now speak a language other than English at home.
- State reports provided by the Department of Health indicate that the county ranks last (worst) in the state in the percentage of adults with Type II diabetes, obesity, and heart disease.

Each of these community colleges is in a different place regarding developing business models and student value propositions. In one case, the desire to improve student success came from within the college (VC), while in the other two cases it was the result of external pressure. Even in the cases of external pressure, one institution saw an opportunity to grow and took the process seriously (CCC) while the other (OCC) continues to fight the change. These approaches align with the cultures, leadership types, and histories provided in Chapters 4 and 5. As community colleges move to develop redesigned business models, it is imperative to remember that culture types, cultural values, institutional histories, and approaches to leadership matter.

As demonstrated with the aforementioned hypothetical examples, the student value proposition must be understood based on the student population being served. The value proposition is central to the development of each element of the business model and the next three chapters illustrate its importance. To demonstrate the role of the value proposition in improving organizational effectiveness, Amarillo College is provided as an example of what understanding your students can do for effectively serving and supporting them.

Real Life Case Study—Amarillo College[19]

So how does a community college improve its three-year graduation rate from 26 percent to 48 percent (85 percent) in just five years? It does so by evaluating the totality of its operations to ensure that it is a student-ready institution. It does so by turning a program, the No Excuses Poverty Initiative, into an intentionally designed instrument for deep culture change. It does so by getting to know its students and responding both empathetically and comprehensively to address their needs and remedy their problems. It does so by determining that the college provide every support and service necessary to keep students engaged, connected, and enrolled. It does so by living out a culture of caring where, in the words of President Russell Lowery-Hart "we love our students to success."

Yes, this college loves its students and is not only unashamed to admit it, but has provided national convenings to help other colleges learn how to do the same. To love somebody, however, you must know them, and Amarillo College knows more about its students than most colleges.

Amarillo College (AC) is a community college of just over ten thousand students located in Amarillo, Texas, a city of around two hundred thousand. The institution is majority–minority (55 percent) and no racial/ethnic group constitutes a majority of the student population. The population is also overwhelmingly female (65 percent) first generation (71 percent), and placed in developmental education (68 percent). Additionally, about half of the students receive Pell Grants, one-quarter have dependent children, and 15 percent are married. The demographics provide a surface-level understanding of who AC serves, but it does not offer the insight necessary to impact their lives. Through efforts detailed shortly, the college now understands who their students are. Her name is "Maria," she is twenty-seven years old, a mother with two part-time jobs, and a first-generation student. Yes, they know the demographics, but to understand how to serve her, the college needed much, much more information.

Amarillo College participated in the Wisconsin HOPE Lab survey to better understand the needs of their students and what they found was a scope and scale of poverty that required an immediate and extensive response. Nearly 60 percent of the students had been housing insecure, 33 percent had been unable to pay their full utilities, 25 percent were unable to pay their full rent or mortgage, 13 percent had moved two or more times, and 11 percent had experienced homelessness in the last year. Although significant resources for students through the No Excuses Poverty Initiative and the Advocacy and Resource Center (ARC) exist, AC students are still struggling with their basic needs. So, in this environment and with this level of need, how has the graduation rate increased so much so fast? How has Maria done this?

The answer is that the campus community accepts no excuses, and so AC continues to leverage partnerships, raise awareness in the community and beyond, and encourage collaboration on campus to improve student lives and opportunities for success. An examination of student success some years ago revealed, in Russell's words, "information about student success that was just embarrassing."

He nor the institution were satisfied with the retention or graduation numbers and the decision was made to begin utilizing predictive analytics to better understand the barriers to, and facilitators for, student success. With the reassignment of the Math Department chairman, Collin Witherspoon, into the role of executive director of decision analytics and institutional research, Amarillo College conducted deeper analyses on why students were not being successful.

While the demographics and basic needs information could have been used to explain away the lack of student success, accepting low success rates was unacceptable and did not reflect a culture of caring. Under Witherspoon's leadership, the college has developed an analytics system and uses an early alert system to help guide students to success. The faculty and staff of the college are the main engines of the changing culture and increasing student success. In the classroom and in the support units, the faculty and staff who engage with students daily have developed strong relationships that embolden them to ensure that Maria is receiving the care, support, and services necessary to keep her enrolled until graduation. How did this culture of caring start, and how has the college been able to so effectively understand who Maria is and what she needs?

One of the first steps was to get the college to admit that it did not really know who their students were. Previously the college was a true junior college and served a more affluent, White population that did not need as many supports. By assuming they were serving the same population, the college was "placing judgements that were inaccurate and irresponsible" on its students. Faculty, staff, and administrators made judgements on why students struggled academically, fell asleep in class, did not seek educational support, and dropped out, and when they found out who Maria really was, the "judgements dropped away."

The college was confronted with the fact that the current AC student is one who "needs an advocate looking out for them" and the college community needs to "be patient and be their advocates." The college was simply not structured to serve Maria and rather than trying to tweak the then-current business model, the decision was made to overhaul and redesign.

The decision was made to look at customer service in the corporate world because they were "not going to reimagine [AC] by looking at higher education" due to the fact that "higher education does a lot of naval gazing." Although several companies were examined, the primary company that was used to reframe the college values was Zappos due to the feeling from students that the values were a better representation of what the ideal college would look and feel like. As a result, Amarillo College established five institutional values that are unlike those typically found in higher education, and that is precisely the point.

As explained by Russell, "the previous college values were defined by us and didn't have anything to do with our students." The values, all of which are connected to caring, are wow, fun, innovation, family, and yes. Interactions with faculty and students should lead to a wow moment, celebration and fun are intentional, barriers can be removed through innovative thinking and actions, treating each other as family requires empathy in action, and whenever possible, the answer should be yes.

The college also utilized the Zappos team challenge concept and developed a competition where groups of faculty, staff, and students (integrated) were tasked with solving a specific problem that was linked with one of the new college values. The faculty and staff are invested in, and look forward to, these challenges. By getting to know who Maria is, not accepting excuses for failing to meet her needs, amplifying the student voice, distributing leadership over the culture modification to all subcultures, and looking outside of higher education, the Amarillo College culture of caring was born.

Culture of caring at Amarillo College is about "creating an environment of support where students are seen, loved, and cared for until they have the confidence to succeed." To support this view, the institution has eliminated boutique programs and only directs resources, with one exception, to programs that can be scaled to support at least 20 percent of the population. Whether regarding changes like the eight-week accelerated classes, expansion of tutoring support, or the anti-poverty programs, the goal is to provide as many opportunities as possible as often as possible for student success.

Culture of caring is also about relationships and empathy. For the faculty and staff to truly understand the students, they must understand how students experience the college. President Lowry-Hart had frontline staff go through the processes, including filling out the applications, within their individual units. The level of frustration felt by the staff enabled them to better understand how the students feel and as a result, changes were made, which included access to a coach that can come to financial aid and other offices as a student advocate.

An additional change—and one borrowed from corporate America—is the use of greeters in all major buildings and parking lots during the beginning of each semester to ensure that students are not left to wander. The college also initiated a large-scale student shopper program with more than fifty students. President Lowry Hart notes that the project was so successful that one unit, which never was secret shopped, reported over twenty secret shoppers in one day. In his words, "staff went from ignoring our students to seeing our students and then caring for our students." As an example of how the secret shopper program itself represented culture of caring, each of the individuals received a "scholarship" and the thirty-four who joined the redesign think-tank over three meetings received an additional "scholarship."

Although the term *student value proposition* was new to President Lowry-Hart, he agreed with the concept and indicated that at AC, the value proposition is for students to "walk away with a credential leading to a living wage and to walk away knowing they are loved. It is about the credential and love." Lowry-Hart readily admits that not all colleges embrace the term *love* or, as he has noted, events like "bring your dog to work day." He notes that the culture of caring has been uniquely labeled, established, and implemented in alignment with the historical values, in conjunction with recent modifications to the culture, and based on the words of the students who have been fully engaged.

This methodology is a perfect representation of the intentionally redesigned community college business model. Amarillo College engaged all subcultures in a culture modification process that established a business model which provides access to the key resources required for success, optimizes the student experience, and pursues needed financial resources to graduate students who know they are loved. Many populations benefit from the education, workforce development, and outreach provided by AC; however, nobody benefits more than Maria. She is leaving with a degree, the opportunity to pursue her career, and the start of a better life for her and her children. Through implementing a business model that focuses on the student value proposition, Amarillo College is creating a college that demonstrates a commitment to human development and societal improvement.

CONCLUSION

While many colleges consider the unique needs of student populations, engaging in business model development and implementation requires a structured approach to determine the needed resources, appropriate products, and finances necessary to deliver on the value proposition. Building on the information in the first two sections of this book, community colleges should consider the following when developing their own student value propositions:

- Determining optimal value proposition requires an understanding of potential benefits, problems to be addressed, and needs to be met for each student subset. A singularly focused proposition does not equip the college with the framework to adequately and effectively serve students.
- Regardless of who is being provided with educational opportunities, training, or other programming, the individuals being served are students. Customizing the value proposition enhances the overall effectiveness of the model.
- While the initial pressure to develop a model may come from external pressure, the college—based on culture type, governance structures, management approaches, and leadership—can design an appropriate, uniquely designed business model.
- Colleges should consider utilizing multiple data sources and working directly with students where possible to develop the value proposition. Colleges should also consider how data analytics can be used to target key resources and evaluate product effectiveness.

- There are opportunities and challenges within all cultures and leadership approaches, but engaging in major organizational change that fails to account for the unique history of the college limits the effectiveness of model development.

In summary, the "value proposition [represents] an aggregation, or bundle, of benefits that a company offers customers."[20] Within the community college business model, the value proposition allows colleges to determine the effectiveness of their key resources, key processes, and resourcing in achieving the benefits proposed within the value proposition. The primary and foundational question that must be answered by the reinvented community college business model, however, is also the foundational challenge faced by community colleges today.

How does the community college achieve organizational effectiveness given the particular needs of its students? How is this done in a manner that efficiently makes use of college resources in an environment characterized by greater accountability, intensified oversight, and reduced funding? And how is this accomplished within an increasingly dynamic environment without pricing out students? Engaging in the development of a reinvented CCBM positions colleges to address these challenging and complex questions through intentional design and a focus on optimizing operations. The next chapter starts this exploration by delving into the key resources required to solve problems and meet student needs.

NOTES

1. Alexander Osterwalder and Yves Pigneur, *Business Model Generation: A Handbook for Visionaries, Game Changers, and Challengers* (Hoboken, NJ: John Wiley & Sons, Inc., 2010), 14.

2. Osterwalder and Pigneur, *Business Model Generation*, 23.

3. Osterwalder and Pigneur, *Business Model Generation*, 20.

4. Osterwalder and Pigneur, *Business Model Generation*, 21.

5. Mark W. Johnson, Clayton M. Christensen, and Henning Kagermann, "Reinventing Your Business Model," *Harvard Business Review* (December 2008), 54.

6. Keith Hampson, "Business Model Innovation in Higher Education: Part I," February 2014. http://acrobatiq.com/business-model-innovation-in-higher-education-part-1/.

7. Louis Soares, Patricia Steele, and Lindsay Wayt, "Evolving Higher Education Business Models: Leading with Data to Deliver Results." Report, American Council on Higher Education and Center for Policy Research and Strategy, Washington, DC, 2016. https://www.acenet.edu/news-room/Documents/Evolving-Higher-Education-Business-Models.pdf.

8. Lloyd A. Armstrong, "A Business Model View of Changing Times in Higher Education," 2014. https://www.changinghighereducation.com/2014/12/new_business_model_view_of_change_in_higher_education.html.

9. Camilo Maldonado, "Price of College Increasing Almost 8 Times Faster than Wages," *Forbes* (July 24, 2018). https://www.forbes.com/sites/camilomaldonado/2018/07/24/price-of-college-increasing-almost-8-times-faster-than-wages/#3744a0a566c1; Abby Jackson, "This Chart Shows How Quickly College Tuition has Skyrocketed Since 1980," *Business Insider* (July 20, 2015). https://www.businessinsider.com/this-chart-shows-how-quickly-college-tuition-has-skyrocketed-since-1980-2015-7; Emmie Martin, "Here's How Much More Expensive It is for You to Go to College than It was for Your Parents," *CNBC Money* (November 29, 2017). https://www.cnbc.com/2017/11/29/how-much-college-tuition-has-increased-from-1988-to-2018.html.

10. Gary King and Maya Sen, "The Troubled Future of Colleges and Universities," *Political Science and Politics* 46(1) (2013): 84.

11. King and Sen, "The Troubled Future of Colleges and Universities," 87.

12. David Breneman, "Is the Business Model of Higher Education Broken?" Miller Center of Public Affairs – National Discussion and Debate Series White Paper, University of Virginia, April 27, 2010. http://web1.millercenter.org/debates/whitepaper/deb_2010_0427_ed_cost.pdf.

13. Sara Goldrick-Rab, *Paying the Price: College Costs, Financial Aid, and the Betrayal of the American Dream* (Chicago: University of Chicago Press, 2016), 235.

14. Goldrick-Rab, *Paying the Price*, 233.

15. Breneman, "Is the Business Model of Higher Education Broken?," 6.

16. Goldrick-Rab, *Paying the Price*, 235.

17. Sara Goldrick-Rab, Christine Baker-Smith, Vanessa Coca, and Elizabeth Looker, et al. *College and University Basic Needs Insecurity: A National #RealCollege Survey Report* (Philadelphia: The Hope Center for College, Community, and Justice, 2019), 20.

18. Goldrick-Rab et al., *College and University Basic Needs Insecurity*, 7–9.

19. Russell Lowery-Hart and Collin Witherspoon, Amarillo College Interview, August 14, 2019; Sara Goldrick-Rab and Clare Cady, "Supporting Community College Completion with a Culture of Caring: A Case Study of Amarillo College." Report, Temple University and Wisconsin HOPE Lab, Philadelphia, 2018, 5–6. https://hope4college.com/wp-content/uploads/2018/09/wisconsin-hope-lab-case-study-amarillo-college.pdf.

20. Osterwalder and Pigneur, *Business Model Generation*, 26.

Chapter Seven

Managing Key Resources

Within the CCBM, key resources are "the most important assets required to make a business model work [and] allow an enterprise to create and offer a value proposition."[1] Put another way, these resources represent the aspects of the organization necessary for the realization of an exceptional value proposition. They are "reflective of all of the tangible and intangible resources, human, physical, and technological, maintained and grown by the business to ensure that the expectations of the customer are met."[2]

Within the traditional business model framework, the goal is not to develop key resources, but rather to build up the resources necessary to ensure value delivery and, in the case of corporations and for-profit entities, to maximize profit. For social businesses, however, key resources have to be framed differently. The goal is to build up and develop the key resources because the value proposition *is* the mission, not profit maximization. Contextualized for the CCBM, key resources include the people, physical structures, technology, and partnerships required to educate and support students as they begin, continue, and complete their educational journey at the community college. These resources provide the college with the capabilities to address problems, meet needs, and optimize the educational experience for the benefit of the students, the college, and external stakeholders.

Key resources can either be tangible or intangible, but what makes them key is their centrality in impacting student educational experiences. Given the scope and breadth of what constitutes a key resource, Table 7.1 details the three categories of resources available, and necessary, to implement the CCBM.

In examining the table, it may be surprising that important organizational assets and artifacts, such as organizational plans, academic curriculum, syllabi, and cocurricular/ extracurricular programming, are not identified. These elements are better understood as *key products* associated with an exceptional educational experience. It is the faculty, staff, and administrators (human

Table 7.1. Contextualizing Key Resources for Community Colleges

	Corporate Context	Community College Context
Physical	The purely tangible assets such as facilities, buildings, machines, and systems that enable the work of the organization to be completed	The physical resources that allow for an educational experience to occur including buildings, classrooms, grounds, and the technological infrastructure
Intellectual	Primarily intangible assets that include brand, reputation, patents partnerships, information lists, and tacit knowledge within the employee base; these resources provide a competitive advantage	Primarily intangible resources such as partnerships, consortia arrangements, brand and reputation, and the tacit knowledge within the college community; when aligned with the mission and leveraged, they provide learning, knowledge creation, and value enhancement opportunities
Human	Employees who ensure that the customer value proposition is enhanced to ensure profit maximization	Faculty and staff responsible for providing the education and support responsible for optimizing the student value proposition and educational experience

Source. Osterwalder and Pigneur 2010.

resources) at the college who are responsible for developing these products, and by addressing resources and educational products separately community colleges are better prepared to develop a model built to recognize, develop, and leverage both.

It is also important to explain that financial resources are identified as a part of the profit formula rather than as a key resource. Finances are generated and expended in the community college to achieve the mission, not to generate a profit. As noted previously, the business model is not a financial or economic model. Discussions about cost, both regarding containment and development of new fiscal resources, are primarily addressed in Chapter 9.

Equally important is the distinction between managing finances and managing key resources. The purpose of the redesigned business model is to prioritize student success, which requires commitment to developing, supporting, and leveraging key resources. Community colleges must be cognizant, however, of appearances that dollar values are being placed on the key resources. While cost containment and fiscal optimization is vital for leveraging overall organizational capacity, colleges would be wise to avoid approaches that in any way communicate that the human resource base is expendable. While fiscal cuts are a reality, community colleges as social businesses rely on substantial investments in, and support of, the college community charged with supporting student success.

Even as community colleges are increasingly challenged by public divestment, the greatest fiscal barrier is the uncontrolled rising cost of operations. The community college business model implores colleges to target and grow support for student learning and success; however, the cost of doing business is increasing faster than new resources are available. This tension, between the increasing costs and requirements to increase expenditures to student success, is addressed in detail later in this publication.

The redesigned community college business model's key resources must work to solve problems and meet student needs. There are three variations of resource deployment that are instructional in considering how key resources can be deployed to improve the student value proposition.[3] These include the following:

- Solution shops—each student population subset possesses unique and either differentially structured or unstructured problems or needs that must be understood before key resources can be effectively deployed to provide solutions. Human resources are the most important single resource, and, as a result, it is up to the faculty, staff, and administration to work together to effectively serve students and achieve organizational effectiveness.
- Value-adding process—Key resources must address problems and needs with the goal of transformation, not simply problem solving. With a comprehensive understanding of where students are when entering the community college must seek to *increase* the equity of student outcomes regardless of student preparedness upon entry.
- Facilitated networks—the development of partnerships is essential for producing the support necessary to implement a successful business model. When the college partners with the secondary beneficiaries of the value proposition, student needs are more effectively addressed, and the college is better positioned as an engine of social and economic mobility.

The CCBM provides community colleges with the ability to utilize all three approaches in deploying key resources.

Without an intense, critical, and intentional focus on developing and leveraging these resources for student success, the business model, even with a well-designed student value proposition, cannot be implemented. Accordingly, the essential, key resources offered by the community college for the delivery of the student value proposition are human (faculty and staff), physical (facilities and technology), and intellectual (partnerships and tacit knowledge).

Human Resources—The Community College Faculty and Staff

Faculty, staff, and administration interactions with students shape beliefs about the college's commitment to their growth and success.[4] Faculty and staff responsible for the teaching and learning environment and support for student success must have a solid understanding of who the students are, and this awareness begins not at the point of admission, but in the preenrollment characteristics that have been shown to impact student success.[5] The most significant factors include the following:

- Cultural capital—As a result of exposure to different educational, community, and familial environments, students ascribe different levels of importance to education. This factor reflects the degree to which students are nurtured for educational success, and college students from lower socioeconomic status (SES) groups often do not perceive the same value from a college degree.
- College plans—Reflective of college preparedness, this factor addresses student understanding about the college-going experience. This includes awareness of elevated expectations of rigor, an understanding of the processes and systems associated with admission and enrollment, and knowledge about the economic return on investment. Given the high percentage of first-generation community college students, these students are less likely to have conducted college planning.
- Academic preparation—In contrast to college preparedness, academic preparation reflects academic study skills, exposure to a rigorous curriculum, access to high-performing secondary education, and academic mindset. Students who attended lower resourced primary and secondary educational institutions tend to be academically underprepared, and this is evidenced through achievement gaps.

Faculty and staff can also discover more effective ways to support student success by learning more about students who have earned their associate degree. In a recent study, community college graduates were interviewed to identify common characteristics of their success.[6] The four themes that emerged are as follows:

- Clear goals—This characteristic refers to how well students have articulated criteria for their success. These goals are not platitudes, but expectations that lead to intentional, conscious actions by students acting as their own best advocates.
- Strong desire to succeed—This factor reflects intrinsic motivation to succeed and is evidenced by sacrifices students make to attend college. This motivation pushes them past obstacles and barriers. These students often

credit and are appreciative of college community members who help them overcome problems and find solutions.
- Ability to manage external demands—Given busy and demanding schedules, students who successfully completed their program avoided academic derailment. These skills reflect agency and help-seeking behavior, both of which are noncognitive factors often associated with student success.
- Self-empowerment—This factor represents internal awareness of one's ability to achieve and succeed. This characteristic is important for students who deal with nonacademic struggles or who are aware of academic unpreparedness. Students with a high level of self-empowerment only need access to the resources necessary for their success.

What is clear from these characteristics is that some reflect skills (establishing goals and managing demands) while others reflect behaviors and attitudes. From the perspective of the student value proposition, these variables provide insight into problems to be solved and needs to be met. Students who are unable to articulate clear goals, do not possess a strong desire to succeed, are unable to manage demands, and lack self-empowerment are less likely to succeed. These shortcomings offer opportunities for faculty and staff to step in and provide solutions.

Although community college students are not a homogeneous group, they are more likely to be first generation, socioeconomically disadvantaged, and from poorer performing secondary education institutions. As a result, they tend to be less academically prepared for higher education and more dependent on members of the college community to address issues of transition and adjustment, academic underpreparation, negative self-concept, and psychological/emotional issues. These issues are exacerbated for Black and Latino students, populations more likely to attend community college and less likely to attain success.[7]

Delivery of the student value proposition requires that faculty, staff, and administrators reject deterministic views of students' chances for success. The support, care, and validation of students from members of the college community are essential to a successful educational journey.[8] In speaking directly with students identified as high-risk who were academically successful, they attributed their success to the following faculty and staff behaviors:[9]

- a desire to connect with students,
- a primary focus on positively impacting student learning and success,
- wanting to make a difference in the lives of students,
- acting authentically, and
- intentionally developing connections with students.

These behaviors referred to both faculty and staff, but the students also identified behaviors specific to faculty. Students felt that faculty members enthusiastic about teaching, those who challenged and supported students, and those who adapted their teaching approaches to students in the classroom most impacted their success. These characterizations were shared by faculty who described their desire to energize and engage students within a welcoming environment. Students also identified behaviors specific to staff, which included commitment, support, encouragement, caring, helpfulness, engagement, and effective communication.

These next sections provide an in-depth examination of faculty and staff members as the most important resource for student success. It is important to note that administration was not included as a key resource for several reasons. The main reason is that the primary role of administration is to work with faculty and staff in developing the business model and establishing the value proposition. Upon development, the role and responsibility of administration is to ensure faculty and staff are supported as the model is implemented. While administration is ultimately responsible and held accountable for organizational effectiveness, this goal is only achievable through the growth, development, and support of faculty and staff. The administration must be intentional and work within the designed model to remove barriers, provide support and guidance, and communicate to the college community. (Chapters 4 and 5 were largely written as a guide for community college administrators as they relates to managing and leading the development of the business model.)

Faculty

The commitment and dedication of the faculty who instruct, support, and guide students is central to their success. When major organizational change efforts and activities lack significant faculty input, an opportunity to build a more informed process is lost. The leadership of faculty during discussions, framing, and implementation contribute to the development of an authentic, effective business model.

The faculty must be a primary and substantial partner in this work because empirical evidence demonstrates that high-quality faculty–student interactions and dynamics are fundamental to student development as they increase sense of belonging, academic development, and personal growth.[10] Evidence also shows that positive relationships lead to improved educational skills and grade point averages as well as increased retention, graduation, and transfer rates.[11] In fact, one study has even documented that faculty and student relationships better predict overall success than student characteristics.[12]

In an examination of national datasets, another study found that significant gains regarding perceptions of student learning are based on active and collaborative classroom interactions.[13] Faculty engagement, encouragement, support, and understanding have all been shown to improve learning and retention. Some effective behaviors include the following:

- Interacting regularly with students—By presenting their authentic selves, faculty provide opportunities for the development of deeper relationships with students, which in turn increases overall commitment toward, and engagement in, their classwork.
- Encouraging engagement with the college community—Positive interactions with faculty help build expectations for greater engagement with faculty, staff, and students and lead to increased feelings of belonging and the development of supportive communities.
- Focusing on increasing academic skills—By creating an academically rigorous and supportive environment, faculty help students develop and strengthen reading, writing, reasoning, and analytical skills, which increases success in subsequent coursework.
- Focusing on higher-order learning—Through the use of activities and the creation of experiences that focus on higher-order cognitive development and growth, faculty members intentionally design a classroom where student learning is enhanced.
- Creating enriching educational experiences—Faculty who cocreate powerful educational experiences engage students in their own learning, help expand critical nonacademic skills, and support personal growth.
- Adaptability in teaching—Through the use of active, collaborative, and culturally relevant pedagogies, faculty connect with students and can develop high-quality relationships that allow for academic, emotional, and social growth.

Central to these effective behaviors, however, is a strengths-based, philosophy regarding to student capabilities and abilities. This approach rejects deficit thinking and takes the stance that all students can learn when immersed in a supportive, engaging, and affirming environment. Students take their cues from faculty, and faculty members who believe in students help students believe in themselves. It is important to remember that

> the educational context created by faculty behaviors and attitudes has a dramatic effect on student learning and engagement. Institutions where faculty create an environment that emphasizes effective educational practices have students who are active participants in their learning and perceive great gains from their undergraduate experience . . . faculty do matter.[14]

In considering how faculty engage with students, formal and informal roles must both be examined. This distinction is clarified when considering the difference between advisor, mentor, and developer roles.[15] While one is formal and designed to help students navigate their academic journey (advisor), the other two are based on deeper relationships. The role of mentor requires an emotional attachment between the faculty member and the student. The mentor–mentee relationship allows for academic, personal, and professional development to all be addressed in a trusting, caring environment. The role of developer is the most robust informal relationship as it involves conversations that integrate academic, psychosocial, career support, and future planning. These roles are all important because each represents a different level of connection with students. As faculty engage and relationships strengthen, the likelihood of student success grows.

Growing, Developing, and Leveraging Faculty as a Key Resource for Student Learning and Success

While growing a resource is not solely about increasing numbers, community colleges must look at their full-time (FT) faculty to full-time equivalent (FTE) ratios. Budget cuts and financial constraints are real concerns for many colleges and the idea of holding these ratios level, let alone reducing them, may seem impractical and unattainable. Research demonstrates that greater student outcomes are achieved with full-time faculty and with part-time (PT) faculty who are provided with resources and integrated into the departmental culture.[16] Colleges must also disaggregate data on student success to understand which departments have had the greatest and least success regarding student outcomes.

If community colleges are serious about implementing a business model intentionally designed for student success, difficult decisions must be made regarding the deployment of resources. Increasing student success requires not only fully engaged faculty, but enough full-time and fully supported part-time faculty to provide the exceptional support outlined within this chapter. It also means holding departments accountable for poor outcomes and working with the faculty and academic administrators to address problems.

College considerations:

- Overall full-time faculty to student FTE ratios
- FT to PT faculty ratios by college, department, and program
- Student success by department/program and student subgroup

Most community colleges support faculty development, however, development opportunities need to include education, training, and structures aligned with student success as an institutional priority. Building on the student value proposition, faculty benefit from exposure to different teaching approaches, classroom management techniques, pedagogies, theories, and literature on culture of care. Many colleges have pockets of faculty innovation, but for the CCBM to deliver an optimized student value proposition, innovation needs to be scaled so that all students have access to the benefits of a supportive teaching and learning environment.

College considerations:

- Provide financial support for attendance at external conferences/development of internal conferences that address the faculty role in improving student success
- Provide administrative support for the teaching and learning center including expansion of programming on the faculty role in student success
- Engage faculty and staff in joint opportunities for learning about developing a culture of care and the role of relationships in student success
- Increase communication so that faculty are aware of, and can share, information regarding support services

Given the importance of the faculty role in student learning and success, the CCBM must provide leadership opportunities regarding the student value proposition. Equally important is the role that faculty play in the delivery of the product (the educational experience, Chapter 8), so failing to leverage the knowledge, experience, and commitment of faculty reduces the relevance and effectiveness of the model. Informal leadership is important and must be recognized, but the college needs to intentionally design meaningful and relevant formalized roles as well.

College considerations:

- Provide faculty with opportunities to lead major institutional efforts (e.g., strategic planning) and initiatives designed to improve student learning and student success
- Examine and change the policies, practices, and procedures that create barriers for student success within the classroom, department, or college
- Develop/expand faculty leadership development programs with a focus on the student experience and student success
- Provide space, time, financial support, and incentives for faculty to develop workshops and trainings for and with colleagues

- Utilize and leverage the appropriate governance processes to embed culture of care philosophies and actions into the academic programs

Staff

Regardless of whether staff directly support student learning, the environment for teaching and learning, or provide administrative and operational support, they impact the educational experience. For those in student facing roles, establishing high-quality connections, listening to students, and adapting approaches are key to enhancing the value proposition. Often these behaviors are described as maintaining a culture of care, which has been shown to improve student success.[17] Students impacted by a culture of care feel respected and heard; perceive that the college is committed to their success; and demonstrate higher levels of social integration, commitment to their academic work, greater persistence, and self-advocacy.[18]

The roles and responsibilities of staff are diverse given the range of educational and student support services available to students. While beyond the scope of this publication to address each area individually, the following provides a helpful classification of services:[19]

- Enrollment management—These are the services focused on enrollment from preadmission to admission, registration, and continuing until graduation. The primary focus of these units is support for the transition from high school to college, managing the systems that track academic progress, and working to ensure retention.
- Learning support—These services focus on supporting academic success, and in collaboration with the academic programs, they provide discipline-based and general support for development of the knowledge, skills, and behaviors necessary for success.
- Student support—These services address the emotional, mental, physical, and societal needs that often derail community college students. Of particular importance is counseling, which, when proactive, significantly enhances student success.[20]
- Cocurricular—Research has consistently demonstrated the importance of providing cocurricular services that establish communities, provide opportunities for high-quality connections, and create climates of productive dissonance.

Outside of faculty, the community college staff who interact most frequently with students are often their advisors. Academic advising has been associated with greater persistence and retention, improved GPA, student satisfaction, and an improved educational experience.[21] One recent study found that centralized advising staffed with trained, dedicated advisors was responsible for significant gains in first semester, second semester, and first year GPA, as well as year-to-year retention.[22] To deliver an exceptional advising experience to the students, consider the following generally accepted practices:[23]

- utilizing a caseload approach to ensure that students get to know their advisors,
- mandating regular check-ins with the advisor,
- providing group advisement to supplement individual advisement sessions,
- ensuring regular collaboration with faculty regarding student progress, and
- delivering both standard and emergent topic workshops and seminars.

When these practices are integrated, advising becomes intrusive and proactive. This approach benefits students by requiring connection, allowing for co-facilitation of academic planning, and providing access to individualized support. This comprehensive advisement approach helps alleviate advisement stigma and provides more definitive pathways for degree completion, increased confidence, and agency.[24]

Whether for advising or any of the other educational, student, or administrative functions that support students, staff should utilize tactics associated with student success. Staff members who work directly with students should incorporate the following actions into their support practice:[25]

- Create social relationships—Staff should assist students in establishing meaningful relationships that create a sense of belonging. Community college students typically have greater demands on their time and often require structured and formalized opportunities to develop the communities so important for persistence.
- Clarify aspirations and secure commitment—Community college students are often unclear about the value of the college experience. Developing goals without substantial assistance is difficult and students left to drift are more likely to attrite when confronted with barriers or obstacles. Staff must help bridge the knowledge and expectation gaps.
- Provide a sensemaking function regarding college—Community college students often enter higher education unsure about expectations, processes, structures, and responsibilities. It is the responsibility of staff to assist students with understanding unwritten rules, institutional culture, and the norms and mores of the teaching and learning environment.

- Assist students with balancing competing demands—Community college students are more likely to have extensive familial, employment, and other life demands not conducive to taking courses, studying, or taking advantage of educational and social support resources. Community college staff must communicate the importance and availability of resources, work to remove the stigma of seeking assistance, and support the development of help-seeking behaviors, life-balancing skills, growth mindset, and agency in support of persistence and overall student success.

Growing, Developing, and Leveraging Staff as a Key Resource for Student Learning and Success

Research has demonstrated that the "commitment of the institution to the welfare of its students "directly impacts student persistence and overall success."[26] The relationships that students have with frontline support staff form the basis for how they experience institutional commitment. Given the importance of staff support, budgetary issues cannot be used as a reason to underfund student supports. The constraints are real and at times severe, but a commitment to a business model designed for student success requires a commitment to supporting the units and staff charged with enhancing the out-of-classroom educational experience.

College considerations:

- Data, both unduplicated and duplicated, regarding the utilization of educational and student support services (e.g., tutoring center, computer labs, writing center)
- Advisor to advisee ratios
- Examination of educational, student, and administrative support unit budgets to determine the adequacy of resources expended in support of the student value proposition

As with faculty, opportunities exist for staff development in most community colleges. Typically, however, these opportunities are offered less frequently than for faculty. Inequitable staff development opportunities communicate a double standard and that support for student success outside of the classroom is not a priority. College staff need to be provided with the education, training, and structures necessary to help them support student learning and success. Staff members need the administration to work with their divisions, departments, and units to provide the tools and opportunities to learn and grow so that they can support student success.

College considerations:

- Provide financial support for attendance at external conferences/development of internal conferences that address the staff role in improving student success (e.g., advisor conferences, tutoring conferences, etc.)
- Develop or strengthen support for professional development from the human resources/employee relations office
- Engage faculty and staff in joint opportunities for learning about a culture of care and the role of relationships in student success
- Increase communication so that staff are aware of, and can share, information regarding support services

In addition to understanding the importance of the staff role in the CCBM design, staff must be leveraged if the model is to be fully implemented. Positive interactions between staff and students enhance student success. Accordingly, they need to be engaged as respected leaders in the development of the value proposition. These opportunities should be structured, intentional, and meaningful for both staff and the students.

College considerations:

- Provide staff with opportunities to lead major institutional efforts (e.g., strategic planning) and initiatives designed to deliver the student value proposition
- Examine and change the policies, practices, and procedures that create barriers for the support of student success within the divisions, departments, and units responsible for the educational, student, or administrative support for students
- Develop/expand staff leadership development programs with a focus on the student experience and student success
- Provide space, time, financial support, and incentives for staff to develop workshops and trainings for and with their colleagues and student leaders
- Introduce statements and procedures that reflect a culture of care within the divisions, departments, and units through the appropriate governance processes

Students

Although students are not identified as a key human resource, they play an important role in supporting their peers' learning and success. While human development is greatly enhanced by peer-to-peer relationships, this is especially true within community colleges.[27] Literature on the topic documents that informal and formal opportunities for peer-to-peer interactions enhance the student experience and improve student success.[28] So, while students are the primary beneficiaries of the value proposition and consumers of the education and services provided, they are also a potential resource in delivering on the value proposition. Some benefits to the student value proposition that emerge from peer support include the following:[29]

- Community—Building peer leadership programs allows for the development of community among students, which establishes social networks, increases sense of belonging, and destigmatizes the need for assistance and support.
- Resource and referral—With so many first-generation and traditionally underserved student populations, these networks provide opportunities for information sharing and guidance. When student leaders are provided with formalized training, access to resources, and information, they become a valuable support for student success.
- Academic support—Peer leaders, with the appropriate training and academic skills, can contribute to the work of educational support programs by promoting and supplementing the work of faculty and staff. Students also experience increased gains in learning and student success through modified academic support processes.

To realize these benefits, however, community colleges must be intentional when designing peer-to-peer programming for academic support, student support, and cocurricular opportunities.[30] A major part of the intentional design must include adequate training and opportunities to interact with, and learn from, faculty, staff, and administrators.

An added benefit to purposefully designing and growing peer-to-peer programming is that both the students being tutored and mentored, as well as those supporting their peers, enjoy an enhanced educational experience. It is important to remember that students gauge the community college's commitment to their success through connections, support, and relationships. By engaging students in the support of their peers as a key aspect of business model redesign, the likelihood of optimizing the value proposition and enhancing the educational experience for all students is enhanced.

Physical Resources—Community College Facilities

How does the college design for the creation and utilization of facilities in support of the student value proposition? Community colleges must consider the range of facilities available to students, which include physical structures, campus grounds, and the utilization/availability of space. They must also understand the ways in which these elements contribute to solving student problems and addressing needs. The student educational experience is significantly impacted through the facilities since individuals live their experiences within physical spaces, but have the physical spaces been intentionally constructed to enhance student learning and success?[31]

Informal learning has become increasingly important for overall student success. The inclusion of open learning and communal space for students has been shown not only to enhance learning, but also perceptions of support for the educational experience.[32] Two organizational characteristics of community colleges that "wield an indirect influence on student departure decisions" are institutional commitment to student welfare and institutional integrity.[33] While institutional commitment reflects perceptions of deep, authentic support for student learning and success, institutional integrity addresses the degree to which students believe that the college lives out its ideals. Students who perceive that the college is committed to their success are more likely to experience a strong sense of belonging and community. Additionally, indications are that as students continue to perceive an institutional commitment to their success at different points in their educational journey, retention increases.

Since facilities represent the most tangible mechanism for experiencing institutional commitment and authenticity, the intentional leveraging of facilities for student success must remain central to the model. Community colleges already have several tools available to determine the degree of satisfaction with facilities and overall use of space. These include:

- nationally normed student satisfaction and engagement instruments;
- entering student, graduate, and course completion surveys;
- college focus groups;
- faculty and staff satisfaction surveys; and
- academic program/administrative unit reviews.

The issue is not the lack of data regarding facilities, but rather whether this information is being used in the decision-making process. Impressions about the degree to which the campus environment, including facilities, communicates a commitment to student success impacts success. Accordingly, colleges must utilize this information and reevaluate impressions after making changes to ensure that campus facilities are supporting the delivery of the student value proposition.

Over years of conducting focus groups for strategic planning and organizational change efforts, one finding continues to emerge. Community colleges rarely understand how the state of the facilities, perceived inequities regarding space allocation, the physical location of student services, and absence of information regarding facilities planning and deferred maintenance communicate a lack of commitment and institutional integrity. Faculty, staff, and especially students take note of the infrastructure, and more importantly, the utilization of space. In a vacuum, these stakeholders come to their own conclusions about institutional priorities. Community college must be more intentional regarding their facilities and consider, through a redesigned business model, how to address the following questions:

- How are decisions about facilities upkeep and deferred maintenance made? What groups are involved in these discussions?
- How are decisions made regarding location of space? What groups are involved in these discussions?
- What departments and units are in the most desirable space? Which are in the least desirable?
- Are the decisions regarding upkeep and space allocation viewed as congruent with the institutional mission and values?

Table 7.2 provides examples of unintended consequences that can emerge when failing to consider the messages sent to the college community regarding the facilities. Beyond bad optics, each illustration demonstrates situations that, while unintentional, do not reflect a commitment to students. These are all situations that could bring the institution's authenticity about valuing students into question. When developing the business model, it is imperative that community colleges address facilities as a key resource.

Physical Resources—Community College Technology

As a key resource, *technology* refers to the electronic tools, systems, and equipment utilized by community colleges to increase the efficiency of operations, ensure the completion of complex tasks, expand access to data and information, and support the functions of a modern institution of higher education. Engaging in the business of higher education would be impossible today without access to personal computers; the Internet; or myriad information systems that allow faculty, staff, students, and administrators to operate.

While a driver of efficiency and access point for better service to students, technology is also a disruptive force that "dramatically shifts business models over time."[34] Technology on college campuses is ubiquitous, and its pervasiveness has created challenges and opportunities.[35] When the college intentionally designs for student success through technology, it becomes an

Table 7.2. Lack of Intentional Design of Physical Space for Student Success

	Situation	Issues	Potential Corrections
Academic Space—Classroom	Technology has been updated in classrooms, but the setup is not conducive to more interactive teaching methods.	The command center with the standard podium and the traditional tables and chairs do not allow for movement of equipment.	Work with faculty and student groups to determine what class setups should be considered during a pilot phase of classroom renovation efforts.
Educational Support Space—Tutoring Center	For thirty years, the tutoring center has been in the center of the main building on campus.	The college has numerous new facilities and many students do not have classes in the main building.	Work with faculty, staff, and students to determine where the tutoring spaces should be located across the campus.
Student Support Space—Veterans Center	Due to limited available space, the newly established Veteran's Center is in the basement of the Student Center.	Space is at a premium, but the veterans are the only student group located on the basement level.	Work with the faculty and staff to examine the current utilization of alternative space and determine if other offices can move to the basement.
Congregating Space—Cafeteria	Given its central location within the primary academic and educational support building, the cafeteria is used to study, hold meetings, and socialize.	Although classes run from 7:00 a.m. to 9:00 p.m. and from 8:00 a.m. to 5:00 p.m. on weekends, the cafeteria closes at 6:00 p.m. during the week and noon on weekends.	Work with faculty, staff, and students to document the hardships created by not having the space open (hunger, access to communal space) and recommend changes through the governance process.

agent that allows the college to enhance "student learning, build a sense of community, increase student engagement, and facilitate communication."[36] As was the case with facilities, this key resource represents an opportunity to build an environment that increases organizational effectiveness.

Fundamentally, technology offers solutions to problems, but the implementation of technology often creates a unique set of problems. Table 7.3 documents some of the challenges that come with the use of technological tools and the opportunities provided by the CCBM to effectively meet these challenges.

Table 7.3. Challenges and Opportunities to Leverage Technological Tools

	Opportunities
The Information Systems are not Effectively Integrated	Implementation of the CCBM will require the integration of the students' information system, learning management system, course management system, and other database systems to provide the information necessary to evaluate and redesign, as necessary, the student educational experience.
Resistance to New Technology	The implementation of the CCBM will provide a focus point for all technology conversations. The college needs to then demonstrate how the problems raised by the campus community will be addressed by the tools along with support and resources for continued training.
Overall Cost of Technological Infrastructure	The CCBM will provide a framework for prioritizing which elements of the infrastructure are central to the student experience, where redundancies and siloing exist, and opportunities to develop economies of scope and scale.
Underutilization of Technology Effectiveness	When technology is incorporated as a recognized key resource within a business model, the necessity of the tools will become apparent and the tools will gain relevance when understood to be a priority.
Lack of College IT Strategy	The business model provides the opportunity to develop an IT strategic plan focused on the deployment of technological resources for the purpose of enhancing the student value proposition.

It is up to the administration and college leadership to ensure effective utilization of technology to improve student success; however, technology alone is never the solution. Rather, technological tools must be effectively leveraged to provide actionable information. When considering how community colleges employ technology, the most substantial element is the computing equipment. This is also among the most expensive technology costs at the college. Computing equipment includes all the hardware, software, and supporting tools that enable students, faculty, staff, and administrators to accomplish their daily activities. Without strong principles to guide the requisition, deployment, and life-cycle management, however, the college is not positioned to leverage the computing equipment for an improved student learning experience. To more effectively leverage these resources, community colleges, in alignment with the business model principles, should[37]

- focus on short-term technology plans that increase flexibility in deploying technology,
- consult with students to better understand their needs and allow for leadership opportunities regarding the use of technology fees,

- consult with faculty on computing equipment and software in classrooms and labs,
- consult with staff in educational and student support offices on technology needs,
- align technology purchases and deployment with student learning and academic program objectives (e.g., laser cutters and engravers, 3D printers, Adobe software, etc.),
- build out the technology support program based on student wants and needs (e.g., mobile computing, 100 percent WIFI connectivity, mobile charging stations), and
- ensure sufficient bandwidth so that wireless networks remain fast.

It is not enough just to have the equipment and infrastructure, leveraging this technology means ensuring that the equipment and systems are optimized to improve the educational experience.

Another aspect of technology that is increasingly important is the student support systems that provide divisions, departments, and units with data and information that guide operations, planning, and decision making. Community colleges depend on the information from these systems to assist students with information on their progress and to respond to external mandates and reporting requirements. The systems alone cannot provide solutions and answers. However, with the proper integration, support, and use of analytical tools, these powerful systems are among the most important tools for improving student success—and the overall educational experience—for students.[38] While not a comprehensive list, Table 7.4 provides an analysis of how the various systems possess tremendous potential to deliver an enhanced value proposition.

Finally, leveraging technology requires a deeper examination of utilization. Technology provides opportunities for learning in and outside of the classroom, and, accordingly, should be understood as a mechanism for providing exceptional learning opportunities.[39] The majority of our students are digital natives and are not only comfortable with technology, but have the expectation that it is a fundamental part of their educational experience. Some ways in which community colleges can leverage technology to enhance the educational experience are to provide opportunities for students to

- work with programmers and content experts on the redesign of the college website or program/department webpages,
- work with faculty and staff on the development of college applications,
- utilize digital sandboxes by expanding the capabilities of technology in the labs,

Table 7.4. Leveraging the Institutional Information Systems to Enhance the Student Value Proposition

	Data Available	Opportunities to Leverage
Student Information System (SIS)	Gender/Race, Grades, Academic Record, Attendance, Financial Aid Information, Admissions Data, etc.	As a result of integration, and with the support of analytics, this system provides opportunities to better understand the entering student characteristics, impact of course grades, and academic behaviors impacting student success. Information can also be used to review the impact of policies, practices, and procedures.
Learning Management System (LMS)	Student log ins, Engagement, Grades, Communication, Learning Outcomes, Assignment Completion, etc.	As a result of integration, and with the support of analytics, the impact of communication with faculty, student engagement, and course participation can be examined to understand the effects on student success. Information can also be used to review the impact of policies, practices, and procedures.
Course Management System (CMS)	Courses Taken, Course Needed, Grades, GPA, Major, Interaction with Support Services, etc.	As a result of integration, and with the support of analytics, the impact of course combinations, adherence to program maps, and gateway/major courses can be examined to understand impacts on success. Information can also be used to review the impact of policies, practices, and procedures.
Enrollment Management System (EMS)	Student Demographics, Grades, Nonacademic Work and Life Characteristics, Communication, Student Progress, Utilization of Support Services	As a result of integration, and with the support of analytics, nonacademic and noncognitive factors, utilization of support services, and effectiveness of communication along student progression points can be examined to understand the impact on success. Information can also be used to review the impact of policies, practices, and procedures.

- participate as leaders or co-facilitators with the college's social media team,
- participate in internships with technology-based companies and entrepreneurs, and
- participate in technology-mediated service-learning projects.

Intellectual Resources—Community College Partnerships

Given the tri-mission of the community college, the pursuit, development, and growth of partnerships is not new. Whether through the development of articulation agreements with four-year colleges, contract training with local businesses, or collaborating with a local non-profit on a community enhancement project, community colleges have long depended upon connections with external stakeholders. And while the development and implementation of these partnerships have certainly focused on mission achievement, they have likely not been guided by an overarching framework focused on the student value proposition.

When viewing partnerships as a key resource, however, the partnering entities are positioned as one of the "cornerstones" essential for "mak[ing] the business model work."[40] Given the essential nature of partnerships, community colleges must ensure that partnering organizations possess shared values, not just shared goals. Any partnerships that do not enhance the college's ability to provide an exceptional educational experience in support of student success should be avoided. Among the many benefits of operating from an intentionally designed business model is that colleges avoid forming misaligned partnerships. By its nature, the redesigned business model guides colleges toward the development of long-term relationships designed to improve the student experience and opportunities for success.

Some guiding principles should be considered, however, when pursuing partners. The three primary motivations for forming long-term relationships include the following:[41]

- Optimization and economy of scale—These partnerships are designed to optimize the development, support, and allocation of resources and activities. Within the community college environment, this motivation is typically associated with reducing redundancies and costs and results in the development of consortia and formalized partnerships with other higher education institutions.
- Reduction of risk and uncertainty—These partnerships are designed to reduce volatility. Within the community college environment, these partnerships are reflected in the establishment of relationships that shield the college from the impacts of, or increase the college's influence over,

political and competitive pressures. This motivation leads to establishing relationships with local and state representatives; gaining institutional membership on civic, industry, and commerce boards; and connecting with K–12 providers and four-year colleges.
- Acquisition of resources and activities—These partnerships are designed to improve access to resources that enhance current operations, strengthen the ability to deliver on the mission, or open up new markets and opportunities to provide services and support. For community colleges, the motivation in raising revenues is to provide greater resources to support current students and identify individuals who would benefit from the college's offerings. Examples include contract training, workforce development, adult and basic education training, dual enrollment, and greater industry participation.

Based on an understanding of the classification of partnership types as well as the three underlying motivations, this publication identifies three types of partnerships that community colleges should consider pursuing in support of the business model. These include educational pipeline, workforce development, and consortia partnerships.

The education pipeline partnership is designed to improve access to higher education and overall student success. This brand of partnership focuses on high school and adult learner access to the community college and transfer institutions. Examples of offerings established through these partnerships include college preparatory training, dual enrollment, articulation agreements, and joint admissions. Each partner receives benefits in the form of improved success metrics and the students, most importantly, are provided with a more seamless education at each transition point. Some innovative examples include the following:

- Northern Virginia Community College (NOVA) and George Mason University (GMU)—This partnership provides community college students entering NOVA with the opportunity to be dually enrolled at GMU. There is only one admission, advising, and financial aid process, and students are paired with success coaches who follow them throughout the process. As a result, nearly half of the entering class for GMU comes from NOVA, and as has been demonstrated nationally, community college transfers are more successful than the native freshmen.
- Prince George's County Public Schools (Maryland)—The Pathways in Technology Early College High (P-TECH) offers high school students the chance to participate in dual enrollment, and, if college ready, begin courses in the 10th grade. In six years, and in partnership with Prince George's Community College, these students can earn two- and four-year

degrees in health information management or hospitality services management with transportation, mentoring from business and industry, and paid internships included.

As a result of changing funding dynamics and an intensified focus on student outcomes, community colleges are experiencing greater pressure to develop certificate programs; enhance science, technology, engineering, and math (STEM) majors; involve business and industry leaders in academic programs' advisory boards; and increase the number of workforce contracts. While the major focus of chambers of commerce, workforce investment boards, and politicians is jobs, reduction of the skills gap, and economic growth, the community college must balance these priorities with the college mission, goals, and values. Some examples of innovative workforce partnerships include the following:

- Central Piedmont Community College (North Carolina)—Long recognized as one of the workforce leaders in the community college sector, Central Piedmont Community College (CPCC) works individually with workforce providers to ascertain short-term and long-term strategies that serve the college, the company, and the county. In addition to the traditional contract training work, CPCC offers apprenticeships, work-based learning/co-ops, and internships that are focused on meeting company needs while also positioning students for long-term economic gains.
- Shelton State Community College (Alabama)—In partnership with Mercedes Benz, the college maintains a formal partnership for a mechatronics program that provides students with both a certificate and an associate in applied science (AAS) degree in industrial electronics. By building a partnership with a large, technologically advanced workforce partner that provides both a certificate and an associate degree, the college, company, and students all receive substantial benefits.

Consortia arrangements reflect the development of long-term relationships with multiple partners and can include higher education and external stakeholders. These partnerships are amorphous, established for varying amounts of time, can be specific to one area of interest, and can be limited to states or regions. Among the main reasons to establish consortiums are to share knowledge, increase operational efficiencies, reduce costs, and/or increase influence and advocacy. Some innovative examples include the following:

- Community College Consortium for Open Educational Resources (CCCOER)—Based on a partnership of more than two hundred fifty

community and technical colleges in seventeen states and Canada, this network is designed to expand the effective use of open educational resources (OER) pedagogy, course design, and student support. The colleges involved in the consortium share best practices, develop capacity for OER materials to reduce costs and increase efficiencies, and operate as an advocacy bloc to increase financial and philosophical support for OER, which is a significant tool in the battle to increase college affordability.
- Community College Consortia to Education Health IT Professionals in Health Care Program—Through the support and coordination of the Office of the National Coordinator for Health Information Technology (ONC), more than eighty community colleges across all fifty states worked to increase the number of health IT specialists with expertise in electronic health record (EHR) transitions. While some consortia are designed to continue, others, like this one, were designed to address an important problem and reflect the reliance on community colleges to adapt to changing societal demands.

The key to the success of these partnerships is that tangible benefits are realized for each of the invested entities. This has, historically, been a guiding principle for community colleges, but not necessarily with the students' educational experience as a driving force. In considering partnerships as a key resource, students must be one of the primary beneficiaries of the relationship. Establishing partnerships as one of the central mechanisms for delivering on the student value proposition strengthens the business model framework and creates additional opportunities to enhance organizational effectiveness.

Intellectual Resources—Tacit Knowledge

Knowledge lives within the faculty, staff, administration, and the students, and overall organizational effectiveness is impacted by the application of knowledge in support of the student value proposition. Since it lives within one of the key resources (human resources) associated with the CCBM, it is of central importance to the student value proposition.

The facts, information, education, training, and skills that faculty and staff bring into their daily activities help shape the college environment, guide educational processes, and frame the overall student experience. This form of knowledge is explicit in nature and, accordingly, has been addressed throughout the publication. A form of knowledge that is powerful, underleveraged, and amorphous, however, is tacit knowledge. In fact, estimates are that as much as 90 percent of the knowledge available to organizations is in the form of tacit knowledge.[42]

Simply stated, *explicit knowledge* is that which has been communicated, captured, and codified while *tacit knowledge* has not been articulated, lives inside of individuals, and has yet to be utilized.[43] "[It] covers knowledge that is unarticulated and tied to the senses, movement skills, physical experiences, intuition, or implicit rules of thumb."[44] This knowledge is connected with specific points in people's lives and reflects the practical knowledge that has been developed through implicit learning, often intentionally, and accrued over time. It is situationally based; contextually bound; and intricately interwoven into the experiences, information, and philosophies of the individual. Tacit knowledge is especially important because it has a rareness to it. As this often unspoken, perhaps even unrealized base of knowledge lives inside individuals, the exact form in which it takes is "irreplaceable."[45] This form of knowledge has also been studied frequently in design thinking research due to its situationally based and organic nature.[46]

Some of the important features of tacit knowledge include[47]

- an amplifying effect when discrete (individual) tacit knowledge is transformed into community tacit knowledge as individuals combine knowledge,
- a networked quality where the combination of tacit knowledge creates an entirely new and potentially different storehouse of explicit knowledge, and
- the ability to be grown exponentially since the more it gets used, the greater the access to additional knowledge.

The major issue with tacit knowledge is that it often remains abstract to the organization and thereby difficult to leverage. Regardless of the different theories and definitions of tacit knowledge, *organizations never possess* tacit knowledge, but rather, it must be *offered by individuals*. Moving from tacit knowledge to explicit knowledge reflects movement along a continuum rather than integrating an entirely new form of knowledge. This "knowledge conversion" is the process of individuals becoming aware of personal knowledge that would improve a situation or choosing to provide knowledge that was previously codified internally, but not yet shared.[48] The power of tacit knowledge is apparent during this transition—when it evolves from a potential resource to an actualized resource for organizational improvement.

The faculty, staff, administration, and students possess potentially sector transforming knowledge, but how does the community college benefit if it is not shared? What are the circumstances that would encourage individuals to share?[49] Several conditions impact the willingness to offer tacit knowledge, but the central theme is that alignment between person and organization is key. Some important conditions include an organizational environment that

- an individual is committed to improving,
- values, supports, and encourages innovation and risk-taking,
- prioritizes people through formal recognition and appreciation, and
- feels like a community and supports a sense of belonging.

The transfer from tacit to explicit is not an automated process—the institutional conditions must encourage it. Depending on the cultural factors, culture types, and leadership approaches addressed previously, tacit knowledge is more likely to be transformed. The following is a real-life example—with a hypothetical name—of how tacit knowledge was transformed into explicit knowledge at one community college.

Real Life Case Study—Iota College

Iota College, a suburban community college located in the eastern United States, is an institution with a culture that is a model of adhocracy. The college is a partnership hub and incubator, the senior management team is viewed as authentic and people centric, innovation and risk-taking are highly valued, professional development is a priority, and student success is an institutionally agreed upon focus. This institution has experienced ten-year student graduation rate improvements of more than 100 percent, transformed curricula and programs to align with jobs, and established itself as the key partner in its region. While studying Iota College, one artifact emphasized how the college environment encourages individuals to offer their tacit knowledge in support of organizational success.

Two female directors disclosed that during discussions about what role they could play in advancing the college mission, they discovered that they each had a love of horses. As they talked some more, they decided to find a way to integrate their love of horses into a program that would benefit the college. On their own time, they investigated leadership programs involving horses and came across a horse sense for leaders program. With their own resources, they both drove to visit a farm and learn more. They were impressed with what they saw and drafted a plan. The president at Iota College maintained a recommendation box outside their door and they delivered their plan. It was discussed at a cabinet meeting and was later piloted. The following excerpt from the study provides a bit more context:[50]

> One thing that I'm doing in partnership with a person that I have worked with in the skills area is that we both have an interest in horses . . . so we, together, are both searching for the correct mix of people and beasts to bring to this campus or make available to this campus. A horse sense for leaders program and it's fascinating, not just because of my interest in animals, but because they so mir-

ror your ability to communicate and so we are looking at a couple of trainers and people who are doing similar work to see if it's a good fit with our culture here. So that is an extension of my personal interests and it's tangentially related to what I do . . . I definitely think that this will be encouraged.

Both directors had an interest in horses and were riders with substantial knowledge. It was their knowledge and experience communicating with horses that led them to pursue the opportunity. It was the environment that encouraged new ideas that provided them with the freedom to pursue the opportunity. It was the welcoming atmosphere that made them want to pursue the opportunity. Iota College encourages its college community to convert their tacit knowledge into explicit knowledge.

CONCLUSION

Without a sound understanding of what the key resources are and their centrality to the business model, community colleges cannot implement an effective business model. These resources—human, physical, and intellectual—are foundational to the model and delivery of the student value proposition. In fact, without intentional development, growth, and leveraging of these resources, implementation of the model is impossible. Additionally, as noted, the most important resource is the community of individuals, faculty, staff, students, and administrators who support access, success, and the environment for learning and student outcomes. While this chapter addressed the who and what behind delivery of the value proposition, the next chapter addresses the following question: How is the student value proposition delivered? The answer is through the key products that must be intentionally designed to enhance the student educational experience.

NOTES

1. Alexander Osterwalder and Yves Pigneur, *Business Model Generation: A Handbook for Visionaries, Game Changers, and Challengers* (Hoboken, NJ: John Wiley & Sons, Inc., 2010). 34-35.
2. Osterwalder and Pigneur, *Business Model Generation*, 14.
3. Clayton M. Christensen, Michael B. Horn, Louis Soares, and Louis Caldera, "Disrupting College: How Disruptive Innovation can Deliver Quality and Affordability to Postsecondary Education." Report, Center for American Progress, Washington, DC, February 8, 2011. https://www.americanprogress.org/issues/economy/reports/2011/02/08/9034/disrupting-college/.

4. John M. Braxton, Amy S. Hirschy, and Shederick A. McClendon, *Understanding and Reducing College Student Departure–ASHE-ERIC Higher Education Report: Volume 30, Number 3* (San Francisco: Jossey-Bass, 2004), 47–52.

5. Kimberly Martin, Richard Galentino, and Lori Townsend, "Community College Student Success: The Role of Motivation and Self-Empowerment," *Community College Review* 42 (2014): 238–240; Braxton, Hirshy, and McClendon, *Understanding and Reducing College Student Departure*, 36–41.

6. Martin, Galentino, and Townsend, "Community College Student Success," 238–240.

7. Center for Community College Student Engagement, "Aspirations to Achievement: Men of Color and Community Colleges: Special Report," 2014. http://www.ccsse.org/docs/MOC_Special_Report.pdf.

8. Elisabeth A. Barnett, "Validation Experiences and Persistence among Community College Students," *The Review of Higher Education* 34(2) (2010): 212; Esau Tovar, Merril A. Simon, and Howard B. Lee, "Development and Validation of the College Mattering Inventory with Diverse Urban College Students," *Measurement and Evaluation in Counseling and Development* 42 (2009): 157–158.

9. Laurie A. Schreiner, Patrice Noel, Edward Anderson, and Linda Cantwell, "The Impact of Faculty and Staff on High-Risk College Student Persistence," *Journal of College Student Development* 52(2) (2011): 325–336.

10. Schreiner et al., "The Impact of Faculty and Staff on High-Risk College Student Persistence," 334–336.

11. George D. Kuh and Shouping Hu, "The Effects of Student-Faculty Interaction in the 1990s," *Review of Higher Education* 24(3) (2001): 309–332; Guadalupe Anaya and Darnell G. Cole, "Latina/o Student Achievement: Exploring the Influence of Student-Faculty Interactions on College Grades," *Journal of College Student Development* 42(1) (2001): 9–11.

12. Carol A. Lundberg and Laurie Schreiner, "Quality and Frequency of Faculty-Student Interaction as Predictors of Learning: An Analysis by Student Race/Ethnicity," *Journal of College Student Development* 45(5) (2004): 562–564.

13. Paul D. Umbach and Matthew R. Wawrzynski, "Faculty do Matter: The Role of College Faculty in Student Learning and Engagement," *Research in Higher Education* 46(2) (2005): 173–176.

14. Umbach and Wawrzynski, "Faculty do Matter," 173.

15. Vicki L. Baker and Kimberly A. Griffin, "Beyond Mentoring and Advising: Toward Understanding the Role of Faculty 'Developers' in Student Success," *About Campus: Enriching the Student Learning Experience* 14(6) (2010): 3–8.

16. Florence Xiaotao Ran and Di Xu, "How and Why do Adjunct Instructors Affect Students' Academic Outcomes? Evidence from Two-Year and Four-Year Colleges." CAPSEE Working Paper, Center for Analysis of Postsecondary Education and Employment, New York, 2017, 22–33; Di Xu, "Academic Performance in Community Colleges: The Influences of Part-Time and Full-Time Instructors," *American Educational Research Journal* 56(2) (2018): 398–404.

17. Schreiner et al., "The Impact of Faculty and Staff," 325–331.

18. John M. Braxton, Willis A. Jones, Amy S. Hirschy, and Harold V. Hartley III, "The Role of Active Learning in College Student Persistence," *New Directions for Teaching and Learning* 115 (2008): 77–81; Braxton, Hirschy, and McClendon, *Understanding and Reducing College Student Departure*, 47–52.

19. Joan B. Hirt and Tara E. Frank, "Student Development and Consumerism: Student Services on Campus," *Understanding Community Colleges*, John S. Levin and Susan T. Katar, eds. (New York: Routledge, 2013), 50–51.

20. Perry C. Francis and Aaron S. Horn, "Campus-Based Practices for Promoting Student Success: Counseling Services." Research Brief, February 2016, 1–5. https://files.eric.ed.gov/ fulltext/ED566750.pdf.

21. Joseph B. Cueseo, *Igniting Student Involvement, Peer Interaction, and Teamwork: A Taxonomy of Specific Cooperative Learning Structures and Collaborative Learning Strategies* (Stillwater, OK: New Forums Press, 2002), 47–48.

22. Felly Chiteng Kot, "The Impact of Centralized Advising on First-Year Academic Performance and Second-Year Enrollment Behavior," *Research in Higher Education* 55(6) (2014): 539–540.

23. Zineta Kolenovic, Donna Linderman, and Melinda Mechur Karp, "Improving Student Outcomes via Comprehensive Supports: Three-Year Outcomes from CUNY's Accelerated Student in Associate Programs (ASAP)," *Community College Review* 41(4) (2013): 274–277.

24. Adena Young-Jones, Tracie D. Burt, Stephanie Dixon, and Melissa J. Hawthorne, "Academic Advising: Does it Really Impact Student Success?" *Quality Assurance in Education* 21(1) (2013): 14–16; Paul Donaldson, Lyle McKinney, Mimi Lee, and Diana Pino, "First-Year Community College Students' Perceptions of and Attitudes Toward Intrusive Academic Advising," *NACADA Journal* 36(1) (2016): 34–38.

25. Melinda Mechur Karp, "Toward a New Understanding of Non-Academic Student Support: Four Mechanisms Encouraging Positive Student Outcomes in the Community College." CCRC Working Paper No. 28, Teachers College, New York, 2011, 6–20.

26. Braxton, Hirschy, and McClendon, *Understanding and Reducing College Student Departure*, 47.

27. Jaime L. Shook and Jennifer R. Keup, "The Benefits of Peer Leader Programs: An Overview from the Literature," *New Directions for Higher Education* 157 (2012): 7–14.

28. Stephanie R. Ganser and Tricia L. Kennedy, "Where It All Began: Peer Education and Leadership in Student Services," *New Directions for Higher Education* 157 (2012): 25–28; Ian Brissette, Michael F. Scheier, and Charles S. Carver, "The Role of Optimism in Social Network Development, Coping, and Psychological Adjustment During a Life Transition," *Journal of Personality and Social Psychology* 82(1) (2002): 107–110.

29. Jennifer A. Latino and Catherine M. Unite, "Providing Academic Support through Peer Education," *New Directions for Higher Education* 157 (2012): 39–42; Shook and Keup, "The Benefits of Peer Leader Programs," 7–14.

30. Pat Esplin, Jenna Seabold, and Fred Pinnegar, "The Architecture of a High-Impact and Sustainable Peer Leader Program: A Blueprint for Success," *New Directions for Higher Education* 157 (2012): 93–98; Brian M. Wooten, Joshua S. Hunt, Brian F. LeDuc, and Phillip Poskus, "Peer Leadership in the Cocurriculum: Turning Campus Activities into an Educationally Purposeful Enterprise," *New Directions for Higher Education* 157 (2012): 54–57.

31. Peker Ender, "Campus as an Integrated Learning Environment: Learning on Campus Open Spaces." MS Thesis, Middle East Technical University, Ankara, Turkey, 2010, 34–61.

32. Ender, "Campus as an Integrated Learning Environment," 34–61; Diana Oblinger, "Leading the Transition from Classrooms to Learning Space," *Educause Quarterly* 1 (2005): 14–18.

33. Braxton, Hirschy, and McClendon, *Understanding and Reducing College Student Departure*, 47.

34. Michael Zavelle, "The Bifurcating Higher Education Business Model," *Change We Must: Deciding the Future of Higher Education*, Matthew Goldstein and George Otte, eds. (New York: Rosetta Books, 2016), 7.

35. Reynol Junco and Dianne M. Timm, eds., *Using Emerging Technologies to Enhance Student Engagement*, New Directions for Student Services, 124 (Winter 2008) (San Francisco: Jossey-Bass, 2009), 1.

36. Junco and Dianne M. Timm, *Using Emerging Technologies to Enhance Student Engagement*, 1.

37. Meghan Bogardus Cortez, "3 Ways Community Colleges Leverage Tech Successfully," *EdTech* (March 12, 2018). https://edtechmagazine.com/higher/article/2018/03/3-ways-community-colleges-leverage-tech-successfully.

38. Beth Dietz-Uhler and Janet E. Hurn, "Using Learning Analytics to Predict (and Improve) Student Success: A Faculty Perspective," *Journal of Interactive Online Learning* 12(1) (2013): 21–25; Paul Fain, "Logging Off, Dropping Off," *Inside Higher Ed* (June 13, 2016). https://www.insidehighered.com/news/2016/06/13/data-student-engagement-lms-key-predicting-retention.

39. Laura W. Perna and Roman Ruiz, "Technology: The Solution to Higher Education's Pressing Problems?" *American Higher Education in the 21st Century: Social, Political, and Economic Changes 4th Ed*, Michael N Bastedo, Philip G. Altbach, and Patricia J. Gumport, eds. (Baltimore: Johns Hopkins Press, 2016), 435–443.

40. Osterwalder and Pigneur, *Business Model Generation*, 38.

41. Osterwalder and Pigneur, *Business Model Generation*, 38.

42. Elizabeth A. Smith, "The Role of Tacit Knowledge in the Workplace," *Journal of Knowledge Management* 5(4) (2001): 313. https://pdfs.semanticscholar.org/8433/09e392e6a2144c41fa643e699c0ae2bb6a9f.pdf.

43. Dick Stenmark, "Leveraging Tacit Organizational Knowledge," *Journal of Management Information Systems* 17(3) (Winter 2000–2001): 12–13.

44. Ikujiro Nonaka and Georg von Krogh, "Tacit Knowledge and Knowledge Conversion: Controversy and Advancement in Organizational Knowledge Creation Theory," *Organization Science* 20(3) (2009): 635.

45. Jamal Shamsie and Michael J. Mannor, "Looking Inside the Dream Team: Probing into the Contributions of Tacit Knowledge as an Organizational Resource," *Organization Science* 24(2) (2013): 514.

46. Claudia Mareis, "The Epistemology of the Unspoken: On the Concept of Tacit Knowledge in Contemporary Design Research," *Design Issues* 28(2) (2012): 61–64.

47. Shamsie and Mannor, "Looking Inside the Dream Team," 517–520.

48. Nonaka and Krogh, "Tacit Knowledge and Knowledge Conversion," 642.

49. Stenmark, "Leveraging Tacit Organizational Knowledge," 12–13.

50. Christopher Shults, "The Impact of Presidential Behaviors on Institutional Movement toward Greater Abundance in Community Colleges: An Exploratory Study." PhD dissertation, University of Michigan, Ann Arbor, 2009, 292–293.

Chapter Eight

Delivering the Product

Community college missions reflect a duty to serve students and provide them with the academic and support systems to meet their needs. Thus far, the concept of the model has been provided, the value proposition has been described, and the key resources necessary to deliver the proposition have been detailed. This chapter provides insight into the next important element of the business model, the product.

To recap, higher education is an industry. Community colleges are in the business of human development and societal improvement, and education is utilized to achieve these aims. Within the social business model approach, the goal is to maximize societal impact. To accomplish this task, as a fundamental aspect of their redesigned business models, community colleges must provide a product to students that meets their needs and addresses identified problems. To better understand the product construct as it relates to higher education, consider the following, which provides a traditional understanding of the product as well as a modified description for community colleges:[1]

- The product (the offer)—Reflective of whatever deliverable is expected from the customer as understood through interactions with the business. Based upon the nature of the business, the deliverable can reflect a tangible product that has been built, a tangible service that has been provided, or a deliverable that is both tangible and intangible and is, therefore, difficult to measure.

This definition, when operationalized for community colleges is as follows:

- The product (the educational experience)—Reflective of student impressions, expectations, and assessments of effectiveness as they engage with academic, educational, and student support services as well as faculty, staff, and programming. The various experiences that students have along their educational journey at the community college contribute to the perceived value of the product and are, in fact, the deliverable at the core of the student value proposition.

While the credential is the ultimate evidence of a successful experience for most students, what the community college must provide, and what students are seeking, is an optimized educational experience. This experience encompasses all interactions with the institution and the college community from pre-entry through completion of a workshop, course, or program.

To understand how the notion of product relates to the community college business model, it is helpful to reconceptualize the student's educational experience as an educational good. This means that while students approve or disapprove of facets of their journey toward their goals, they are often only aware of the true value of the experience after completion.[2] Given the percentage of community college students who are first generation, low income, and from high schools with lower college-going rates, the majority likely cannot conceptualize the full value outside of the credential until after they have experienced the journey themselves. As colleges seek to improve the student value proposition, they must evaluate how to deliver an educational experience (the product) that is foundational to future education, career, and life success.

The key activities to be considered are the levers that drive the delivery of the product.[3] To avoid confusion, the key activities are not simply activities. They are features of the community college that students experience directly or indirectly. It is up to the faculty, staff, and administration to intentionally design these levers to enhance the overall educational experience. These levers, all of which are critical to the student's experience, include the following:

- Mechanisms—these represent the physical, tangible elements of the educational experience that students interact with directly. Some are associated with academic offerings and include departments, majors, and curriculum while others reflect interactions with student services and include educational support units, student support units, and cocurricular programming. Students also engage with units, systems, and individuals responsible for administrative and backbone support including information technology, financial aid, facilities, and public safety.
- Processes—Teaching is the primary process associated with the CCBM; however, support processes such as tutoring, advisement, counseling, and career development play a direct role in improving organizational effectiveness. Organizational effectiveness, however, is also enhanced by

myriad operational services, such as human resources, public safety, buildings and grounds, and institutional effectiveness.
- Structures—The structures not only include mandatory activities, such as assessment and evaluation of student learning, educational support, and planning, but also management processes such as governance and long-range planning. In building an effective business model, the community college must ensure continuous evaluation and enhancement of operational structures, which include strategic and operational planning, backbone administrative systems, and accreditation.

While the product of the college is the students' educational experience, financial solvency is a critical, secondary consideration that affects any conceptualization of product development, delivery, and enhancement.[4] As detailed in previous chapters, the threat to continued operations resulting from a lack of available funding is greater than at any point in history. As a result of changing expectations and increasing competition for tax dollars, fewer traditional financial resources are available.

Community colleges must also be aware that the intensifying emphasis on reducing overall expenditures has, and continues to, produce external pressure to "increas[e] higher educational productivity on the learning side."[5] Despite this pressure, community colleges must avoid wholesale changes to the mechanisms, processes, and structures for the sole purpose of reducing costs. The educational experience is paramount and the CCBM will assist colleges in leveraging knowledge, technology, infrastructure, and available financial resources to strengthen the student value proposition despite a challenging environment.

The impact of economic factors is reflected not only in the increased scrutiny from external stakeholders or reduced state and local financial support, but also in the changing public perceptions of higher education. As a result of the rise and decline of the for-profit sector, the historically severe economic downturn, legislation emphasizing the workforce education mission, and the increasing unaffordability of a sector education, students are questioning the essential role of college and the importance/necessity of a traditional college education.

In addition to students, workforce partners, government officials, and society at large are not offering the same level of deference to higher education institutions. Expectations that traditional students be retained, graduate, and either transfer or enter the workforce with a degree that ensures family-sustaining wages have increased. Expectations that the community college demonstrate the flexibility of a for-profit college in providing short-term certificates and other nondegree-based career options are prevalent. Even expectations that the community outreach mission results in an enhanced quality of life for the community have intensified. Community colleges must consider how to deliver an increasingly relevant and powerful student experience with reduced traditional funding and greater expectations from all external stakeholders.

MECHANISMS

The most visible aspects of the students' educational experience are those that they interact with daily. The frameworks that organize and coordinate these experiences are referred to as "mechanisms." In considering the redesigned business model, community colleges must be willing to look at the infrastructure created against the changing conditions and expectations required to deliver the value proposition. At issue in many community colleges, however, is that too many traditional approaches are simply accepted without examining effectiveness or the degree to which these mechanisms meet the needs of students.

Higher education has benefited from innovations to the teaching and learning environment through learning science. What has not kept pace, however, are the ways in which colleges have managed operational structures. Community colleges are better positioned then at any other time in history to provide outstanding value propositions to students given that "the efficacy of higher education business models continue to improve as technology innovations refine and redefine the teaching and learning experience."[6]

Enhancements to technology, in conjunction with greater knowledge about student needs, provide exceptional opportunities for improvements. Nevertheless, colleges need to ensure they are guided by a student-centric, rather than a faculty- and staff-centric, approach. In other words, the redesigned business model leads to the restructuring of questions. Rather than asking if the students are college ready, this model requires that the institution conduct a self-analysis to determine if the college is student ready. Are academic programs, course schedules, teaching methods, office hours, club hours, college hours, and other aspects of the educational experience based on student needs and wants? Or are they designed to meet the needs and wants of faculty and staff?

In considering academic programs and majors; the organization of academic, educational, and student support services; and the backbone administrative functions critical for continued operations, some important questions must be addressed:

- To what degree have college mechanisms changed in the last thirty to forty years?
- Have changes been proactive and intentional or reactive and unplanned?
- Have changes occurred commensurate with the evolving dynamics impacting colleges?
- Are the mechanisms guided primarily by desires and expectations of faculty, staff, and administrators or by approaches designed to meet student needs and provide solutions?

These contextual questions are important for community colleges to consider, but one question is even more important: How do the various mechanisms support the development and delivery of an exceptional product to students?

Programming

The student's most tangible and direct connection to the college occurs through educational programming. Community colleges serve a diverse student population, each with a unique set of needs, and must ensure that each group is supported while also establishing institutional priorities. For many colleges, however, this has led to serving the academic, but not the workforce, mission. For instance, some within colleges continue to differentiate between education and training, and some of the ineffectual practices that come along with this false dichotomy include the following:

- siloing academic, workforce, and community outreach programming;
- establishing an "academic" side of the house and an "occupational" side of the house;
- disrupting opportunities for collaboration and partnering; and
- reducing the human, physical, and intellectual resources available to support students.

These distinctions are most relevant to the faculty, staff, and administration at the colleges, not the students, employers, community organizations, nonprofits, and governmental entities served by the college. If the community college is going to establish and implement a business model designed to enhance the educational experience, it must reevaluate and redevelop notions regarding academic, occupational, and community programming—*all of which should be understood and delivered as educational programming.*

In thinking about the educational programming available to students, it is important to note that "occupational programs no longer prevent students from seeking higher degrees [and] they add an interim credential that yields quick job payoffs on the way to higher degrees."[7] Another benefit of these programs is that they help students gain greater awareness of the fields they are entering. Philosophically, colleges must view workforce development programs as providing different, but not inferior, academic and technical skills.

When effectively designed and operated with connections to traditional academic programming, workforce programming allows for a different form of academic inquiry that can be relevant and meaningful to students. Workforce development programs need to be viewed as more than just skills training, which is often an externally imposed label. The beauty of developing a unique business model for the institution is that the college can ensure intentionality in the design and terminology of all programs. The curriculum itself is based on meeting a variety of needs, but the conceptualization of the programming should align with the college vision and be driven by the business model.

Among the most important benefits of educational programming for non-matriculating community members is exposure to the college and opportunities for further learning. Whether the programming occurs offsite with the faculty or staff or on-site within academic and educational spaces, opportunities exist to introduce community-based students to the value offered by the institution. When the community college operates from an intentionally designed business model that establishes an exceptional student experience as its primary objective, educational programming can be understood as a collaborative, comprehensive process that integrates all student subgroups. Some benefits from this approach are

- reduced time to matriculation for students entering from non-credit programs,
- more impactful internship opportunities,
- greater alignment between academic programs and careers,
- greater connections between academic departments and workforce partners, and
- deeper connections between the college community and the external community.

In support of an optimized value proposition, community colleges should reevaluate programming philosophies regarding traditional seat time and credit hour requirements.[8] Students enter the college with diverse life experiences, knowledge bases, and skill sets and colleges have largely been reactive in addressing these changes. Traditional metrics associated with learning in the classroom remain important and essential to meet financial aid requirements and ensure policy compliance. Governmental entities and accreditors, however, have worked to increase flexibility so that colleges can consider new approaches, offer credit for learning outside the classroom, and increase the convenience of educational offerings. Some proven practices designed to enhance the student educational experience include the following:

- Competency-based education (CBE)—This approach to academic programming allows for students to engage in a more personalized educational process. Guided by flexible scheduling, learning modules, self-paced assignments, and competency exams, this approach is based on evidence of content mastery.
- Credit for life experiences/prior learning assessments—In an acknowledgment that students bring knowledge into the classroom, some colleges provide students with the opportunity to receive credits for certain experiences. Often these include language skills (CLEP), military service, and professional licenses.
- Stackable credentials—Students who take noncredit coursework and earn credentials can transfer some of the hours associated with the certificate into a select group of courses. Acting as pseudo articulation agreements, these arrangements allow for students to utilize some of the time and money spent on noncredit programming for college credits.

In considering these changes, it is important that faculty lead the conversations about how to reconceptualize educational programming at the college. Faculty possess the discipline, knowledge, and expertise required to determine how programming must be contextualized within the academic departments and majors.

Academic Departments and Majors

Questions about the appropriateness of academic departments and majors are not new to higher education. Some of the challenges have come from accrediting bodies and external regulators; some from within disciplines; some from the administrators, faculty, and staff; and still others have come from students.[9] Over time, these questions have increased as has the need to review the status of departments and majors.

One reason that colleges review the status of departments and majors is very practical—declining enrollments within some of the traditional academic fields (liberal arts, history, education, music, etc.). Community colleges can no longer simply increase enrollments in major courses by adding them to the general education program, but must consider merging or closing programs and cross-listing or outsourcing courses to reduce operational budgets. This haphazard approach, however, can prove problematic as demonstrated by the reduction in humanities departments and majors and Middle East studies and languages programs (which led to a dearth of experts in Middle East studies after 9/11).

Related to the issue of declining enrollments is the opposite situation—the addition of new departments and majors. When the list of academic majors available across higher education was updated in 2010, the number had increased by an astounding three hundred from a decade earlier, with "a third of the new programs . . . in just two fields: health professions and military technologies/applied sciences. Other fast-growing fields included biology/biological sciences and foreign languages . . . indeed, nearly four in ten majors on today's government list didn't exist in 1990."[10]

These changes reflect economic and societal shifts, much like the focus on increasing the number of scientists during the Cold War. A similar pattern has emerged recently as evidenced by the focus on STEM (science, technology, engineering, and mathematics), STEAM (STEM + art), and STREAM (STEAM + reading and wRiting). Enabled by technological shifts, the number and scope of majors has grown and traditional majors have undergone significant changes.

Entire disciplines like journalism, music and art, and communications have been fundamentally and permanently impacted. Now, students can enter departments and enroll in majors that include

- digital humanities,
- music technology,
- digital journalism,
- social media marketing, and
- environmental/sustainable engineering.

While these changes have often occurred in reaction to external pressures, community colleges have also experienced substantial internal pressure to adjust educational programming. Consider the work of faculty, student groups, and individual students that led to the development of ethnic, gender, and LGBTQIA (lesbian, gay, bisexual, transgender, queer or questioning, intersex, and asexual or allied) studies departments and majors. Colleges across the country, starting with the civil rights and women's rights movements in the 1960s and 1970s and continuing with the gay rights and equality movements today, have led to fundamental shifts in departments and majors. While impactful and directly associated with the student experience, these shifts have historically been addressed in a reactive, unplanned manner.

In moving toward greater organizational effectiveness, community colleges must work to develop a business model that intentionally evaluates the relevancy and efficacy of departments and majors against changing dynamics, student needs, and institutional capabilities and resources. This is one of the great challenges that needs to be addressed by the community college when seeking to design and implement a redesigned business model. Successfully responding to this challenge is essential for student success.

Curriculum

Although higher education, as an industry, is slow to adapt to changing conditions that does not mean that change is not a constant. Even in community colleges that operate based on tradition and internal control (clan and hierarchy cultures), changes to curriculum are routine. Whether in individual classes, across sections, within departments, or throughout colleges and systems, curricular change is a normal, albeit sometimes controversial, practice. The following statement helps place curriculum change within the proper historical context:

> The curriculum in American higher education is often characterized as a pendulum swinging from one extreme to another . . . [and] conflict over these issues has often been intense within academic communities. The need for curriculum reform can be understood as emanating from changes in the broader society, such as scientific advancement, evolving conceptions of knowledge, changing student demographics, and, more recently, labor market demands. These have often provided competing rationales for some forms of curricular change.[11]

Undoubtedly, tension continues between the conservation of practices, principles, and academic values and the push from internal and external stakeholders to offer innovative academic programming. The model must ensure regular engagement of faculty, teaching assistants, and educational support staff in conversations about intentionally designed, proactive changes to the curriculum that support student success. Curricular changes community colleges are making to enhance learning, increase overall affordability, and improve retention include the following:

- Self-paced developmental coursework—Instead of completing a developmental education course, students are provided with opportunities to test out of the course upon demonstrating college-level preparedness with the subject matter.
- Corequisite courses (including Accelerated Learning Program [ALP])—These courses incorporate academic support and developmental content into a for-credit course so that students can gain academic credits, preserve financial aid, and avoid the stigma associated with developmental education.

- Open educational resources (OER)—This curricular approach is based on the utilization of freely accessible material from myriad sources rather than costly textbooks and other copyrighted materials, resulting in a significantly reduced cost of attendance for students.

Two curricular changes that have profoundly impacted community colleges include online education and hybrid courses. Both exist in their current scale and scope due to external pressure created from for-profit colleges, but have largely been fully integrated into the student experience in most community colleges. Despite extensive research, no consensus exists on whether student learning and student outcomes differ by modality, however, online education, hybrid courses, and "flipped classrooms" remain contentious on many community college campuses.[12] Community colleges need to examine student learning and outcomes on their campuses to determine the degree to which these curricular approaches effectively support student success.

Support for the Educational Experience

Delivering an exceptional value proposition to students requires that the educational support, student support, and operational mechanisms at the college be understood as equally important to student success as the in-classroom experience. Building out an effective business model must ensure that all the functional facets of the college in which students interact add to the value proposition and support overall success.

To provide some context and guidance, consider how the assessment and evaluation movement has redefined the role of nonacademic areas in student outcomes and improving outcomes. The phrase "administrative, educational, and student support units"—sometimes referred to as AES—includes the nonacademic areas of the community college that support student success directly or indirectly. The specific actions and activities of these units are addressed fully in the next section of this chapter (processes), but the rationale for redesign is offered below.

The educational support mechanism is made up of the various units and processes charged with supporting student learning. While collaboration with academic departments and programs is a necessity, these areas hold primary responsibility over the support provided. The critical functions provided are designed to ensure that students are equipped to succeed academically, both in the classroom and beyond. The community college needs to utilize the business model approach to ensure that these functions are augmented through an intentionally designed web of support that communicates student success as the primary mission of the college. Some of the more important educational supports include the following:

- Advising—Outside of college faculty, advisors arguably play the most vital role in offering guidance and direction to students. To ensure effective support, however, the college needs to examine advisement approaches, advising requirements, and the systems provided so that advisors can advise, not simply operate as schedulers.
- Tutoring—Effective tutoring has been shown to significantly impact not only grades, but retention, graduation, and transfer. Community colleges need to consider tutoring resources, policies, availability, and practices to ensure that students are gaining the supplemental educational support necessary to succeed in the classroom.
- Library/learning resource centers—In addition to providing access to physical and electronic publications and scholarly resources, the library offers physical space, academic programming, and educational support associated with student success. The community college needs to evaluate the degree to which the librarians and support staff are developed, empowered, and incorporated into the larger student success conversations.
- Student activities—Student engagement is directly associated with increased learning and success. The cocurricular staff are responsible for integrating nonacademic learning, skills development, and personal growth into the learning environment, and colleges must ensure this programming is not neglected or undervalued.
- Internships—The internship opportunities made available to students increase the relevance and meaningfulness of coursework while also providing practical experience that contextualizes learning. Considering the student populations served, these opportunities can provide additional income, thereby reducing the need for students to maintain multiple jobs.

The student support mechanisms include the range of services provided to assist students with their social, emotional, and life needs. As was the case with the educational support framework, these services are best delivered when included as part of a greater support network intentionally designed to meet student needs and solve problems throughout the educational journey. Community colleges must understand the students they serve and provide comprehensive assistance to ensure that, where possible, issues outside the control of the college do not prevent continued attendance at the college. Some of the more important student supports include the following:

- Counseling/health services—Whether the college maintains professionally trained and licensed counselors or individuals with the professional expertise and education to refer, these individuals are the frontline support for student mental, emotional, and physical health. Given their roles, these individuals

are the most knowledgeable members of the community regarding student health and, accordingly, need to be provided with leadership opportunities that include programming, policies, and institutional practices.
- Basic needs support—Community colleges serve populations more likely to require assistance with food, housing, finances, and legal services. Accordingly, this support function is often the difference between continued enrollment and attrition. Colleges need to work to better understand the scope and scale of student needs and develop the resources required to support students dealing with immediate, and often severe, life crises. As with other support areas, these individuals need to be integrated into the business model and provided with significant leadership opportunities.
- Financial aid—The vast majority of community college students depend on a mix of federal, state, and local grants and loans to attend college. Often this office is among the most criticized on campus, in many cases due to issues outside their control. Community colleges need to evaluate the degree to which the practices, policies, and attitudes align with supporting student success, and make changes when the results indicate that student success is hampered.
- Learning communities/cohort programs—Research has indicated that learning communities/cohort models are an effective support system for students due to the development of community, increased sense of belonging, and peer supports. Consequently, community colleges need to ensure that as many students as possible are provided with cohort experiences. Of particular importance are the services and support made available to the disabled, veteran, LGBTQIA, and minority student populations.

The administrative support mechanisms consists of the operations, functions, and activities that provide backbone support to the college community. Despite their visibility, these areas are often overlooked and undervalued when considering student learning and improving the environment for student success. It is a mistake, however, to underestimate the importance of administration on the student value proposition. The space in which the students live and the physical aspects of the college with which they interact provide both tangible evidence of how students are or are not served and communicate the degree to which they are valued by the college.

Given the importance of this element to the student experience, overlap exists between the concept as a resource (Chapter 7) and as a mechanism for delivering an exceptional product. In developing the business model, community colleges would be wise to consider it as both—a resource to be developed, deployed, and leveraged as well as a key factor in ensuring an extraordinary educational experience. Some of the more important administrative supports include the following:

- Facilities (structure and space)—In considering the impact of the physical plant on the student experience, community colleges often focus on the aesthetics and capabilities relative to competition and a desire to increase enrollments. Within the community college business model framework, however, it is important to consider how the structures provide opportunities for greater engagement, effective support for learning, a welcoming environment, and informal spaces for congregating. The use of structures and space communicate value to students in a powerful way. Colleges should prioritize the usability and welcoming nature of the structures and space as a key method for supporting student learning and success.
- Facilities (equipment and information technology)—Students benefit from access to classrooms, labs, libraries, and student activities spaces with equipment designed to support their engagement and learning. Community colleges have spent significant time and resources redesigning classrooms, building labs, and adjusting computer and software lifecycles. A key strategy for colleges, however, is to ensure that the primary users of the equipment and technology are involved with the teams making decisions. Inequitable or evidence-devoid decisions can unintentionally communicate that certain groups are valued over others. Consequently, these perceptions feed into negative narratives about institutional values as they become part of the institutional mythology and enculturation rituals.
- College website—The website is the community college's public face and serves as much more than a repository of information. It is important to regularly evaluate the effectiveness of the site as a communication tool, both with internal and external stakeholders. The ease with which information can be found by members of the college community, the choice of stories and news items, and the overall look of the site drive perceptions. In developing the business model, the college should evaluate the degree to which the site enhances the value proposition and what messages are sent regarding institutional priorities and values.

PROCESSES

The mechanisms are the frameworks that students interact with, which constitute the *what* of the educational experience. The processes, however, are about *how* things are done. Processes are reflective of the way the educational experience is delivered to students through the mechanisms discussed previously. They are the tools utilized by faculty, staff, and administrators to directly impact student learning, support the environment for learning and success, or support institutional operations.

They represent the activities in which faculty, staff, and administrators engage in daily to educate, support learning, and nurture an environment conducive to student success. Processes are important not only for student learning and success, but are often deeply meaningful to faculty and staff. The processes, it is important to remember, are deeply personal.

While described in greater detail shortly, processes are at the core of why individuals choose to enter their chosen professions. For faculty, the primary process is teaching. For advisors, the primary process is advising. For librarians, the primary process involves knowledge dissemination and information literacy. For counselors, the primary process is healing. The act of questioning the effectiveness of processes is necessarily personal and, accordingly, must be respected and highly valued by administrators who are often more distanced from direct interactions with students.

While understanding and respecting the unique nature of processes, it is equally important for the college community to understand that external pressures necessitate a continuous evaluation and, where appropriate, reimagining of the processes largely owned by the faculty and staff. The major drivers of change, technology, compliance and regulations; changing student dynamics; and the need to better connect academics and career are no different than for the mechanisms. Processes, however, are the most significant and impactful element of the educational experience. Processes touch students every day, and the faculty and staff supporting students regularly evaluate the degree to which they are benefiting students.

Even outside of institutional assessments, for example, faculty are continually able to evaluate the degree to which their teaching methods and overall pedagogical approaches are helping students learn. While departments, curriculum, and syllabi are important, teaching is the foundation of the educational experience. Depending on organizational policies, advisors are in the position to regularly speak to students and interpret the degree to which they are succeeding and being supported along their educational journey. Even outside of assessments and program reviews, they can navigate, intervene, and alter, positively or negatively, a student's trajectory. Regardless of the specific responsibilities and duties, everyone plays an important role in supporting student success through the delivery of processes.

As the CCBM is built on student success and an optimized educational experience, these individuals are obligated to consider new knowledge, approaches, and understandings relevant to their craft. They are also obligated, where appropriate, to adapt, modify, or redesign the way they understand their professions.

Processes—more than mechanisms—present a peculiar challenge within the business model, and this is due to the organizational architecture of the institutions. It is the very nature of community colleges as professional bureaucracies that make questioning—let alone modifying academic, educational, and operational processes—difficult.[13] The faculty and staff responsible for the delivery of the educational experience live in different, sometimes competing, subcultures and are not necessarily focused on, nor driven by, institutional values. More often, the knowledge and values specific to their subcultures impact their thinking and behaviors. This situation reflects the necessary tension that exists in community colleges—the need for faculty and staff to stay current within their fields while also working as part of a community to ensure that the college is effectively serving students.

Perceived gaps between the language and actions of senior administration and the faculty and staff subcultures—or when the impetus for changing processes is external to the college—will increase the chance that change efforts fall short. As noted in Chapters 4 and 5, the redesigned business model argues for a shared approach to leadership—one that values and leverages the knowledge and talents of faculty and staff; empowers the individuals responsible for the processes to evaluate the effectiveness of the community college, encourages recommendations where appropriate, and sparks positive changes whenever possible.

Teaching

The purpose of this publication is not to deeply examine each of the processes that impact students, but rather to assist community colleges in understanding their importance and value within a redesigned business model. This is especially important to state given the role of teaching in the community college. It would not be an exaggeration to state that teaching is the single most important process in higher education; whether for noncredit quality of life sessions, occupational certificate programs, contract training, or traditional transfer programs, the purpose of the community college is to deliver the instruction that leads to increased awareness, new knowledge and skills, and personal and professional growth.

Significant changes, however, have emerged in the past few decades that must be considered as community college, faculty, evaluate the effectiveness of their teaching. Unquestionably, community college faculty regularly self-evaluate and reflect on the effectiveness of their teaching. They also engage in professional development opportunities that include leading and participating in workshops, working with teaching and learning centers, and exploring discipline specific and pedagogical literature. The intent of this section is not to suggest that faculty are unaware of, or unwilling to, evaluate teaching in the community college, but rather to reinforce the necessity of reevaluation as part of a comprehensive institutional effort to understand and enhance the educational experience of students. Faculty must lead these evaluations and the college must support them as a primary function of a redesigned business model.

Although teaching is intensely personal, is a core principal of academic freedom, and must be valued as central to student success at the community college, it is equally important to examine whether teaching methods are incorporating the lessons learned over decades of research. Significant questions abound as to whether teaching methods, en masse, have evolved sufficiently to incorporate new knowledge or fully leverage the capabilities that exist.[14]

One approach to teaching that has shown not only great promise, but which reflects changing student expectations, is individualized/personalized education. This approach is based on understanding student strengths, weaknesses, and interests and adapting the teaching methods, approaches, and content to optimize the learning experience. It is important to note that institutional policies, class sizes, and complexity of content impact the degree of personalization that is possible.

As part of a business model approach to improving the student experience, however, the focus on individualized teaching represents an opportunity for faculty to consider new approaches and for the college to provide additional resources. Examples of how changing technology and expectations have created greater opportunities for personalizing the student experience include online education, adaptive learning, and retention enhancement systems. Each of these approaches represents opportunities for faculty members to offer individualized attention and support students based on levels of information unavailable in the past. The purpose of the individualized learning approach, within a CCBM, is to enhance the effectiveness of teaching by providing faculty with tools that amplify their teaching practices through intentional self-evaluation and focused institutional support.

Increased student expectations and the prevalence of technology have also transformed classrooms and other learning spaces. As a result, faculty members are better able to create an engaging learning environment that moves away from the traditional lecture model that has proven to be less successful in engaging students.[15] Students, whether in traditional academic majors, occupational programs, or workforce development come into the classroom with elevated expectations of the learning environment. Students often take a transactional approach to higher education and, accordingly, do not differentiate experiences by sector. If they have a positive learning experience through a massive open online course (MOOC), Khan Academy, or an educational app, they expect to find similar experiences within the classroom.[16]

Technology not only expands possibilities for innovative teaching, but also raises the expectations of those being taught. The evaluation of the educational experience not only reflects what is learned, whether students felt cared for, and if a sense of community exists, but also the degree to which the students enjoyed and saw lasting value in the experience. Some examples of technology-enhanced teaching techniques include the following:

- Social media integration—Social media has become a pervasive influence in the lives of students and, therefore, offers opportunities to enhance the learning environment. Faculty have found increasingly innovative methods of incorporating social media into classes that include service-learning videos on Facebook, discourse analysis of tweets, the creation of LinkedIn pages for business courses, and posting projects on Instagram from performing arts programs.
- Games and gaming—Both games and gaming are designed to offer students a more entertaining and engaging way to learn. Whether using actual games (increasingly common in math) or the process of gamification, which includes utilizing gaming inspired motivations to increase student interest in the material, the process of incorporating fun into the curriculum offers new opportunities for enhancing the student educational experience.[17]
- Flipped classrooms—This approach to teaching builds on the notion that the classroom provides an opportunity for interaction and engagement and should not be used as a static environment dominated by lecture. Whether fully or partially flipped, students' time outside the classroom is spent learning about topics while seat time is dedicated to conversation and didactic learning.[18]
- Open pedagogy—This form of teaching encompasses many different aspects that can include all or some of the following: open educational resources (often free to students), interdisciplinary curriculum, team teaching, collaborative syllabi development, and module-based education. In short, this approach to teaching is about adaptability, engagement, and enhancing the student experience.[19]

Numerous techniques are available to faculty in support of innovating teaching practices. When considered as an institutional priority supported with resources as part of an overarching business model, faculty are empowered to explore new ways to engage students, deliver content, and offer resources.

Educational/Student Support

Just as teaching is the purview of the faculty, educational and student support services must be recognized as the responsibility of the staff members tasked with supporting student success. As a core element of the business model, these varied services are designed to supplement classroom learning, enhance personal and professional growth, ensure preparation for transfer and career, and mediate life circumstances. From pre-entry until graduation, students engage offices and personnel at every stage of their educational experience, whether for a course, a defined set of skills, or a credential.

The success of the community college student is intricately tied to the effectiveness of these services. As with teaching, colleges have access to new information on effectively supporting students outside of the classroom. Likely all community colleges can identify pockets of innovation and support where staff are well versed in changing standards, engaged in professional organizations, presenting at conferences, and working to help shape cocurricular and extracurricular experiences. At issue is the degree to which these pockets represent the overarching college culture. Ensuring that the value proposition for all students is enhanced necessitates college-wide prioritization, not innovation bubbles.

In regard to advising, which is a critical support process, student success requires advisors to be advisors, not schedulers. The caseload approach recognizes the importance of advising, from faculty and professional advisors, and is premised on a collaborative relationship as well as communication between advisors.[20] Some high-impact practices include advisors working with the same students, mandatory meetings, and ensuring the lowest student to advisor ratio possible. When the caseload approach is fully supported, students take fewer unnecessary courses, develop greater agency, confidently explore career paths, improve decision making, and demonstrate self-leadership.[21]

Research has indicated that not only is tutoring a necessary and effective support mechanism for college students, but more so for first generation, racial and ethnic minority, and academically underprepared students.[22] Effective tutoring, however, no longer resembles the traditional face-to-face, one assignment at a time, and new tutor every session approach. In addition to certifying tutors, engaging faculty, providing online support, and mandating tutoring for certain populations, other approaches that enhance the student value proposition include the following:

- Academic coaching/success coaches—These coaches are available to help students navigate the nonacademic aspects of their educational experience by focusing on successful behaviors, learning approaches, and academic habits.

- Peer tutoring—Either in a group or one-one-one settings, peer tutors are usually students who have taken the course they are assigned to tutor and have demonstrated content mastery. In contrast to working with a professional tutor, peer tutors offer a sense of community and increased understanding about student lives and circumstances.
- Supplemental instruction (SI)—This approach provides a tutor embedded in the course who works with faculty and students. This approach works best when there is a strong partnership between faculty and the SI leader, when the leader is welcomed into the classroom, and when the leader can offer suggestions regarding classroom management.

Students enrolled in traditional academic programs or continuing education and workforce training programs are focused on careers, so the career services function is an exceptionally important student support service. These offices, however, must provide more than lists of jobs, access to databases, and skill inventories. Although important, students and employers are looking for offices that help establish internships, support job placement, partner with academic departments, support industry advisory boards, increase access to career networks, and amplify employer outreach efforts. Depending on the level of collaboration, these units can also support students in continuing education by providing information about, and supporting, stacked credentials, certifications, apprenticeship models, and on-the-job training. Considering that student success for many students is based on obtaining a career with family-sustaining wages, career services staff must engage in relevant and purposeful processes.

Nearly 25 percent of college students have either a diagnosable mental or psychological illness; however, the percentage of students utilizing counseling services has remained steady at around 10 percent.[23] Whether based on stigma, anxiety, or lack of awareness, counseling units are not reaching many of the students in need of their services.[24] To ensure utilization of these services for students in need, colleges can consider five strategies documented to increase utilization. These include reimagining marketing and outreach through technology and student input; providing a broader range of services, hours, and points of interaction; training students as peer counselors; continually assessing what is working and making changes; and offering a user-friendly referral system that allows for self-referral or notification.[25] Additionally, some counseling centers have developed learning modules; mental health workshops; and academic mindset, behavior modification, and mindfulness programming to provide a holistic approach to student health.

In recent years, community colleges have become increasingly aware of the degree to which students struggle with basic needs. Colleges are now aware that around half of community college students struggle with either food or housing insecurity. This is troubling on a human level, but colleges are also aware that basic needs insecurity leads to significant decreases in graduation rates and retention rates along with substantial increases in failing grades and withdrawals.[26] Food pantries have grown not only in number, but also in size in recent years and have become institutional priorities rather than divisional projects. Addressing basic needs and attempting to remedy the effects of poverty, however, requires a more expansive approach that includes comprehensive wraparound support services.

Among the most important ways to view the student value proposition is the degree to which the community college truly cares for its students. Working not only to provide food through a pantry, but also offering food vouchers, access to meal preparation programming, food scholarships, housing vouchers, pro-bono legal services, tax-preparation assistance, Supplemental Nutrition Assistance Program (SNAP) support, emergency funding, transportation vouchers, and reduced cost childcare provides lifelines that demonstrate that students are the institutional priority. Considering that the social business model is about maximizing social impact and that our business is human development, one of the most profound ways to operationalize the business model is through addressing students' basic needs.

STRUCTURES

Structures represent the philosophical, strategic, and operational elements required for integration of the mechanisms and processes. Students benefit from, or are otherwise impacted by, these structures without the same level of direct interaction. While these frameworks are standard, they often go underleveraged due to the lack of a comprehensive business model that aligns usage. Another limitation is that many of these frameworks are not considered educational, but rather operational. Accordingly, they often operate without an explicit connection to the student experience. Operating within a redesigned business model and focusing on the development of an exceptional educational product provides the incentive to more effectively utilize these structures.

The institutional effectiveness system is a structure that is central to the optimization of the student value proposition. The ability to leverage it, however, is greatly enhanced through the utilizations of an approach that intentionally integrates, compliance, planning, and data/information usage for the purpose of enhancing student success.[27] Community colleges—based on a combination of external mandates and internal needs for evidence to impact decision making—have grown assessment and planning structures to include not only the academic programs, but the Administrative, Educational, and Student Support (AES) units as well.

The mechanisms and processes that govern and reflect the work of faculty and staff are effectively assessed when systems are comprehensive, driven by the content and support experts, supported by the college, and utilized to make decisions that impact student lives. These evaluations represent opportunities for continued improvement and enhancement. When institutional effectiveness is embedded in a business model focused on student success, the college continues to challenge itself and, accordingly, better optimize the student experience.

Moving from the level of program and unit improvements to greater organizational effectiveness, however, requires a comprehensive strategic and operational planning process. All assessment, evaluations, and plans emanating from programs and units must be aligned with the strategic goals and objectives developed through inclusive participation and a shared understanding of the business model. Without the participation and investment of the college community, the college lacks the commitment and urgency to use data to make changes.

Without explicit alignment with, and adherence to, the business model, planning, even if effectual, leads toward drift and away from a commitment to enhancement of the educational experience. Operational planning is directly impacted by annual assessment and the operational activities of the departments and units and allows for utilization of data to redesign the educational experience.[28] Through utilization of a redesigned business model, the product offered to students is enhanced by engaging in the use, and growth of, an IIE structure.

To improve college operations and enhance the educational experience of students, community colleges purchase and utilize a substantial amount of technology. As it pertains to the structures that impact the business model, the most expensive, potentially impactful, and underleveraged are the electronic administrative systems designed to store data and increase efficiency and effectiveness. One of the many reasons these systems have failed to reach their potential is that they have served limited purposes. Often these systems remain the property of divisions and units with limited access granted to those located outside of these areas. If college culture encourages silos, these systems exacerbate divisions based on access, ownership, and budgeting. The product cannot be fully enhanced when the student experience is not the *institutional* priority. Consider the following systems:

- Student information system (SIS)—These systems possess tremendous functionality that not only provides an inventory of all student data, but is the backbone of course scheduling, student transcripts, attendance, and financial information. As a result, many offices have access to these systems; however, access is usually limited to the portions of the system directly related to a unit's responsibilities. Often used as a repository, the SIS holds the potential for better understanding students and their experiences. Using statistical analyses and predictive modeling, colleges can mine the data to identify factors that are positively and negatively impacting students. Fully leveraging this resource requires a review of policies, procedures, and protocols *and* a willingness to allow access to the institutional effectiveness office for analytical support.

- Learning management system (LMS)—These systems provide a potentially powerful interface between students and faculty, but often go underutilized. Often, they only house information about the course, provide a means for assignment upload and grades, and allow faculty a non–email-based communication tool. When educational technology/instructional support, academic affairs, information technology, and institutional effectiveness are partners in the process, faculty members receive the support necessary to elevate their course to include electronic media, fully functional community boards, and interactive content that increases engagement. Additionally, the system offers opportunities to assess system impact on student learning and success, and when integrated, amplifies the power of predicative models.
- Enrollment management system (EMS)—The EMS is designed to provide information on student progression and success from pre-entry through completion. This system is intentionally designed to integrate academic, educational, and student support units. These systems operate enterprise wide with modules for preenrollment, admission, advisement, academic progress, counseling referrals, and the collection and merging of data from other systems. These systems also possess robust analytics engines that create predictive models that grow more precise over time. These systems provide a significant amount of actionable information that can help prevent negative student outcomes. The power of these systems is limited only by culture, creativity, resources, policies, procedures, and protocols.

A final structure that is often overlooked as a key contributor to the development of the student educational experience is the institutional compliance function. Compliance is often viewed negatively due to the external demands placed on both the college and its various academic programs; however, this despised requirement provides opportunities for regular, substantial evaluations of the educational experience.

In recent years each of the seven regional accreditation bodies has intensified its focus on student learning, support for student learning, and student outcomes. By incorporating the standards into yearly assessments, evaluations, and operational planning, the community college is positioned to regularly evaluate and remedy issues that negatively impact students. To provide an example of how the educational experience, the product within the CCBM, can be transformed through intentional design, the Accelerated Study in Associate Programs (ASAP) is provided as a case study.

Real Life Case Study—ASAP

In 2007, the City University of New York (CUNY) partnered with the New York Center for Economic Opportunity to develop the Accelerated Study in Associate Programs (ASAP). This program is funded by the New York City Office of the Mayor, and given its success it has been expanded and now supports more than twenty-five thousand students across the nine CUNY community colleges. The goal is to increase retention, graduation, and transfer rates with a requirement that at least 50 percent of students graduate within three years. Results include the following:[29]

- The average cost per graduate is $6,500 less than for propensity-matched non-ASAP students.
- Three dollars and fifty cents is returned in tax revenues and social service savings for every dollar invested in the program.
- The total net benefits for every one thousand ASAP students are $46.5 million higher than for one thousand non-ASAP students.

Philosophically, the program was established to raise families and communities out of poverty by enhancing economic mobility.[30] Accordingly, students in ASAP are demographically and educationally similar to non-ASAP students. The majority of students in CUNY community colleges come from families with median incomes of less than $30,000 a year; 80 percent of students are Pell eligible; the majority have developmental needs; and 70 percent experience some combination of food insecurity, housing insecurity, or homelessness.[31]

In addition, transportation costs and books provide significant challenges to students, as both require them to work more hours and retain more jobs. In addition to the lack of study time and exhaustion from working, transportation difficulties negatively impact student schedules. It is important to note most CUNY community college students pay little or nothing for tuition and fees, but their non–tuition-based, education-related expenses are over $10,000 for dependent students and over $20,000 for independent students. With these challenges, it is no surprise that the CUNY community college three-year graduation rates hover in the mid-twenties. It is not an issue of will, want, or academic potential from the students, but rather a lack of sufficient wraparound support services, access to student communities, and finances.

Acknowledging the challenges borne by CUNY community college students, the ASAP program is designed to alleviate as many life burdens as possible while also ensuring the academic and educational support to succeed. ASAP provides the following features to its students:[32]

- Cohort experience—Students are provided with flexible schedules, which allow for first-year students to take classes with fellow ASAP students with some colleges maintaining ASAP sections of gateway courses. Students also attend mandatory group advising, academic support, and other engagement activities.
- Financial support—Any gaps between the financial aid awarded and the tuition and fees are waived for students to ensure they have no tuition-related debt. Additionally, students receive an MTA MetroCard and a stipend for books to reduce these burdens.
- Intrusive, individualized advisement—The program maintains a strict advisor to student ratio with additional funding provided by the city to the colleges as program enrollment increases. Advisement sessions are mandatory and through the caseload approach, students can work with the same advisor from entry through graduation.
- Full course load—Research into student retention informed the design of the program and, accordingly, students must attend college full-time. To ensure continual momentum, advisors encourage students to take courses in the winter and summer sessions.
- Academic support services—ASAP students have access to tutoring, usually within a space dedicated to them for review sessions, group study, and general tutoring. The program also encourages significant interaction between faculty and the advisors to ensure communication and a holistic understanding of student progress.
- Career development—Students are provided with career specialists who partner with advisors to help students understand career options, design career plans, and prepare for their future careers. Students are also provided with workshops, assistance with scholarships, and transfer support.

As previously stated, the program has experienced a great deal of success. Based on propensity matching, the student outcomes that demonstrate the overall effectiveness of the program include[33]

- ASAP students have higher completion rates than non-ASAP students (23.6 percentage points higher),

- ASAP students earn their associate degrees faster than non-ASAP students (1.6 fewer semesters),
- ASAP students have both higher transfer and bachelor's attainment rates than non-ASAP students (9.6 and 8.8 percentage points higher), and
- Six years after starting in the community college, the ASAP students were more likely to have earned an undergraduate degree (20.3 percentage points higher).

The success of this program has led to significant interest as well as replication. To this point, three Ohio community colleges have developed programs, colleges in New York and California have implemented similar models, and colleges in Tennessee are also looking to integrate the model. To be clear, ASAP is expensive to implement and maintain as the goal is to go to scale with a comprehensive, cohort-based program. As with any major initiative, some detractors dismiss the program and the limitations as to who the program can serve are real; however, the success of the program to the primary and secondary beneficiaries in the form of enhanced student outcomes and the significant return on investment is unquestionable. This program *reduces* tax expenditures per graduate, increases the number of graduates, and *increases* overall economic output.

College success, especially with traditionally underserved, under supported, and under prepared students does not come without a significant investment. The CCBM argues for increasing the revenue available to support student success because student success is organizational effectiveness. Colleges must find new ways to generate the necessary revenue, not simply reduce expenditures for financial stability, if they are to provide an exceptional educational experience that resembles the ones experienced by ASAP students.

CONCLUSION

In summary, implementing an intentionally redesigned community college business model affords the community college an opportunity to provide an optimized product to students—that being their educational experience. By focusing on the mechanisms, processes, and structures that undergird their educational experience, the community college is positioned to better understand the degree to which it is supporting or impeding student success. Reimagining the educational experience as the product to be delivered also forces faculty, staff, and administration to evaluate the entirety of the student experience, including how the various elements intersect and interact at each progression point.

So far, this publication has provided an in-depth exploration into the student value proposition, the key resources necessary to deliver on the value proposition, and the product provided as a result of the value proposition. The next chapter moves into what is often a significant barrier to optimizing the educational experience of students—financial resources. It should come as no surprise that no silver bullet or single solution to solving this conundrum exists, other than states and counties living up to their funding commitments. Given the unlikelihood of that occurring, community colleges must approach financing with different philosophies, strategies, and tactics than in the past. Indiscriminate cutting provides short-term relief, but may result in long-term problems. The final chapter of the book takes the reader through the journey of enhancing and more effectively deploying financial resources in support of student success.

NOTES

1. Alexander Osterwalder and Yves Pigneur, *Business Model Generation: A Handbook for Visionaries, Game Changers, and Challengers* (Hoboken, NJ: John Wiley & Sons, Inc., 2010), 22.

2. Jeffrey Selingo, *College (Un)bound: The Future of Higher Education and what it Means for Students* (Las Vegas: Amazon Publishing, 2013), 85.

3. Osterwalder and Pigneur, *Business Model Generation*, 36.

4. Keith Hampson, "Business Model Innovation in Higher Education: Part I," February 13, 2014. http://acrobatiq.com/business-model-innovation-in-higher-education-part-1/.

5. Bruce D. Johnstone, "Financing American Higher Education: Reconciling Institutional Financial Viability and Student Affordability," *American Higher Education in the 21st Century: Social, Political, and Economic Changes*, 4th ed., Michael N. Bastedo, Philip G. Altbach, and Patricia J. Gumport, eds. (Baltimore: Johns Hopkins Press, 2016), 336.

6. Michael Zavelle, "The Bifurcating Higher Education Business Model," *Change We Must: Deciding the Future of Higher Education*, Matthew Goldstein and George Otte, eds. (New York: Rosetta Books, 2016), 7.

7. James Rosenbaum, Keenan Cepa, and Janet Rosenbaum, "Beyond the One-Size-Fits-All College Degree," *Contexts* 12(1) (2013): 49.

8. Clayton M. Christensen, Michael B. Horn, Louis Soares, and Louis Caldera, "Disrupting College: How Disruptive Innovation can Deliver Quality and Affordability to Postsecondary Education." Report, Center for American Progress, Washington, DC, February 8, 2011. https://www.americanprogress.org/issues/economy/reports/2011/02/08/9034/disrupting-college/.

9. Michael N. Bastedo, "Curriculum in Higher Education: The Organizational Dynamics of Academic Reform," *American Higher Education in the 21st Century:*

Social, Political, and Economic Changes, 4th ed., Michael N. Bastedo, Philip G. Altbach, and Patricia J. Gumport, eds. (Baltimore: Johns Hopkins Press, 2016), 60.

10. Selingo, *College (Un)bound*, 7.

11. Bastedo, "Curriculum in Higher Education," 60.

12. Laura W. Perna and Roman Ruiz, "Technology: The Solution to Higher Education's Pressing Problems?" *American Higher Education in the 21st Century: Social, Political, and Economic Changes*, 4th ed., Michael N. Bastedo, Philip G. Altbach, and Patricia J. Gumport, eds. (Baltimore: Johns Hopkins Press, 2016), 441–443.

13. Deone Zell, "Organizational Change as a Process of Death, Dying, and Rebirth," *The Journal of Applied Behavioral Science* 39(1) (2003): 73–74.

14. David Breneman, "Is the Business Model of Higher Education Broken?" Miller Center of Public Affairs – National Discussion and Debate Series White Paper, University of Virginia, Charlottesville, April 27, 2010. http://web1.millercenter.org/debates/whitepaper/deb_2010_0427_ed_cost.pdf.

15. Scott Freeman, Sarah L. Eddy, Miles McDonough, and Michelle K. Smith, et al., "Active Learning Increases Student Performance in Science, Engineering, and Mathematics," *Proceedings of the National Academy of Sciences of the United States of America* 23 (2014): 8412–8413. https://www.pnas.org/content/111/23/8410#sec-2; Christopher M. Huggins and Janet P. Stamatel, "An Exploratory Study Comparing the Effectiveness of Lecturing versus Team-based Learning," *Contexts* 43(3) (2015): 231–234.

16. Richard Alfred and Associates, *Managing the Big Picture in Colleges and Universities: From Tactics to Strategy* (Westport, CT: American Council on Education/Praeger, 2006), 115.

17. Kevin Bell, *Game On! Gamification, Gameful Design, and the Rise of the Gamer Educator* (Baltimore: Johns Hopkins University Press, 2017), 150–167.

18. Stephanie Burgoyne and Judy Eaton, "The Partially Flipped Classroom: The Effects of Flipping a Module on 'Junk Science' in a Large Methods Course," *Teaching of Psychology* 45 (2018): 154–157.

19. Open Pedagogy Notebook, "What is Open Pedagogy?" Accessed August 6, 2019. http://openpedagogy.org/open-pedagogy/.

20. Lindsay Pierce, "The Case for a Case Management Approach in Advising Academically Underprepared Students," *Academic Advising Today* 39(4) (2016). https://www.nacada.ksu.edu/Resources/Academic-Advising-Today/View-Articles/The-Case-for-a-Case-Management-Approach-in-Advising-Academically-Underprepared-Students.aspx.

21. Lynn C. Freeman, "Establishing Effective Academic Practices to Influence Student Learning and Success," *Peer Review* 10(1) (2008). https://www.aacu.org/publications-research/periodicals/establishing-effective-advising-practices-influence-student.

22. Lara Kristin Vance, "Best Practices in Tutoring Services and the Impact of Required Tutoring on High-Risk Students," *Online Theses and Dissertations* 441: 91–93. https://encompass.eku.edu/etd/441.

23. Perry C. Francis and Aaron S. Horn, "Campus-Based Practices for Promoting Student Success: Counseling Services," *Research Brief* (February 2016): 1–5. https://files.eric.ed.gov/fulltext/ED566750.pdf.

24. Darcy Gruttadaro and Dana Crudo, "College Students Speak: A Survey on Mental Health." Report, National Alliance on Mental Health, Arlington County, VA, 2012, 12–13. www.nami.org/namioncampus.

25. Correspondence, Caity Lee to Dr. Laura Sponsler, no date, Office of The Vice-President of Student Affairs. https://www.naspa.org/images/uploads/main/Lee_NASPA_Memo.pdf.

26. Sara Goldrick-Rab, Christine Baker-Smith, Vanessa Coca, and Elizabeth Looker, et al., "College and University Basic Needs Insecurity: A National #RealCollege Survey Report." Report, The Hope Center for College, Community, and Justice, Philadelphia, 2019, 20; Sara Goldrick-Rab, Jed Richardson, Joel Schneider, and Anthony Hernandez, et al., "Still Hungry and Homeless in College." Report, The Hope Center for College, Community, and Justice, Philadelphia, 2018, 3.

27. Association for Higher Education Effectiveness, "About AHEE." Accessed August 10, 2019. https://ahee.org/about/; Daniel Seymour and Michael Bourgeois, *Institutional Effectiveness Fieldbook: Creating Coherence in Colleges and Universities (Volume 2)*. (Scotts Valley, CA: CreateSpace, 2018).

28. Association for Higher Education Effectiveness, "About AHEE."

29. City University of New York, "Program Overview." Accessed August 20, 2019. http://www1.cuny.edu/sites/asap/wp-content/uploads/sites/8/2019/08/ASAP_program_overview_web_8.1.19.pdf.

30. Diana Strumbos, Donna Linderman, and Carson C. Hicks, "Postsecondary Pathways Out of Poverty: City University of New York Accelerated Study in Associate Programs and the Case for National Policy," *RSF: The Russell Sage Foundation Journal of the Social Sciences* 4(3) (2018): 100–117. https://www.jstor.org/stable/10.7758/rsf.2018.4.3.06# metadata_info_tab_contents.

31. Sara Goldrick-Rab, Christine Baker-Smith, Vanessa Coca, and Elizabeth Looker, "City University of New York #RealCollege Survey." Report, The Hope Center for College, Community, and Justice, Philadelphia, 2019.

32. City University of New York, "ASAP at a Glance." Accessed August 20, 2019. http://www1.cuny.edu/sites/asap/about/asap-at-a-glance/.

33. Diana Strumbos and Zineta Kolenovic, "Six-Year Outcomes of ASAP Students: Transfer and Degree Attainment." Report, The City University of New York, New York, January 2017, 5–8. http://www1.cuny.edu/sites/asap/wp-content/uploads/sites/8/2017/01/201701_ASAP_Eval_Brief_Six_Year_Outcomes_FINAL.pdf.

Chapter Nine

The Profit Formula

"Profit formula" is a concept rarely used outside of corporate and for-profit culture; however, this publication contends that business modeling should be utilized and contextualized to the community college setting. Business terminology is appropriate, then, and the concept of "profit" is necessary to pursue the development and implementation of a redesigned community college business model. Additionally, an argument can be made that all organizations, for-profit or not-for-profit, have equal right to the use of organizational management language.

While community colleges must operate from a social impact rather than a profit-driven business model, as a business within a growing and dynamic industry, these institutions must apply the constructs and framing necessary to accomplish their mission. The primary reason for a corporate business model is to increase profitability by elevating the customer value proposition. For community colleges, an intentionally designed business model works to ensure that significant margins (profit) exist to deliver the student value proposition. The following statement provides insight into the need for a profit formula within community colleges:[1]

- Profit formula (financial viability)—Reflective of the financial health and well-being of a business, it incorporates both the costs required to operate the business as well as the resources obtained in support of the business. Whether a business is corporate in nature and for-profit, mission-based, and not-for-profit, or anywhere else along the continuum, understanding the principles of financial sustainability is key.

The term "financial strategy" has been offered to contextualize this concept for community colleges. The premise is that "an effective business and finance model adds value to both the college and customer by providing a strategic margin between revenue and cost for investment in future development."[2]

As indicated earlier, the main purpose of considering a profit formula is to ensure sufficient capital to ensure continued operations and, where possible, the development and deployment of slack resources to support operational and strategic priorities. Building on these definitions and operationalizing for integration into a CCBM, the following is offered:

> Within an intentionally designed social business model, the community college's profit formula represents the ratio of all available revenue (restricted and unrestricted) minus overall operational costs.

As mission-driven institutions, community colleges do not exist to increase revenues, maximize profits, or extract maximum resources from students. It is also important to note that the primary purpose of the institution is not to remain financially solvent, although this is a requirement if the college is to deliver an exceptional value proposition. Accomplishment of this goal requires that the college maintain the finances necessary to cover the costs of key resources and processes that ultimately benefit and increase student success. The ratio, which considers both costs (expenditures, containment, efficiencies, etc.) and revenue (current, underleveraged, future, etc.) is essential for financing the model, but must *never* be its driver.

Historically, financial plans have operated as de facto business models with the unintentional result of viewing enrollment through a revenue generation lens. One of the great failures of the traditional business model approach is that financial planning has conceptualized student enrollment as revenue generation for the purpose of continued operation.

The redesigned business model approach is guided by the understanding that student enrollment is the largest single source of operating capital, but it is based in the philosophy that delivering an exceptional education experience to students is the mission, charge, and higher calling of the institution. Student enrollment brings needed financial resources, but these fiscal resources exist to drive a continuously improving experience that increases student learning and success. The organizational effectiveness of the community college is not measured by financial viability, but by the success of students.

Moving toward greater organizational effectiveness requires an intentional approach to resource attainment, development, and allocation that offers a stark contrast to the historical gathering of all of the financial resources you can and spending (unstrategically) all that you get. In short, it is about considering the revenue required to cover the cost of delivering the necessary services and support while ensuring financial stability. The profit formula, necessarily, forces community colleges to prioritize where funds are deployed based on a greater understanding of student needs and problems.

Developing an effective profit formula requires delving deeply into the cost structures, operational costs, and revenue generated. First, the cost structure must identify the major drivers of operational costs, which are the key resources and the product. These elements of the business model include the "most important costs incurred" since they represent both the necessary resources and the product deployed to ensure an optimal student value proposition.[3] Optimizing the first three elements of the redesigned business model—the student value proposition, key resources, and product—all require an understanding of cost structures. Community colleges are high-cost enterprises because human development is a high-cost, resource intensive business.

Once the cost structure is understood, the profit formula allows for a robust evaluation of costs. With most community colleges, personnel costs (salaries and benefits) typically constitute 70 percent or more of the operational budget with infrastructure costs (facilities, technology rent, utilities) adding another 15 percent or more. These are real costs that increase year over year, and the cost structures must consider the relevance and appropriateness of funding. Despite the need to reduce costs, however, community colleges must refrain from operating with a denominator-focused budgeting approach.

This approach reflects indiscriminate, butcher knife cost-slashing to achieve a balanced budget. This undisciplined and arbitrary approach results in the reduction or elimination of resources, services, processes, or activities required to improve student success. Through a thorough examination of overall costs against the student value proposition, the community college is better positioned to strategically cut expenses so that the educational experience is enhanced, or at least not sacrificed at the altar of balanced budgeting.

The final element of the profit formula, "revenue generation," has become an increasingly difficult area to manage given changing funding dynamics. Community colleges must expand the scope of resource generation by considering all sources of revenue, traditional and nontraditional. On the other hand, they must not become so desperate as to chase funding misaligned with the institutional mission. The goal must remain identification of potential revenue streams that support operations and mission fulfillment. This includes redeployment of existing fiscal resources, increasing efficiencies and reducing redundancies, and identifying and securing additional financial resources. Just as denominator-focused budgeting leads to serious problems, the community college must avoid operating with broad numerator-focused management practices. This approach can lead the community colleges, quite unintentionally, into the de facto strategy of increasing enrollment for the purpose of securing additional fiscal resources.

Herein lies the major challenge for community colleges—how to operate in a manner that delivers an exceptional educational experience without allowing the financial conundrum to become the driving force for strategic and operational decision making. "If the climate of austerity that continues to pervade much of U.S. higher education cannot be solved entirely on the revenue side by ever higher tuitions and waiting for the return of generous state appropriations, colleges and universities continue to search for solutions on the cost side by increasing the efficiency and productivity of the enterprise."[4]

This is at the crux of the profit formula—determining how to reduce costs and increase revenue to ensure that financial resources are available to fully and effectively support the delivery of an exceptional value proposition. The remainder of this chapter provides a deeper examination of the cost structures, operational costs, and revenue generation to ensure that community colleges are not operating from a broken business model. A broken business model is one where financial solvency is the primary motivator and goal, and where the colleges "are unable to innovate and alter their production processes as a way to lower costs while sustaining quality."[5]

COST STRUCTURE IN COMMUNITY COLLEGE

Before delving into the cost structure for community colleges, it is important to explain the difference between *cost* and *price*. The student value proposition is premised on student learning and success, and the product is the educational experience. Central to the needs and problems to be solved for students is the price of tuition, fees, and other educational expenses.

In fact, considering the typical demographics of the community college student, it is not the tuition and fees, but their associated educational expenditures of attendance that create an enormous burden.[6] While *price* is a student measure and reflects affordability, *cost* is an institutional measure and represents the fiscal resources required to provide the educational experience. The price of the education never fully covers the cost of the experience. This is a critical distinction and one of the important tenants within the community college cost structure—the acknowledgment that the price *never* covers the cost.

Engaging in the development of the profit formula also requires an understanding that community colleges are both professional bureaucracies and labor-intensive industries. As noted earlier, community colleges have multiple subcultures that constitute the overall culture and organizational infrastructure. The different groups—administrators, faculty, and staff—each maintain unique roles, responsibilities, and contextualized understandings of the student value proposition. Understandings about the intricacies of operational costs and revenue, along with philosophies on institutional spending, can create disagreement and conflict. The development and implementation of an intentionally designed business model, if conducted with awareness and sensitivity to the culture, offers opportunities to find common ground on the need to support student success.

The business of the community college is human development and societal improvement and, accordingly, human labor is the primary method for accomplishing this important calling. When the product being delivered is not a physical good, reduction of operational costs based exclusively on efficiency hampers effectiveness. The reduction of cost is a necessity to ensure that community colleges maintain the fiscal resources necessary to support students, but engaging in the process of decreasing cost without an understanding of the centrality of sufficient labor diminishes opportunities to optimize the student experience.

Another important consideration when exploring the cost structure of community college is which model best represents the institution. In *Business Model Generation*, two distinct models are offered:[7]

- Cost-driven—These models focus on reducing costs where possible and are typified by lean management. These models are typically focused on the customer that is price conscious and is interested in receiving the greatest discount possible. Within higher education, this has been more reflective of the community college strategy designed to ensure that students are afforded a high-value education at a lowered cost.
- Value-driven—These models focus not on cost, but on the product, service, or experience provided. These models are typically focused on less-price-sensitive customers interested in receiving a unique, but not necessarily economical, experience. Within higher education, this is more reflective of selective public and, primarily, private institutions offering high-end amenities, unique experiences, and intangible benefits.

The goal of the community college business model is to provide an exceptional student value proposition that provides an affordable, optimized experience. The CCBM exists between these two traditional approaches with a hybrid cost model. Community colleges are institutions that must consider their cost structure based on a value-driven model. Simply identifying that community colleges are built on a value-driven cost structure is not enough to fully examine the impact of costs and the need for containment. The four primary characteristics that must be explored are as follows:[8]

- Fixed costs—These costs remain the same regardless of changes in overall operations. Total expenditures increase or decrease, but changes are expected and built into the budgets. Examples include full-time salaries and benefits, facilities maintenance costs, and rental/property costs.
- Variable costs—These are costs that increase variably as operations change and the overall impact on the budget is less predictable. These include adjunct salaries, deferred maintenance, and non–personnel-related expenses.
- Economies of scale—This is a cost advantage that occurs as the overall output expands. This is a direct measure of enrollment since, all things remaining constant, the overall cost required to support students decreases on a per-student basis as enrollment increases.
- Economies of scope—This is a cost advantage that occurs as the overall scope of operations expands. When an activity, process, or initiative can be utilized to support multiple efforts, the college receives the benefit of reduced costs. Examples include technology that can be used for multiple purposes, space that can be used for multiple purposes, or services that can support more than just the targeted student population.

It is important to single out economies of scale due to its misuse in financial or de facto business models. Economies of scale, theoretically, have been achieved through continuous growing of enrollments.[9] Since student success is the mission, the model cannot rely solely on achieving economies of scale since increasing enrollment is not the goal. Doing so decreases the likelihood of realizing the goal of enhanced student learning and success.

In addition to the characteristics highlighted above, community colleges must consider the centrality of the cost to the delivery of the product. In other words, both the direct and indirect costs associated with the delivery of the educational experience must be accounted for. This requires an in-depth analysis of the costs associated with the key resources and the product to determine areas where costs must be reduced as well as areas where costs need to *increase* to more effectively support student success. Direct costs are explicitly connected with support for student learning (i.e., faculty and staff salaries, advisement, instructional technology, etc.) while indirect costs support the environment for student success (i.e., departments and majors, planning and assessment, information technology, etc.). It is important to note that the resources, processes, activities, and structures comprising direct and indirect costs are all essential to the value proposition.

Unlike industries that produce tangible products, service-based industries like education and healthcare cannot simply ramp up production and increase productivity. In fact, focusing on increasing the productivity of the faculty and staff responsible for delivering the value proposition can reduce effectiveness and create untenable working conditions. The goal is not efficiency of instruction, but rather effectiveness. In addition to the concern about sacrificing effectiveness, structural characteristics make improving efficiency and productivity within the higher education industry notoriously difficult.

For industries with businesses that produce tangible goods, inputs can be combined, various technologies employed, and managerial approaches utilized to reduce the cost per unit. When the product is an educational experience, however, measures of productivity and efficiencies often remain "unclear and highly idiosyncratic to the institution."[10] Student learning and overall outcomes are impacted both by internal (individual professors, academic and educational services, technology, infrastructure, etc.) and external factors (employment, previous preparation, housing and food insecurity, etc.) and even the factors that are controllable (level of support available, scheduling of courses, etc.) are difficult to measure.

Higher education is also an industry subject to Baumol's cost disease.[11] Industries that can utilize technology to increase outputs are able to increase productivity and efficiency, often without a reduction in the effectiveness of product delivery. In these industries, overall labor costs can be reduced due to the outsourcing of production. In industries such as healthcare, education, and the arts, however, the product is a result of the interaction between those producing the labor and the individuals (students) being served.

Labor-intensive industries with professional bureaucracies find themselves in the difficult position where production costs continue to increase due to a reliance on a highly specialized, highly credentialed, and highly autonomous workforce. Technology and innovation within these industries act to supplement and augment the work of the workforce, not supplant it. The continually rising costs to deliver the product place community colleges in a situation where more and more financial resources are required.

Accordingly, "the problem of unit costs and efficiency (or inefficiency) in higher education is less a function of high unit costs per se and more a function of the seemingly inexorable increase of such costs—and of the resulting tuition increases—at rates considerably in excess of the prevailing rates of inflation."[12] Understanding the cost structure of community colleges requires an understanding of this cost disease. Engaging in the optimization of the student value proposition in the face of an increasingly unsupportive financial environment, however, requires that the community college mediate its effects.

Although improving efficiency and productivity is difficult, this reality does not abdicate community colleges' responsibility to tackle this challenge. In fact, given the difficulties associated with cost-containment, working to establish an effective profit formula that improves resource deployment toward student success is more important than in for-profit and corporate businesses. Again, the goal of reinventing the community college business model is not to emulate corporate or for-profit models, but to define and develop a model rooted in the mission of the community college.

Historically, "the predominate business models in higher education reward spending rather than efficiency as it relates to student outcomes."[13] This has been the principle approach because *efficiency-minded* approaches to achieving student outcomes lead to very difficult conversations. I would argue that the purpose of an intentionally designed community college business model is to ensure *effectiveness-minded* approaches for optimizing student outputs, which necessitates the incorporation of efficiency and productivity.

Cost Containment

A common assumption is that the reason higher education costs have increased is due to "administrative bloat." Given the fact that administrative spending constituted 26 percent and instruction constituted 41 percent of educational spending in 1981, and that the percentages changed to 24 percent and 29 percent respectively in 2015, this appears to be a fallacy.[14] While the percentages were closer, the percentage of operational costs attributable to administration has actually *decreased*. So why have costs continued to skyrocket if the percentage of both instructional and administrative costs decreased?

College budgets have continued to grow, and even with a decreasing percentage of overall cost, instruction still constitutes the largest expense. Community colleges educate students, so instruction should, and does, continue to be the budgeting priority. As the largest contributor to the budget, however, it is logical to consider ways in which these costs can be reduced to provide greater overall financial flexibility and viability.

The educational experience of the student, which at its core is about learning and success, must be a priority, and any reductions to instructional costs must not be at the expense of the student. Community colleges must find ways to reduce cost without sacrificing quality, and one of the approaches used in recent decades has been online courses. The premise that online education is less expensive, however, is not true.

Online courses have significant "hidden costs" not associated with face-to-face courses, including "online instruction and support services, the added cost of online course and program development, and added costs of online program marketing."[15] A substantial cost includes course design, which is a necessity because effective online courses consist of more than a syllabus and content taken directly from a face-to-face course. Since cost cutting should never be the main reason for adding online courses, it is important to look at student learning, which as indicated earlier, does not differ significantly between face-to-face, hybrid, and online courses.

Additionally, given students' busy lives, online courses enhance course-taking flexibility and can contribute to greater student retention. Many of the development costs can also be recouped by achieving economies of scale and scope with the introduction of additional courses, comprehensive online programs, and the incorporation of open educational resources (OER).

The greatest contributor to overall budget growth, even though it is not the largest category, is the substantial increase in student support staff responsible for increasing the standard of care.[16] In addition to increasing the scope and scale of support available to promote student success, many of the increases have been to reduce the noninstructional duties of faculty.[17] Ironically, these increasing costs are directly attributable to college efforts to enhance the student value proposition and the quality of the educational experience. By creating greater specialization, both faculty and staff members are better equipped to fully support student success. Consider the following changes that have occurred over the past ten to twenty years and the impact on overall business costs to the community college:

- an increase in the number of faculty as new academic programs have been added, partnerships with business and industry have expanded, and the focus on early college programs and dual enrollment opportunities have increased;
- a significant increase in the number of counseling staff and academic support personnel tasked with providing the out-of-classroom support necessary for greater student engagement and outcomes;
- an increase in the number of information technology staff required for the implementation, maintenance, and integration of the various technology solutions including the SIS, CMS, LMS, and enrollment management systems;
- an increase in the number of faculty and staff to support the various continuing education and workforce training programs offered;
- an increase in the number of personnel who address increasing compliance requirements, including student learning and assessment, at the federal, state, and regional accreditation levels;
- an increase in the number of staff operationalized as a result of successful grants as well as staff supporting grant writing, implementation, and evaluation;
- an increase in institutional research and planning staff—resulting from access to more data and an increasing focus on the use of digital data

storytelling, data mining, and predictive analytics to inform decision making and direction setting;
- an increase in the number of administrators tasked with overall organizational success and efficiency measures;
- an increase in both marketing/public relations as well as development and alumni-relations staff, both important for engaging former, current, and potential students, better communicating the college's brand, and developing more consistent revenue generation through philanthropy, planned giving, and alumni support;
- the establishment of new academic and student support facilities designed to enhance the overall learning environment and support for cocurricular and extracurricular activities vital to engaging students;
- the development of new instructional space to meet the needs of traditional and new academic programming (research and computer labs, smart classrooms, collaborative space, etc.); and
- costs associated with building and supporting the technology that supports teaching and learning through increased access to information, greater connectivity to digital services, and the ability to support teaching and learning.

The issue, is not necessarily that costs have increased, which is a given, but rather that overall revenues have declined. "With declining revenues, as has been the case in recent years, institutions are forced to make choices that require unpopular tradeoffs."[18] The development of a redesigned business model does not eliminate this reality, but in thinking about the profit formula, community colleges must engage in

- better leveraging existing resources;
- utilization of a focused, mission-centric approach to reductions;
- involvement of the community in a transparent process regarding reductions; and
- uncovering productivity gains and efficiencies that do not reduce effectiveness.

Community colleges must find ways to better manage, and, where possible, constrain the operational costs that continue to increase. Depending on standard approaches to managing cost, even with incremental increases to the revenue stream, is not enough to ensure the financial stability necessary to optimize organizational effectiveness.

A practice that must be avoided in the effort to contain costs is engaging in reactive budgeting. Community colleges must move away from the two reactive approaches to the allocation of financial resources that are most closely associated with crisis management—butcher knife budgeting and denominator management. The first approach involves across the board reductions in the name of equity, sometimes referred to as spreading the pain. If the college mission is financial solvency, then indiscriminate and broad cuts accomplish the task. If, however, the purpose of the college is to ensure human development and societal improvement, then colleges need to take a more strategic, precise approach.

Reflected in the terminology of strategic pruning, reduction tools need to look more like scalpels than butcher knives. The cuts, while necessary, should focus on areas less associated with student success while sparing or, ideally, growing the resources most directly associated with student success. Second, community colleges should resist the common budget reduction approach known as "denominator management." This approach is common within the corporate world because reducing cost as opposed to increasing revenue is the quickest way to begin increasing the return on investment. This tactic is antithetical to the community college mission.

Although a table with a number of cost savings tactics is offered, discussions and decisions made about cost savings should be framed by the business model and focused on the student value proposition. Engaging in cost savings and efficiency-generating activities is not about reducing the cost of doing business. Instead, it is about better deploying resources in support of the educational experience *while* ensuring financial solvency.

Cutting costs is a tactic, not a strategy. The strategy is to optimize the value proposition, and given the need to effectively target and deploy resources, reducing costs is a necessary action. Utilizing an intentional, thoughtful expenditure-reduction approach also requires consideration of a number of factors that have been addressed in this publication. Community colleges must consider the following:

- College culture—How do discussions and actions about cost savings impact the various subcultures independently and the college collectively given institutional history, past practices, and the current environment?
- Culture type—The different primary culture types of clan, adhocracy, hierarchy, and market shape the norms, mores, values, and expectations of the college community.
- Leadership type—The college community has very different expectations regarding conversations and actions based on the predominant leadership style of the president and senior administration as well as the college's governance model.
- Student population served—Given the students who are being served, what are the most important support programs that need to be retained or grown to enhance the educational experience and student value proposition?

- Partnerships—Which partnerships enable the college to collaborate on cost-saving measures that impact instruction, infrastructure, technology, energy, and college administration/management?

Too often, community colleges lack transparency and effective communication regarding budgetary processes. Conversations about cost cutting are particularly difficult. The business model is designed to provide the institution with a shared understanding of the priorities of the institution as well as a framework for guiding resource allocation and delivery of the product. Limiting these discussions and decision making to board, cabinet, or even small group discussions, are antithetical to the philosophies undergirding a comprehensive, institutionally established business model.

Community colleges can look to the practices of effective two- and four-year colleges and universities that have built both efficiency and effectiveness into their strategic planning process and established institutionally representative committees tasked with providing recommendations. Even if an outside firm is convened to provide a comprehensive efficiency and cost reduction audit, the community college should ensure that faculty and staff, not just administrators, are part of the team working with the auditor. Expenditure-reduction processes are both personal and painful to members of the college community. While necessary, these discussions affect the faculty and staff whose passions, life's work, and livelihoods are bound into mechanisms, processes, and structures that drive the student experience. Taking a serious, honest, and empathetic approach that is guided by the business model can make a difficult process less jarring. With these suggestions in mind, Table 9.1 provides a sample inventory of cost-cutting tactics to consider.

This table should not be used like a buffet menu to pick and choose where to cut budgets. Community colleges must first examine all available information to determine what areas of the college need greater financial support to improve the educational experience. Once those prioritized areas are identified, the conversation about where the additional funds come from can commence. Even before the conversations occur, however, the institution should always be looking for available operational efficiency improvements that can provide much-needed financial slack. This is where a campus-wide committee and efficiency audits prove most useful. The next step is to identify available and future fiscal resources.

Revenue Generation

"Financial austerity in higher education has been around for decades, perhaps forever, quite apart from the impact of any slowdown, recession, or turbulence

The Profit Formula

Table 9.1.   Tactics for Cost Cutting and Containment

	Cost-saving Tactics	
Instruction	Reduce low enrollment classes	Consolidate courses based on achieving optimal fill rate
	Mandate that administrators teach	Identify and address reasons for low course pass rates
	Expand the use of OER	Increase class size (if student success is not impacted)
	Reduce program overhead	Consolidate low enrollment/low success programs
Infrastructure	Sell off underutilized assets	Prioritize new construction/redesign to student success/support
	Obtain in-kind space contributions	Reevaluate the master plan to delay non–SVP-related projects
	Partner to share space and costs	Clean buildings at night to save on cleaning costs
Technology	Transition to virtual servers	Eliminate duplicative technologies/leverage capabilities
	Increase computer lifecycle	Integrate systems to avoid duplication and waste
	Dim brightness settings	Institute print limits to save on supplies
Management	Utilize high efficiency lighting	Consolidate operations during low enrollment periods
	Adjust academic calendar	Sign long-term utility contracts during lower price periods
	Consolidate job responsibilities	Automate business work functions and redeploy staff
	Freeze administration salaries	Utilize strategic hiring practices for partial year savings
	Voluntary retirement plans	Partner with other colleges to share faculty and staff costs
	Renegotiate debt service	Establish and empower cost-saving committees
	Collaborative bidding	Determine return on investment for student support operations

Source. Missouri State University n.d., Schulte 2017, Frizzera 2017, Pelletier 2012, Myran 2013, Workman 2014.

in the general economy or in state or federal politics."[19] This statement, while potentially hyperbolic, provides a partial explanation as to why the de facto business model within community colleges has depended upon constant resource gathering and growth. This is the rationale behind the following statement:

> [A]usterity is a function not simply of higher education's high costs, but of the annually increasing trajectory of these costs, and therefore of annually increasing

college and university revenue needs. These increasing revenue needs, in most years, outpace the prevailing rates of inflation, and almost certainly exceed the likely trajectory of available revenues, especially for the state governments.[20]

The fact that resource requirements outpace available resources is symptomatic of the cost disease referred to previously. Even in times of stable financial support from local and state governments, community colleges have been forced to continually generate revenue to ensure sufficient funding for continued operations. What has been demonstrated in the first section of this publication, however, is that the era of stable funding has passed. While overall higher education appropriations have increased after years of reductions (up 2 percent between 2006–2007 and 2016–2017), the overall appropriation per student has decreased by 8 percent. For even more context, total appropriations were up 38 percent from thirty years ago while appropriations per student were down 11 percent.[21]

This reduced support places an even greater burden on students given that equal funding from each major funding stream—students, the locality, and the state—never truly existed for most community colleges. Tuition has often accounted for more than 33 percent of operating revenue and as a result, "the business model of most [colleges] relies primarily on tuition revenue from teaching with some additional funds from sponsored research and philanthropy."[22] Based on earlier descriptions of the traditional community college student, it is clear that as operational costs rise, and state and local funding declines, many students will be completely priced out of the community college unless the profit formula changes.

The major issue has been that real incomes have remained stagnant for decades even as the consumer price index (CPI) has risen. To make matters worse, tuition has increased much faster than the CPI, which makes rising tuitions even more severe by comparison.[23] Community college students are seeing tuition as an ever greater percentage of family income, and even when students come from families with an expected family contribution of zero, the associated rising educational costs (e.g., books, food, transportation) are forcing students into untenable and desperate financial situations. Truly, "many colleges and universities are at a crossroads . . . at a point where relying on continued tuition increases with a backdrop of decreased state support is not viable."[24]

Another tuition-related tactic designed to increase revenue is the push to continually increase enrollment. Revenue generation through enrollment increases is focused primarily, if not exclusively, on financial wellness rather than student success. Another flaw with an unlimited growth strategy is that this approach places increased stress on the college's infrastructure, which leads to the need for new facilities, increased deferred maintenance budgets, and elevated operational costs. Finally, what about optimization? At what point has a college reached the optimal number of students that can be effectively supported given the resources available? What is the optimal number of students that the college can/should serve?

The correct answer to this question is *never* "more." Community colleges need to examine their unique situations and utilize available information to determine if they are attempting to serve too many students. While this question is likely jarring to many, community colleges have been confronted with the reality that within a constrained financial environment, it cannot be all things to all people. This publication is not suggesting community colleges shut the doors or turn away students. Rather, the point is that focusing on increasing enrollment as a financial strategy decreases the institution's ability to effectively serve the students already enrolled. Colleges simply cannot grow infinitely because all resources are finite. Community colleges cannot enroll their way to financial viability. A model premised on unending, continual enrollment increases as the central tactic for financial solvency is, in essence, little more than a planned obsolescence model.

Community colleges have an oft underutilized and underleveraged source of revenue and the great news is that it is 100 percent aligned with the student value proposition and an excellent educational experience. This strategy is to increase student retention—perhaps the single most important metric of student success. Community colleges nationwide maintain an approximately 62 percent retention rate for full-time, first-time freshmen.[25] This means that thirty-eight of every one hundred students who attend college for the first time in the fall do not return the next fall.

The intentional design movement typified by Achieving the Dream and Guided Pathways has encouraged community colleges to identify why students are not returning and to bring successful initiatives to scale to increase overall student success while reducing equity gaps. A major focus of this movement is the culture of care, which charges community colleges with intentionally designing their operations to meet student needs as an institutional priority.

Many of the colleges that have engaged in comprehensive organizational redesign based on student success have seen student outcome increases, with some experiencing greater than 100 percent increases in graduation rates. Retention is the key to graduation and, thereby, central to student success. Ensuring that students continue their enrollment is the main point of the student value proposition, and it just so happens that improving this statistic provides much needed revenue to further fuel student success.

Some of the issues highlighted regarding traditional cost-cutting measures apply to traditional revenue-generating measures as well. When colleges determine that overall expenditures in a given year outpace revenue, a common tactic is to vigorously pursue any and all revenue streams in an attempt to obtain as much funding as possible. Chasing dollars is a recipe for disaster however, as working to accrue resources without clear, explicit alignment with the student value proposition can lead to strategic and operational drift.

A common practice is to apply for grants, even if the funding agency's objectives either do not fully align with operations or require the college to expend resources in a non-prioritized area. Grant funding has become increasingly necessary and, when tailored to prototype activities, can spark innovation and creativity or provide seed funding for an agreed-upon institutional priority. Desperate institutions, however, may inappropriately view these funds as fiscal lifesavers. Grant dollars are not designed to plug budgetary holes or replace operational dollars. Regrettably, colleges in need of a financial boost far too often count on new grants and the associated administrative overhead as a funding source. While the income generation provides short-term relief, grant activities can take faculty and staff away from critical processes that would better support student success.

Finally, partnership pursuit is another activity that, when instituted for the right reasons, can improve the student value proposition. However, when the primary reasons are monetary rather than mission-based, seeking to gain dollars or access to potential students through partnerships can take the college in directions that do not align with the business model. Community colleges need to remember that chasing after additional finances for the purpose of having finances rather than generating additional revenue for the primary purpose of enhancing the educational experience of students creates more problems than it solves.

Before the college entertains discussions or makes decisions about securing additional funding, however, the institution should ensure that the business model is central to the revenue-generation effort. Generating additional revenue, similarly to cost cutting, is a tactic and not a strategy. Therefore, choosing the appropriate tactics is critical to achieving the overarching strategy. Numerous considerations can aid the college in deciding approaches to resource development. Similar to the considerations about cost containment, consider these questions when focused on revenue generation:

- College culture—How do discussions and actions about revenue generation impact the various subcultures independently and the college collectively given institutional history, past practices, and the current environment?
- Culture type—The different primary culture types of clan, adhocracy, hierarchy, and market shape the norms, mores, values, and expectations of the college community.
- Leadership type—The college community has very different expectations regarding conversations and actions based on the predominant leadership style of the president and senior administration.

- Student population served—Given the students who are being served, what are the most important support programs that need to be retained or grown to enhance the educational experience and student value proposition?
- Partnerships—Which partnerships enable the college to collaborate on revenue generation that impacts instruction, infrastructure, technology, energy, and college administration/management?

The community college should consider expanding either the work of a cost containment and efficiencies committee or engage an external body to provide recommendations for revenue generation. As shown in the revenue-generating tactics table (Table 9.2), colleges can pursue traditional and/or nontraditional approaches.

Table 9.2. Tactics for Revenue Generation

	Revenue-generation Tactics	
Instruction	Increase the number of certificates	Identify in-demand programming to be offered as noncredit
	Expand off-peak course offerings	Develop new/market programming to out-of-district students
	Summer session independent study	Partner academic program with for-profit entity (i.e., hospitality)
Infrastructure	Lease underutilized space	Lease prime nonacademic/student support space for revenue
	Sell underutilized facilities	Increase green energy to sell back to energy companies
	Annual surplus sale	Take ownership of foreclosed/undervalued property for rentals
Partnerships	Offer AP courses	Allow mission-aligned advertising on social media platforms
	Increase corporate training	Create entrepreneurship/small business incubators
	Operate summer camps	Create STEM and other academic boot camps
Development	Increase alumni-giving rate	Develop comprehensive planned-giving campaign
	Engage in capital campaigns	Sign long-term utility contracts during lower price periods
	Initiate faculty/staff campaign	Establish significant naming opportunities on prime space
		Establish endowed chairs/professorships
		Utilize a crowdfunding platform to solicit donations

Source. Missouri State University n.d., Schulte 2017, Frizzera 2017, Pelletier 2012, Myran 2013, Workman 2014.

It is important to remember that some traditional approaches can lead to reduced affordability, reduced educational quality, and mission drift. The college must understand that although growing additional revenue is necessary, short-term budget relief is not worth the potential long-term, negative impacts to student access, learning, and success. Some nontraditional tactics might seem plausible, some impractical, and some impossible due to internal or external policies and regulations but community colleges must look to new and different ways to increase their financial slack. This is the essence and importance of the CCBM's profit formula.

CONCLUSION

Both the cost-cutting and revenue-generating tactics provided in this chapter have been used by higher education institutions across the country. It is imperative, however, to remember that the purpose of reducing overall costs, where appropriate, and increasing revenue, where possible, is first and foremost to optimize the student value proposition. By enhancing the educational experience, which requires greater funding, the community college positions itself to progress toward achievement of the mission and organizational success.

Financial stewardship is among the most important responsibilities of the colleges, but again, the stewardship is to ensure continued financial stability for the purpose of targeting finances where they best serve students. Community colleges must also examine the unique human, physical, and intellectual resources and the academic and educational support products to uncover unrealized potential for cost containment and revenue generation. Colleges possess unique elements—including tacit knowledge—that hold the potential for diversifying income streams and monetizing institutional strengths. Thinking differently, and more creatively, about revenue-generating opportunities enable the college to gain access to valuable funding that can be utilized to enhance the student value proposition and product.

NOTES

1. Alexander Osterwalder and Yves Pigneur, *Business Model Generation: A Handbook for Visionaries, Game Changers, and Challengers* (Hoboken, NJ: John Wiley & Sons, Inc., 2010), 41.

2. Gundar Myran, "The New Community College Business and Finance Model," *New Directions for Community Colleges* 162 (Summer 2013): 97.

3. Osterwalder and Pigneur, *Business Model Generation*, 40.

4. Bruce D. Johnstone, "Financing American Higher Education: Reconciling Institutional Financial Viability and Student Affordability," *American Higher Education*

in the 21st Century: Social, Political, and Economic Changes, 4th ed., Michael N. Bastedo, Philip G. Altbach, and Patricia J. Gumport, eds. (Baltimore: Johns Hopkins Press, 2016), 328.

5. David Breneman, "Is the Business Model of Higher Education Broken?" Miller Center of Public Affairs – National Discussion and Debate Series White Paper, University of Virginia, Charlottesville, April 27, 2010, 8. http://web1.millercenter.org/debates/whitepaper/ deb_2010_0427_ed_cost.pdf.

6. Sara Goldrick-Rab, *Paying the Price: College Costs, Financial Aid, and the Betrayal of the American Dream* (Chicago: University of Chicago Press, 2016), 235.

7. Osterwalder and Pigneur, *Business Model Generation*, 40.

8. Osterwalder and Pigneur, *Business Model Generation*, 40.

9. Lloyd Armstrong, "A Business Model View of Changing Times in Higher Education." 2014. http://www.changinghighereducation.com/2014/12/new_business_model_view_of_change_in_higher_education.html.

10. Johnstone, "Financing American Higher Education," 329.

11. William J. Baumol, "Macroeconomics of Unbalanced Growth: The Anatomy of Urban Crisis," *The American Economic Review* 57(3) (1967): 420–422; William J. Baumol and William G. Bowen, "On the Performing Arts: The Anatomy of Their Economic Problems," *The American Economic Review* 55(1/2) (1965): 497–499.

12. Johnstone, "Financing American Higher Education," 330.

13. Louis Soares, Patricia Steele, and Lindsay Wayt, "Evolving Higher Education Business Models: Leading with Data to Deliver Results." Report, American Council on Education and Center for Policy Research and Strategy, Washington, DC, 2016, 7. https://www.acenet.edu/Documents/Evolving-Higher-Education-Business-Models.pdf.

14. Caroline Simon, "Bureaucrats and Buildings: The Case for Why College is So Expensive," *Forbes* (September 5, 2017). https://www.forbes.com/sites/carolinesimon/ 2017/09/05/ bureaucrats-and-buildings-the-case-for-why-college-is-so-expensive/#7e90357e456a.

15. Derek Newton, "Why College Tuition is Actually Higher for Online Programs," *Forbes* (June 25, 2018). https://www.forbes.com/sites/dereknewton/2018/06/25/why-college-tuition-is-actually-higher-for-online-programs/#17e3ebe8f11a.

16. Robert A. Archibald and David H. Feldman, "Drivers of the Rising Price of a College Education." Policy Report, Midwestern Higher Education Compact, August 2018, 15–16. https://www.mhec.org/sites/default/files/resources/mhec_affordability_eries7_ 20180730.pdf.

17. Robert Kelchen, "Is Administrative Bloat Really a Big Problem?" Kelchen on Education (blog), May 10, 2018. https://robertkelchen.com/2018/05/10/is-administrative-bloat-a-problem/.

18. Soares, Steele, and Wayt, *Evolving Higher Education Business Models*, 7.

19. Johnstone, "Financing American Higher Education," 311.

20. Johnstone, "Financing American Higher Education," 311.

21. College Board, "Trends in College Pricing 2018." Report, College Board, 2018, 3–4. https://trends.collegeboard.org/ sites/ default/files/2018-trends-in-college-pricing.pdf.

22. Gary King and Maya Sen, "The Troubled Future of Colleges and Universities," *Political Science and Politics* 46(1) (2013): 83.

23. Armstrong, "A Business Model View."

24. Soares, Steele, and Wayt, *Evolving Higher Education Business Models*, 18.

25. National Center for Education Statistics, "Undergraduate Retention and Graduation Rates." Report, Department of Education, Washington, DC, May 2009. https://nces.ed.gov/programs/coe/indicator_ ctr.asp.

Conclusion

The first chapter tackled the issue of whether higher education is an industry and the community college a business. The answer to both is yes, however, the concept of the social business was introduced to contrast corporate or for-profit business models. The key differentiation is that the community college seeks to maximize social impact through the generation of sufficient revenue to support the operations while the corporation seeks to maximize profit through the generation of a sufficient customer proposition. It is this principle—maximizing social impact—that is at the core of the reimagined community college business model (CCBM).

The community college exists for the purpose of human development and societal impact through the provision of an optimized educational experience that leads to enhanced student learning and outcomes. To assist community colleges with the design and implementation of this intentional business model, Chapter 1 examined how not-for-profit healthcare providers—who are also social businesses with a focus on human development—have developed their models. Finally, the four pillars of the CCBM—the student value proposition, key resources, delivery of the product, and profit formula—were discussed along with how the terminology and concepts have been contextualized for the community college.

Chapter 2 provided insight into the changing dynamics within the higher education industry that have created urgency for change and the need for intentionally designed business models. The impact of changing political, economic, technological, and demographic conditions on community colleges was addressed along with evidence that traditional approaches to operational management prevent community colleges from delivering an optimized student value proposition. The most significant factor is the financial disinvestment from states due to changing expectations and opinions about higher education as well as competition for scarce resources. The impact has been devastating to many colleges and numerous states are looking to merge or close higher education institutions due to the rising cost of education. The result has been increasingly higher tuition rates and the additional burden of tuition combined with stagnant incomes, which is leading to an affordability crisis. The chapter explored multiple forms of disruption and demonstrated how the use of a CCBM can create innovation through urgency and better assess and enhance organizational effectiveness.

Managing within the CCBM was the focus of Chapter 3 with substantial attention given to the inability of current management, operational, and strategic processes to significantly enhance the student value proposition. The business model built on enrollment growth places financial stability at odds with of student success. Even though there are substantial tactics for enhancing organizational effectiveness that include assessment and evaluation, strategic and operational planning, and integrated institutional effectiveness, they do not provide a framework that prioritizes student success. This chapter illustrated how the CCBM allows for the integration and leveraging of these operational and management tactics towards enhanced student learning and success.

Chapter 4 explored the impact of culture on the development and implementation of major organizational changes, like creating an intentionally designed business model. To operationalize the construct of culture within the community college, a framework demonstrating the impact of societal, industry, and sector disruptions as well as the competing value networks of the various college subcultures on organizational change was presented. As professional bureaucracies with administrative and professional classes, community colleges maintain complex dynamics that impact the willingness and ability of the institutions to chart new directions.

Further complicating change efforts are the different types of institutional cultures, which have different loci of control and adaptability. Culture types with a more flexible control base (adhocracy and clan) are better equipped than culture types with a rigid control base (hierarchy and market) to adapt to change. Even with greater natural adaptability, community colleges must also understand the various cultural factors that inhibit or facilitate change. The strongest of these is institutional history, which can be wielded as a tool to build up or tear down change efforts. Four hypothetical community colleges, one for each culture type, were presented to demonstrate how different the model design process looks based on the unique strengths and challenges of each culture type.

The discussion of business model design and implementation would be incomplete without an exploration into who is responsible for the process. Chapter 5 focused on the bureaucratic element of the professional bureaucracy by examining how administration, governance, and leadership each play an essential role in organizational change. For each group, the chapter offered evidence of effective practices, opportunities for growth and development, and techniques for integrating efforts. Leadership constituted the majority of the chapter because the faculty and staff directly responsible for student learning and success must have significant input in building and considerable oversight over the model.

The concepts of leadership style, culture fit, and distributed leadership were provided as foundations for institutional assessment of readiness for organizational change. This chapter concludes with the hypothetical colleges, however, they are now tasked with creating roles for the governing bodies and faculty and staff in the development of a business model.

The purpose of the community college business model is to optimize the student value proposition and that was the focus of Chapter 6. The community college has multiple missions and, accordingly, a diverse group of students to educate. The CCBM requires that the college consider all individuals who are engaging in an educational experience as their students. It is essential that the institution understand each student subset so the educational experience can be designed to meet needs, solve problems, and deliver on or exceed expectations.

To assist with understanding the process of building out the value proposition, three of the hypothetical colleges offered the reader the chance to consider the process of building out models for academic, workforce development, or continuing education students. This chapter also provided a case study of Amarillo College, an institution in Texas that has worked for years to better understand and serve the students—a process which has led to an 85 percent increase in college completion.

Providing an optimized student value proposition requires intentional design and an understanding of the key resources available to the student. These resources are central to the student value proposition and were addressed in detail in Chapter 7. With the mission of human development and as a labor-intense industry, human resources were identified as the most important resource for supporting student learning and success. The chapter considered how the college—through an effective business model—can work to grow; develop; and leverage the capabilities, expertise, and commitment of the faculty and staff to meet student needs and support their success.

The physical resources are the aspects of the college that students interact with directly including the facilities, space, and technology. The chapter emphasized that colleges must understand the degree to which these resources support students as well as the messages that are delivered to students about their value to the college. Finally, the intangible intellectual resources offer support to students by the development of knowledge and relationship-based support for success. In the development of partnerships and the transition from tacit to explicit knowledge, the community college is presented with the opportunity to amplify the support offered by faculty and staff in support of student success.

Social businesses, like all business, produce a product for the benefit of those they serve. In the case of the CCBM, the product is the educational experience and its design and delivery was the focus of Chapter 8. In examining the mechanisms, processes, and structures that encompass the educational experience, the chapter provided insight into how each element supports the student value proposition. The mechanisms frame the student experience and include the academic programs, student support services, and backbone operations that must be evaluated for impact on student learning and success.

Processes represent the activities that directly impact students, and which are central to the way faculty, staff, and administrators work in the community college. These include teaching, counseling, tutoring, and associated activities and the chapter charged community colleges with assisting faculty and staff in the examination and evaluation of these activities. Structures are the organizational and administrative supports, which include institutional effectiveness and technology, and they must integrate the mechanisms and processes for the purpose of enhancing the value proposition. The chapter ended with a case study of the Accelerated Study in Associate Programs (ASAP), a cohort-based model developed within the City University of New York (CUNY). Through intentional design, comprehensive wraparound supports, and basic needs support, the program has significantly increased retention, graduation, and transfer rates.

The profit formula is presented in Chapter 9 and details both sides of the resource formula—cost containment and revenue generation. The chapter argued against the practices of denominator management and butcher knife budgeting in the name of greater efficiency and financial viability. The reason is that these approaches disproportionately impact areas critically important to student success.

The CCBM provides a focal point that should be at the center of all budgetary discussions and actions that impact student learning and success. It allows for a scalpel budget approach, where areas less directly connected to the value proposition are subjected to greater levels of cost containment. On the revenue side, the chapter argued against chasing revenue to reduce the short-term pain of budgetary struggles. While student enrollment must never be prioritized as a revenue stream, community colleges that improve retention accrue revenue and gain economies of scale by *meeting their mission.*

Examples of cost cutting and revenue generation, along with guidelines for colleges to consider, closed out the chapter.

Community colleges operating without a comprehensive framework designed to improve student outcomes are not positioned to significantly improve organizational effectiveness. Not only is our mission one of access, success, and affordability, but the changing dynamics, greater pressures, and changing expectations demand better outcomes. The traditional business model approaches, which are siloed and designed to address different objectives, have not delivered the necessary levels of effectiveness and success demanded by students or that colleges should demand of themselves.

Community colleges must not shy away from their role as social businesses operating in a highly competitive and increasingly volatile market. Community colleges should use this publication as a guidebook for design and implementation of these frameworks, but should create their own vocabulary so that the frameworks celebrate their uniqueness. It is my sincere hope that this publication sparks impassioned conversations about student success and inspires community colleges to evaluate and redesign for greater effectiveness.

Bibliography

Achieving the Dream. "About Us." Accessed August 10, 2019. https://www.achievingthedream.org/about-us.

Adelman, Cliff. *Answers in the Toolbox: Academic Intensity, Attendance Patterns, and Bachelor's Degree Attainment.* Washington, DC: Department of Education, 1999. https://www2.ed.gov/pubs/Toolbox/index.html.

Alfred, Richard, Christopher Shults, Ozan Jacquette, and Shirley Strickland. *Community Colleges on the Horizon: Challenge, Choice, or Abundance.* Lanham, MD: Rowman & Littlefield, 2009.

Alfred, Richard, and Associates. *Managing the Big Picture in Colleges and Universities: From Tactics to Strategy.* Westport, CT: American Council on Education/Praeger, 2006.

Altbach, Philip G. "Patterns of Higher Education Development." In *American Higher Education in the 21st Century: Social, Political, and Economic Changes*, 4th ed., edited by Michael N. Bastedo, Philip G. Altbach, and Patricia J. Gumport, 191–211. Baltimore: Johns Hopkins Press, 2016.

American Association of Community Colleges. "AACC Pathways Project." Accessed August 10, 2019. https://www.aacc.nche.edu/programs/aacc-pathways-project/.

Anaya, Guadalupe, and Darnell G. Cole. "Latina/o Student Achievement: Exploring the Influence of Student-Faculty Interactions on College Grades." *Journal of College Student Development* 42(1) (2001): 3–14.

Angeli, Frederica, and Anand Kumar Jaiswal. "Business Model Innovation for Inclusive Health Care Delivery at the Bottom of the Pyramid." *Organization and Environment* 29(4) (2016): 486–507.

Apel, Aaron, Phil Hull, Scott Owczarek, and Wren Singer. "Transforming the Enrollment Experience Using Design Thinking." *College and University* 93(1) (2018): 45–50.

Archibald, Robert B., and David H. Feldman. "Drivers of the Rising Price of a College Education." Policy Report, Midwestern Higher Education Compact, Minneapolis, MN, August 2018. https://www.mhec.org/sites/default/files/resources/mhec_affordability_series7_20180730.pdf.

Armstrong, Lloyd. "A Business Model View of Changing Times in Higher Education." 2014. http://www.changinghighereducation.com/2014/12/new_business_model_view_of__change_in_higher_education.html.

Association of Community College Trustees. "A Guide to the Election and Appointment of Community College Trustees." Accessed June 24, 2019. https://www.acct.org/article/guide-election-and-appointment-community-college-trustees.

Association for Higher Education Effectiveness. "About AHEE." Accessed August 10, 2019. https://ahee.org/about/.

Baker, Vicki L., and Kimberly A. Griffin. "Beyond Mentoring and Advising: Toward Understanding the Role of Faculty 'Developers' in Student Success." *About Campus: Enriching the Student Learning Experience* 14(6) (2010): 2–8.

Barnett, Elisabeth A. "Validation Experiences and Persistence among Community College Students." *The Review of Higher Education* 34(2) (2010): 193–230.

Bastedo, Michael N. "Curriculum in Higher Education: The Organizational Dynamics of Academic Reform." In *American Higher Education in the 21st Century: Social, Political, and Economic Changes*, 4th ed., edited by Michael N. Bastedo, Philip G. Altbach, and Patricia J. Gumport, 60–83. Baltimore: Johns Hopkins Press, 2016.

Baumol, William J. "Macroeconomics of Unbalanced Growth: The Anatomy of Urban Crisis." *The American Economic Review* 57(3) (1967): 415–426.

Baumol, William J., and William G. Bowen. "On the Performing Arts: The Anatomy of Their Economic Problems." *The American Economic Review* 55(1/2) (1965): 495–502.

Beck, Melinda. "How Telemedicine is Transforming Health Care." *The Wall Street Journal*, June 26, 2016. https://www.wsj.com/articles/how-telemedicine-is-transforming-health-care-1466993402.

Bell, Kevin. *Game On! Gamification, Gameful Design, and the Rise of the Gamer Educator*. Baltimore: Johns Hopkins University Press, 2017.

Bennis, Warren G. *On Becoming a Leader*. New York: The Perseus Book Group, 1989.

Birnbaum, Robert. *How Colleges Work: The Cybernetics of Academic Organization and Leadership*. San Francisco: Jossey-Bass Publishers, 1988.

Bok, Derek. *Universities in the Marketplace: The Commercialization of Higher Education*. Princeton, NJ: Princeton University Press, 2004.

Bolden, Richard. "Distributed Leadership in Organizations: A Review of Theory and Research." *International Journal of Management Reviews* 13 (2011): 251–269.

Bolman, Lee G., and Terrence E. Deal. *Reframing Organizations*, 3rd ed. San Francisco: Jossey-Bass, 2003.

Bransberger, Peace, and Demarée K. Michelau. *Knocking at the College Door: Projections of High School Graduates*, 9th ed. Boulder, CO: Western Interstate Commission for Higher Education, 2016.

Braxton, John M., Willis A. Jones, Amy S. Hirschy, and Harold V. Hartley III. "The Role of Active Learning in College Student Persistence." *New Directions for Teaching and Learning* 115 (2008): 71–83.

Braxton, John M., Amy S. Hirschy, and Shederick A. McClendon. *Understanding and Reducing College Student Departure–ASHE-ERIC Higher Education Report* 30(3). San Francisco: Jossey-Bass, 2004.

Breneman, David. "Is the Business Model of Higher Education Broken?" Miller Center of Public Affairs – National Discussion and Debate Series White Paper, University of Virginia, Charlottesville, April 27, 2010. http://web1.millercenter.org/debates/whitepaper/deb_2010_0427_ed_cost.pdf.

Brissette, Ian, Michael F. Scheier, and Charles S. Carver. "The Role of Optimism in Social Network Development, Coping, and Psychological Adjustment During a Life Transition." *Journal of Personality and Social Psychology* 82(1) (2002): 102–111.

Brown, Tim, and Barry Katz. "Change by Design." *The Journal of Product Innovation Management* 28(3) (2011): 381–383.

Burgoyne, Stephanie, and Judy Eaton. "The Partially Flipped Classroom: The Effects of Flipping a Module on 'Junk Science' in a Large Methods Course." *Teaching of Psychology* 45 (2018): 154–157.

Cameron, Kim S., and Deborah R. Ettington. "The Conceptual Foundations of Organizational Culture." In *Higher Education: Handbook of Theory and Research Volume V*, edited by John C. Smart, 356–396. New York: Agathon, 1988.

Cameron, Kim S. "Effectiveness as Paradox: Conflict and Consensus in Conceptions of Organizational Effectiveness." *Management Science* 32(5) (1986): 539–553.

———. "Measuring Organizational Effectiveness in Institutions of Higher Education." *Administrative Science Quarterly* 23(4) (1978): 604–632.

Carlson, Scott. *Sustaining the College Business Model: How to Shore up Institutions Now and Reinvent Them for the Future*. Washington, DC: Chronicle of Higher Education, 2018.

Carter, Min Z., Achilles A. Armenakis, Hubert S. Field, and Kevin W. Mossholder. "Transformational Leadership, Relationship Quality, and Employee Performance During Continuous Incremental Organizational Change." *Journal of Organizational Behavior* 34(7) (2013): 942–958.

Center for Community College Student Engagement. "Aspirations to Achievement: Men of Color and Community Colleges: Special Report." Report, Center for Community College Student Engagement, Austin, TX, 2014. https://www.ccsse.org/docs/MoC_Special_Report.pdf.

Chait, Richard P., William P. Ryan, and Barbara E. Taylor. *Governance as Leadership: Reframing the Work of Nonprofit Boards*. Hoboken, NJ: Wiley, 2004.

Chandler, Nick. "Braced for Turbulence: Understanding and Managing Resistance to Change in the Higher Education Sector." *Management* 3(5) (2013): 243–251.

Christensen, Clayton M., Michael B. Horn, Louis Soares, and Louis Caldera. "Disrupting College: How Disruptive Innovation can Deliver Quality and Affordability to Postsecondary Education." Center for American Progress, Washington, DC, February 8, 2011. https://www.americanprogress.org/issues/economy/reports/2011/02/08/9034/disrupting-college/.

City University of New York. "ASAP at a Glance." Accessed August 20, 2019. http://www1.cuny.edu/sites/asap/about/asap-at-a-glance/.

———. "Program Overview." Accessed August 20, 2019. http://www1.cuny.edu/sites/asap/wp-content/uploads/sites/8/2019/08/ASAP_program_overview_web_8.1.19.pdf.

Clark, Burton R. "The Organizational Saga in Higher Education." *Administrative Science Quarterly* 17(2) (1972): 178–184.

Cohen, Arthur M., Florence B. Brawer, and Carrie B. Kisker. *The American Community College*. San Francisco: Jossey-Bass, 2014.

Cohen, William A. *The Art of the Leader*. Englewood Cliffs, NJ: Prentice Hall, 1990.

College Board. "Trends in College Pricing 2018." Report, College Board, New York, 2018. https://trends.collegeboard.org/sites/default/files/2018-trends-in-college-pricing.pdf.

Cortez, Meghan Bogardus. "3 Ways Community Colleges Leverage Tech Successfully." *EdTech*, March 12, 2018. https://edtechmagazine.com/higher/article/2018/03/3-ways-community-colleges-leverage-tech-successfully.

Coster, Joanne E., Janette K. Turner, Daniel Bradbury, and Anna Cantrell. "Why do People Choose Emergency and Urgent Care Services? A Rapid Review Utilizing a Systematic Literature Search and Narrative Synthesis." *Academic Emergency Medicine* 24(9) (2017): 1137–1149.

Cueseo, Joseph B. *Igniting Student Involvement, Peer Interaction, and Teamwork: A Taxonomy of Specific Cooperative Learning Structures and Collaborative Learning Strategies.* Stillwater, OK: New Forums Press, 2002.

Cusumano, Michael, Steve Kahl, and Fernando F. Suarez. "Produce, Process, and Service: A New Industry Lifecycle Model." Center for eBusiness@MIT, Paper 228, Massachusetts Institute of Technology, Cambridge, June 2006. http://web.mit.edu/sis07/www/cusumano.pdf.

Dafny, Leemore S., and Thomas H. Lee. "Health Care Needs Real Competition." *Harvard Business Review* (December 2016). https://hbr.org/2016/12/health-care-needs-real-competition.

Deal, Terrence E., and Allan A. Kennedy. "Culture: A New Look Through Old Lenses." *Journal of Applied Behavioral Science* 19(4) (1983): 498–505.

Deena, Eric. "The Business Model of Higher Education." *Educause Review* (March/April, 2014): 62–63. https://er.educause.edu/articles/2014/3/the-business-model-of-higher-education.

Dietz-Uhler, Beth, and Janet E. Hurn. "Using Learning Analytics to Predict (and Improve) Student Success: A Faculty Perspective." *Journal of Interactive Online Learning* 12(1) (2013): 17–26.

DiSalvo, Daniel, and Jeffrey Kucik. "Pensions are Killing Higher Education: States are Opting to Fund Pensions and other Obligations over Education." *U.S. News and World Report*, June 2, 2017. https://www.usnews.com/opinion/articles/2017-06-02/public-pensions-are-killing-higher-education.

Donaldson, Paul, Lyle McKinney, Mimi Lee, and Diana Pino. "First-Year Community College Students' Perceptions of and Attitudes Toward Intrusive Academic Advising." *NACADA Journal* 36(1) (2016): 30–42.

Drury, Richard L. "Community College in America: A Historical Perspective." *Inquiry* 8(1) (2003). https://files.eric.ed.gov/fulltext/EJ876835.pdf.

Dunagan, Alana. "College Transformed: Five Institutions Leading the Charge in Innovation." Report, Clayton Christensen Institute, Redwood City, CA, February 2017. https://files.eric.ed.gov/fulltext/ED586366.pdf.

Ebersole, John. "The Unexamined Factors Behind the Student Debt 'Crisis.'" *Forbes*, September 15, 2016. https://www.forbes.com/sites/johnebersole/2015/09/15/the-unexamined-factors-behind-the-student-debt-crisis/#5123ac334b89.

Eckel, Peter D., and Adrianna Kezar. "The Intersecting Authority of Boards, Presidents, and Faculty: Toward Shared Leadership." In *American Higher Education in the 21st Century: Social, Political, and Economic Changes*, 4th ed., edited by Michael N. Bastedo, Philip G. Altbach, and Patricia J. Gumport, 155–190. Baltimore: Johns Hopkins Press, 2016.

Ehrenberg, Ronald G. "American Higher Education in Transition." *The Journal of Economic Perspectives* 26(1) (2012): 193–216.

Emmanouilidou, Lydia. "Sen. Warren Introduces Legislation to Fix 'Broken' Accreditation System." *WGBH News* (blog), September 22, 2016. http://blogs.wgbh.org/on-campus/2016/9/22/sen-warren-introduces-legislation-fix-broken-accreditation-system/.

Ender, Peker. "Campus as an Integrated Learning Environment: Learning on Campus Open Spaces." Manuscript Thesis, Middle East Technical University, Ankara, Turkey, 2010.

Esplin, Pat, Jenna Seabold, and Fred Pinnegar. "The Architecture of a High-Impact and Sustainable Peer Leader Program: A Blueprint for Success." *New Directions for Higher Education* 157 (2012): 85–100.

Fain, Paul. "Moody's Downgrades Higher Education Outlook." *Inside Higher Ed*, December 6, 2017. https://www.insidehighered.com/quicktakes/2017/12/06/moodys-downgrades-higher-educations-outlook.

———. "Rubio Reintroduces Accreditation Bill." *Inside Higher Ed*, March 15, 2017. https://www.insidehighered.com/quicktakes/2017/03/15/rubio-reintroduces-accreditation-bill.

———. "Logging Off, Dropping Off." *Inside Higher Ed*, June 13, 2016. https://www.insidehighered.com/news/2016/06/13/data-student-engagement-lms-key-predicting-retention.

Flanagan, Christine. "Business Model Innovation: A Blueprint for Higher Education." *Educause Review* (November/December 2012): 12–20. https://er.educause.edu/articles/2012/11/business-model-innovation—a-blueprint-for-higher-education.

Francis, Perry C., and Aaron S. Horn. "Campus-Based Practices for Promoting Student Success: Counseling Services." Research Brief, Midwestern Higher Education Compact, Minneapolis, MN, February 2016. https://www.mhec.org/sites/default/files/resources/20160215SS7_counseling_services.pdf.

Freeland, Richard M. "Yes, Higher Ed is a Business – but it's also a Calling." *Chronicle of Higher Education*, March 18, 2018. https://www.chronicle.com/article/Yes-Higher-Ed-Is-a-Business/242852.

Freeman, Lynn C. "Establishing Effective Academic Practices to Influence Student Learning and Success." *Peer Review* 10(1) (2008). https://www.aacu.org/publications-research/periodicals/establishing-effective-advising-practices-influence-student.

Freeman, Scott, Sarah L. Eddy, Miles McDonough, Michelle K. Smith, Nnadozie Okoroafor, Hannah Jordt, and Mary Pat Wenderoth. "Active Learning Increases Student Performance in Science, Engineering, and Mathematics." *Proceedings of the National Academy of Sciences of the United States of America* 23 (2014): 8410–8415. https://www.pnas.org/content/111/23/8410#sec-2.

Frizzera, John. "Colleges and Cash Crops – Creating New Revenue Streams." idFive, Baltimore, October 13, 2017. https://idfive.com/ideas/college-revenue-streams/.

Ganser, Stephanie R., and Tricia L. Kennedy. "Where It All Began: Peer Education and Leadership in Student Services." *New Directions for Higher Education* 157 (2012): 17–29.

Geertz, Clifford. *The Interpretation of Cultures*. New York: Basic Books, 1973.

Gilde, Christian. *Higher Education: Open for Business*. Lanham, MD: Lexington Books, 2007.

Goldrick-Rab, Sara. *Paying the Price: College Costs, Financial Aid, and the Betrayal of the American Dream*. Chicago: University of Chicago Press, 2016.

Goldrick-Rab, Sara, Christine Baker-Smith, Vanessa Coca, and Elizabeth Looker. "City University of New York #RealCollege Survey." Report, The Hope Center for College, Community, and Justice, Philadelphia, 2019. https://hope4college.com/wp-content/uploads/2019/03/HOPE_realcollege_CUNY_report_final_webversion.pdf.

Goldrick-Rab, Sara, Christine Baker-Smith, Vanessa Coca, Elizabeth Looker, and Tiffani Williams. "College and University Basic Needs Insecurity: A National #RealCollege Survey Report." Report, The Hope Center for College, Community, and Justice, Philadelphia, 2019. https://hope4college.com/wp-content/uploads/2019/04/HOPE_realcollege_National_report_digital.pdf.

Goldrick-Rab, Sara, and Clare Cady. "Supporting Community College Completion with a Culture of Caring: A Case Study of Amarillo College." Report, The Hope Center for College, Community, and Justice, Philadelphia, 2018. https://hope4college.com/wp-content/uploads/2018/09/wisconsin-hope-lab-case-study-amarillo-college.pdf.

Goldrick-Rab, Sara, Jed Richardson, Joel Schneider, Anthony Hernandez, and Clare Cady. "Still Hungry and Homeless in College." Report, The Hope Center for College, Community, and Justice, Philadelphia, 2018. https://hope4college.com/wp-content/uploads/2018/09/Wisconsin-HOPE-Lab-Still-Hungry-and-Homeless.pdf.

Grawe, Nathan D. *Demographics and the Demand for Higher Education*. Baltimore: Johns Hopkins University Press, 2018.

Gronn, Peter. "Distributed Leadership as a Unit of Analysis." *The Leadership Quarterly* 13(5) (2002): 423–451.

Gruttadaro, Darcy, and Dana Crudo. "College Students Speak: A Survey on Mental Health." Report, National Alliance on Mental Health, Arlington County, VA, 2012. www.nami.org/namioncampus.

Hampson, Keith. "Business Model Innovation in Higher Education: Part I." February 2014. http://acrobatiq.com/business-model-innovation-in-higher-education-part-1/.

Harney, John O. "Exploring Higher Education Business Models – If Such a Thing Exists." *The New England Journal of Higher Education* (October 8, 2013). https://nebhe.org/journal/exploring-higher-education-business-models-if-such-a-thing-exists/.

Hirt, Joan B., and Tara E. Frank. "Student Development and Consumerism: Student Services on Campus." In *Understanding Community Colleges*, edited by John S. Levin and Susan T. Katar, 37–52. New York: Routledge, 2013.

Hogan, Tory H., Christy Harris Lemak, Nataliya Ivankova, Larry R. Herald, Jack Wheeler, and Nir Menachemi. "Hospital Vertical Integration into Subacute Care as a Strategic Response to Value-Based Payment Incentives, Market Factors, and Organizational Factors: A Multiple-Case Study." *Inquiry* 55 (2018). https://www.ncbi.nlm.nih.gov/pmc/articles/PMC6047235/.

Horton, Joann. "Identifying At-Risk Factors that Affect College Student Success." *International Journal of Process Education* 7(1) (2015): 83–101.

Huggins, Christopher M., and Janet P. Stamatel. "An Exploratory Study Comparing the Effectiveness of Lecturing versus Team-based Learning." *Contexts* 43(3) (2015): 227–235.

Hussar, William J., and Tabitha M. Bailey. "Projections of Education Statistics to 2027: Forty-Sixth Edition." Report, National Center for Education Statistics, Washington, DC, 2019. https://nces.ed.gov/pubs2019/2019001.pdf.

Jackson, Abby. "This Chart Shows how Quickly College Tuition has Skyrocketed Since 1980." *Business Insider*, July 20, 2015. https://www.businessinsider.com/this-chart-shows-how-quickly-college-tuition-has-skyrocketed-since-1980-2015-7.

Johnson, Mark W., Clayton M. Christensen, and Henning Kagermann. "Reinventing Your Business Model." *Harvard Business Review* (December 2008): 51–59.

Johnstone, D. Bruce. "Financing American Higher Education: Reconciling Institutional Financial Viability and Student Affordability." In *American Higher Education in the 21st Century: Social, Political, and Economic Changes*, 4th ed., edited by Michael N. Bastedo, Philip G. Altbach, and Patricia J. Gumport, 310–344. Baltimore: Johns Hopkins Press, 2016.

Joliet Junior College. "History." Accessed July 23, 2019. https://www.jjc.edu/about-jjc/history.

Jones, Juli A. "Foundation of Corporatization: Lessons from the Community College." *Society for History Education* 41(2) (2008): 213–217.

Junco, Reynol, and Dianne M. Timm, eds. *Using Emerging Technologies to Enhance Student Engagement* 124 (Winter 2008). San Francisco: Jossey-Bass, 2009.

Kaiser, Laura S., and Thomas H. Lee. "Turning Value-Based Health Care into a Real Business Model." *Harvard Business Review* (October 8, 2015). https://hbr.org/2015/10/turning-value-based-health-care-into-a-real-business-model.

Karp, Melinda Mechur. "Toward a New Understanding of Non-Academic Student Support: Four Mechanisms Encouraging Positive Student Outcomes in the Community College." CCRC Working Paper No. 28, Teachers College, New York, 2011.

Katar, Susan T. "Community College Faculty Conceptualizations of Shared Governance: Shared Understandings of a Sociopolitical Reality." *Community College Review* 45(3) (2017): 234–257.

Keenan, Boyd R. "The Need for Closer Conformity to the Business Model." *The Journal of Higher Education* 32(9) (1961): 513–515. https://www.jstor.org/stable/1979688.

Kelchen, Robert. "Is Administrative Bloat Really a Big Problem?" Kelchen on Education (blog), May 10, 2018. https://robertkelchen.com/2018/05/10/is-administrative-bloat-a-problem/.

Keller, George. *Academic Strategy: The Management Revolution in American Higher Education*. Baltimore: Johns Hopkins University Press, 1983.

Khan, Muhammad Saqib, Irfanullah Khan, Qamar Afaq Qureshi, Hafiz Muhammad Ismail, Hamid Rauf, Abdul Latif, and Muhammad Tahir. "The Styles of Leadership." *Public Policy and Administration Research* 5(3) (2015): 87–92.

King, Gary, and Maya Sen. "The Troubled Future of Colleges and Universities." *Political Science and Politics* 46(1) (2013): 83–89.

Kolenovic, Zineta, Donna Linderman, and Melinda Mechur Karp. "Improving Student Outcomes via Comprehensive Supports: Three-Year Outcomes from CUNY's Accelerated Study in Associate Programs (ASAP)." *Community College Review* 41(4) (2013): 271–291.

Kot, Felly Chiteng. "The Impact of Centralized Advising on First-Year Academic Performance and Second-Year Enrollment Behavior." *Research in Higher Education* 55(6) (2014): 527–563.

Kretschmer, Rainer, and Michael Nerlich. "Assessing the Impact of Telemedicine on Health Care Management." In *The Impact of Telemedicine on Health Care Management,* edited by Michael Nerlich and Rainer Kretschmer, 46–51. Amsterdam: IOS Press, 1999.

Kroll, Keith. "Teaching in the Commercialized Community College." *The Radical Teacher* 93 (Spring 2012): 12–21.

Kuh, George D., and Shouping Hu. "The Effects of Student-Faculty Interaction in the 1990s." *Review of Higher Education* 24(3) (2001): 309–332.

Kuh, George D., and Elizabeth J. Whitt. *The Invisible Tapestry: Culture in American Colleges and Universities*, ASHE-ERIC Higher Education Report No. 1. Washington, DC: Association for the Study of Higher Education, 1988.

Lansky, David, and Jeff Micklos. "Sustainable Financing for Complex Care Management is Critical to a Value-Driven Health Care System." January 31, 2019. https://catalyst.nejm.org/sustainable-financing-complex-care-management/.

Lapovsky, Lucie. "The Higher Education Business Model: Innovation and Financial Sustainability." Accessed November 17, 2018. https://www.tiaa.org/public/pdf/higher-education-business-model.pdf.

———. "The Changing Business Model for Colleges and Universities." *Forbes*, February 6, 2018. https://www.forbes.com/sites/lucielapovsky/2018/02/06/the-changing-business-model-for-colleges-and-universities/.

Larrat, Paul E., Rita M. Marcoux, and F. Randy Vogenberg. "Impact of Federal and State Legal Trends on Health Care Services." *Pharmacy and Therapeutics* 37(4) (2012): 218–226.

Latino, Jennifer A., and Catherine M. Unite. "Providing Academic Support through Peer Education." *New Directions for Higher Education* 157 (2012): 31–43.

Lee, Caity, and Laura Sponsler. "Improving Student Access & Utilization of Campus Mental Health Resources: A Memo for Vice President for Student Affairs." No date. https://www.naspa.org/images/uploads/main/Lee_NASPA_Memo.pdf.

Liu, Yuen Ting, and Clive Belfield. "Evaluating For-Profit Higher Education: Evidence from the Educational Longitudinal Student." A CAPSEE Working Paper, Center for Analysis of Postsecondary Education and Employment, New York, 2014.

Lowe, William J. "Can Business Learn from Higher Education?" *Change* 32(2) (2000): 4.

Lundberg, Carol A., and Laurie Schreiner. "Quality and Frequency of Faculty-Student Interaction as Predictors of Learning: An Analysis by Student Race/Ethnicity." *Journal of College Student Development* 45(5) (2004): 549–565.

Maldonado, Camilo. "Price of College Increasing Almost 8 Times Faster than Wages." *Forbes*, July 24, 2018. https://www.forbes.com/sites/camilomaldonado/2018/07/24/price-of-college-increasing-almost-8-times-faster-than-wages/#3744a0a566c1.

Malone, Thomas W., Peter Weill, Richard K. Lau, Victoria T. D'urso, George Herman, Thomas G. Apel, and Stephanie L. Woerner. "Do Some Business Models Perform Better than Others?" MIT Sloan Working Paper 4615-06, MIT Sloan School of Management, Boston, 2006.

Mareis, Claudia. "The Epistemology of the Unspoken: On the Concept of Tacit Knowledge in Contemporary Design Research." *Design Issues* 28(2) (2012): 61–71.

Martin, Emmie. "Here's How Much More Expensive It is for You to Go to College than It was for Your Parents." *CNBC Money*, November 29, 2017. https://www.cnbc.com/2017/11/29/how-much-college-tuition-has-increased-from-1988-to-2018.html.

Martin, Kimberly, Richard Galentino, and Lori Townsend. "Community College Student Success: The Role of Motivation and Self-Empowerment." *Community College Review* 42 (2014): 221–241.

McGahan, Anita M., Nicholas Argyris, and Joel A. C. Baum. "Context, Technology and Strategy: Forging New Perspectives on the Industry Life Cycle." In *Business Strategy over the Industry Lifecycle*, edited by Joel A. C. Baum and Anita M. McGahan, 1–24. United Kingdom: Emerald Group Publishing, 2004.

McMillan Cottom, Tressie. *Lower Ed: The Troubling Rise of For-Profit Colleges in the New Economy*. New York: The New Press, 2017.

Mellor, Jennifer, Michael Daly, and Molly Smith. "Does it Pay to Penalize Hospitals for Excess Readmissions? Intended and Unintended Consequences of Medicare's Hospital Readmissions Reductions Program." *Health Economics* 26(8) (2017): 1037–1051.

Miller, Danny. "Configurations Revisited." *Strategic Management Journal* 17(7) (1996): 505–512.

Mintzberg, Henry. *The Structuring of Organizations*. Englewood Cliffs, NJ: Prentice Hall, 1979.

Missouri State University. "Long Range Plan." Accessed July 17, 2019. https://www.missouristate.edu/assets/longrangeplan/cost_reduction_strategies.pdf.

Mitchell, Michael, Michael Leachman, and Kathleen Masterson. "Funding Down, Tuition Up: State Cuts to Higher Education Threaten Quality and Affordability at Public Colleges." Report, Center on Budget and Policy Priorities, Washington, DC, August 15, 2016. https://www.cbpp.org/research/state-budget-and-tax/funding-down-tuition-up.

Myran, Gundar. "The New Community College Business and Finance Model." *New Directions for Community Colleges* 162 (Summer 2013): 93–104.

National Center for Education Statistics. "Undergraduate Retention and Graduation Rates." Department of Education, Washington, DC, May 2009. https://nces.ed.gov/programs/coe/indicator_ctr.asp.

Newton, Derek. "Why College Tuition is Actually Higher for Online Programs." *Forbes*, June 25, 2018. https://www.forbes.com/sites/dereknewton/2018/06/25/why-college-tuition-is-actually-higher-for-online-programs/#17e3ebe8f11a.

Nonaka, Ikujiro, and Georg von Krogh. "Tacit Knowledge and Knowledge Conversion: Controversy and Advancement in Organizational Knowledge Creation Theory." *Organization Science* 20(3) (2009): 635–652.

Northhouse, Peter G. *Leadership: Theory and Practice*. Thousand Oaks: Sage, 2007.

Obergfell, MacGregor. "Performance Based Funding is Here to Stay." *New America*, June 21, 2018. https://www.newamerica.org/education-policy/edcentral/performance-based-funding-here-stay/.

Oblinger, Diana. "Leading the Transition from Classrooms to Learning Space." *Educause Quarterly* 1 (2005): 14–18.

Open Pedagogy Notebook. "What is Open Pedagogy?" Accessed August 6, 2019. http://openpedagogy.org/open-pedagogy/.

Osterwalder, Alexander, and Yves Pigneur. *Business Model Generation: A Handbook for Visionaries, Game Changers, and Challengers*. Hoboken, NJ: John Wiley & Sons, Inc., 2010.

Patterson, James. "Connecticut Community Colleges to Merge in Two Stages." *EducationDive*, June 20, 2018. https://www.educationdive.com/news/connecticut-community-colleges-to-merge-in-two-stages/526111/.

Pelletier, Stephen G. "Rethinking Revenue." *Public Purpose* (Summer 2012). https://www.aascu.org/WorkArea/DownloadAsset.aspx?id=5569.

Perna, Laura W., and Roman Ruiz. "Technology: The Solution to Higher Education's Pressing Problems?" In *American Higher Education in the 21st Century: Social, Political, and Economic Changes*, 4th ed., edited by Michael N. Bastedo, Philip G. Altbach, and Patricia J. Gumport, 432–461. Baltimore: Johns Hopkins Press, 2016.

Pierce, Lindsay. "The Case for a Case Management Approach in Advising Academically Underprepared Students." *Academic Advising Today* 39(4) (2016). https://www.nacada.ksu.edu/Resources/Academic-Advising-Today/View-Articles/The-Case-for-a-Case-Management-Approach-in-Advising-Academically-Underprepared-Students.aspx.

Porter, Michael E. "How Competitive Forces Shape Strategy." *Harvard Business Review* (October 1979). https://hbr.org/1979/03/how-competitive-forces-shape-strategy.

Quinn, Robert, and John Rohrbaugh. "A Spatial Model of Effectiveness Criteria: Toward a Competing Values Approach to Organizational Analysis." *Management Science* 29 (1983): 363–377.

Ran, Florence Xiaotao, and Di Xu. "How and Why do Adjunct Instructors Affect Students' Academic Outcomes? Evidence from Two-Year and Four-Year Colleges." CAPSEE Working Paper, Center for Analysis of Postsecondary Education and Employment, New York, 2017.

Rosenbaum, James, Keenan Cepa, and Janet Rosenbaum. "Beyond the One-Size-Fits-All College Degree." *Contexts* 12(1) (2013): 48–52.

Rubin, Beth. "University Business Models and Online Practices: A Third Way." *Online Journal of Distance Learning Administration* 25(1) (2013).

Sabol, Andrija, Matej Sander, and Durdica Fuckan. "The Concept of Industry Life Cycle and Development of Business Strategies." Paper presented at the Management, Knowledge, and Learning International Conference, Zadar, Croatia, June 2013.

Schein, Edgar. *Organizational Culture and Leadership*. San Francisco: Jossey-Bass, 1992.

Schreiner, Laurie A., Patrice Noel, Edward Anderson, and Linda Cantwell. "The Impact of Faculty and Staff on High-Risk College Student Persistence." *Journal of College Student Development* 52(2) (2011): 321–338.

Schroeder, Charles C. "Collaborative Partnerships: Keys to Enhancing Student Learning and Success." In *Challenging and Supporting the First-Year Student*, edited by M. Lee Upcraft, John N. Gardner, and Betsy O. Barefoot, 204–220. San Francisco: Jossey-Bass, 2004.

Schulte, Liz. "6 Alternative Revenue Streams for Colleges." *Direct Network*, June 9, 2017. https://directnetwork.mbsdirect.net/6-alternative-revenue-streams-for-colleges.

Schultz, David. "From the Editor – Public Affairs Education and the Failed Business Model of Higher Education." *Journal of Public Affairs Education* 19(2) (2013): ii–vii.

Selingo, Jeffrey. *College (Un)bound: The Future of Higher Education and what it Means for Students*. Las Vegas: Amazon Publishing, 2013.

Seymour, Daniel, and Michael Bourgeois. *Institutional Effectiveness Fieldbook: Creating Coherence in Colleges and Universities (Volume 2)*. Scotts Valley, CA: CreateSpace, 2018.

Shamsie, Jamal, and Michael J. Mannor. "Looking Inside the Dream Team: Probing into the Contributions of Tacit Knowledge as an Organizational Resource." *Organization Science* 24(2) (2013): 513–529.

Sharan, Alok D., Gregory D. Schroeder, Michael E. West, and Alexander R. Vaccaro. "Understanding Business Models in Health Care." *Clinical Spine Surgery* 29(4) (2016): 158–160.

Sheets, Robert, Stephen Crawford, and Luis Soares. "Rethinking Higher Educational Business Models: Steps Toward a Disruptive Innovation Approach to Understanding and Improving Higher Education Outcomes." Report, Center for American Progress, Washington, DC, 2012. https://cdn.americanprogress.org/wp-content/uploads/issues/ 2012/03/pdf/ higher_ed_business_models.pdf.

Shook, Jaime L., and Jennifer R. Keup. "The Benefits of Peer Leader Programs: An Overview from the Literature." *New Directions for Higher Education* 157 (2012): 5–16.

Shults, Christopher. "The Impact of Presidential Behaviors on Institutional Movement toward Greater Abundance in Community Colleges: An Exploratory Study." PhD dissertation, University of Michigan, Ann Arbor, 2009.

———. "Making the Case for a Positive Approach to Improving Organizational Performance in Higher Education Institutions." *Community College Review* 36(2) (2008): 133–159.

Simon, Caroline. "Bureaucrats and Buildings: The Case for Why College is So Expensive," *Forbes*, September 5, 2017. https://www.forbes.com/sites/carolinesimon/2017/09/05/bureaucrats-and-buildings-the-case-for-why-college-is-so-expensive/#7e90357e456a

Smart, John C. and Russell E. Hamm. "Organizational Effectiveness and Mission Orientations of Two-Year Colleges." *Research in Higher Education* 34(4) (1993a): 489–502.

———. "Organizational Culture and Effectiveness in Two-Year Colleges." *Research in Higher Education* 34(1) (1993b): 95–106.

Smart, John C., George D. Kuh, and William G. Tierney. "The Roles of Institutional Cultures and Decision Approaches in Promoting Organizational Effectiveness in Two-Year Colleges." *The Journal of Higher Education* 69(3) (1997): 256–281.

Smircich, Linda. "Concepts of Culture and Organizational Analysis." *Administrative Science Quarterly* 28(3) (1983): 339–358.

Smith, Elizabeth A. "The Role of Tacit Knowledge in the Workplace." *Journal of Knowledge Management* 5(4) (2001): 311–321. https://pdfs.semanticscholar.org/8433/09e392e6a2144c41fa643e699c0ae2bb6a9f.pdf.

Soares, Louis, Patricia Steele, and Lindsay Wayt. "Evolving Higher Education Business Models: Leading with Data to Deliver Results." Report, American Council on Education and Center for Policy Research and Strategy, Washington, DC, 2016. https://www.acenet.edu/news-room/Documents/Evolving-Higher-Education-Business-Models.pdf.

Soliz, Adela. "College Completion: The Effects of the Expansion of For-Profit Colleges on Student Enrollments and Outcomes at Public Colleges." EdD Thesis, Harvard University, Cambridge, MA, 2016.

Spillane, James P., and John B. Diamond. "Taking a Distributed Perspective." In *Distributed Leadership in Practice,* edited by James P. Spillane, John B. Diamond, and Joseph F. Murphy, 1–15. New York: Teachers College Press, 2007.

Spillane, James P. *Distributed Leadership.* San Francisco: Jossey-Bass, 2006.

Stenmark, Dick. "Leveraging Tacit Organizational Knowledge." *Journal of Management Information Systems* 17(3) (Winter 2000–2001): 9–24.

Strumbos, Diana, Donna Linderman, and Carson C. Hicks. "Postsecondary Pathways Out of Poverty: City University of New York Accelerated Study in Associate Programs and the Case for National Policy." *RSF: The Russell Sage Foundation Journal of the Social Sciences* 4(3) (2018): 100–117. https://www.jstor.org/stable/10.7758/rsf.2018.4.3.06#metadata_info_tab_contents.

Strumbos, Diana, and Zineta Kolenovic. "Six-Year Outcomes of ASAP Students: Transfer and Degree Attainment." Report, The City University of New York,

New York, January 2017. http://www1.cuny.edu/sites/asap/wp-content/uploads/sites/8/2017/01/201701_ASAP_Eval_Brief_Six_Year_Outcomes_FINAL.pdf.

Suddaby, Roy, and William M. Foster. "History and Organizational Change." *The Journal of Management* 43(1) (2017): 19–38.

Swanger, David. "Innovation in Higher Education: Can Colleges Really Change?" White Paper, Fulton-Montgomery Community College, Fulton County, NY, June 2016. https://www.fmcc.edu/about/files/2016/06/Innovation-in-Higher-Education.pdf.

Thompson, Derek. "This is the Way the College 'Bubble' Ends: Not with a Pop, but a Hiss." *The Atlantic*, July 26, 2017. https://www.theatlantic.com/business/archive/2017/07/college-bubble-ends/534915/.

Tierney, William G. "Organizational Culture in Higher Education: Defining the Essentials." *The Journal of Higher Education* 59(1) (1988): 2–21.

Toner, Mark. "The Highly Endangered Business Model (and How to Fix It)." Report, American Council on Education, Washington, DC, June 12, 2015. https://www.acenet.edu/the-presidency/columns-and-features/Pages/The-Highly-Endangered-Higher-Education-Business-Model.aspx.

Tovar, Esau, Merril A. Simon, and Howard B. Lee. "Development and Validation of the College Mattering Inventory with Diverse Urban College Students." *Measurement and Evaluation in Counseling and Development* 42 (2009): 154–178.

Umbach, Paul D., and Matthew R. Wawrzynski. "Faculty do Matter: The Role of College Faculty in Student Learning and Engagement." *Research in Higher Education* 46(2) (2005): 153–184.

Vance, Lara Kristin. "Best Practices in Tutoring Services and the Impact of Required Tutoring on High-Risk Students." *Online Theses and Dissertations* 441. https://encompass.eku.edu/etd/441.

VanWagoner, Randall. *Competing on Culture, Driving Change in Community Colleges*. Lanham, MD: Rowman & Littlefield, 2018

Vaughan, George B. *The Community College Story*. Washington, DC: Community College Press, 2006.

Weick, Karl E. *Making Sense of the Organization*. Hoboken, NJ: Wiley-Blackwell, 2000.

———. *Sensemaking in Organizations*. Los Angeles: Sage Publications, 1995.

———. "Educational Organizations as Loosely Coupled Systems." *Administrative Science Quarterly* 21(1) (1976): 1–19.

Wooten, Brian M., Joshua S. Hunt, Brian F. LeDuc, and Phillip Poskus. "Peer Leadership in the Cocurriculum: Turning Campus Activities into an Educationally Purposeful Enterprise." *New Directions for Higher Education* 157 (2012): 45–58.

Workman, John. "200 Ideas from the Frontier: Alternative Revenues in Higher Education." EAB, January 6, 2014. https://eab.com/insights/infographic/business-affairs/alternative-revenues-in-higher-education/.

Xu, Di. "Academic Performance in Community Colleges: The Influences of Part-Time and Full-Time Instructors." *American Educational Research Journal* 56(2) (2018): 368–406.

Young-Jones, Adena D., Tracie D. Burt, Stephanie Dixon, and Melissa J. Hawthorne. "Academic Advising: Does it Really Impact Student Success?" *Quality Assurance in Education* 21(1) (2013): 7–19.

Yunus, Muhammad, Bertrand Moingeon, and Laurence Lehmann-Ortega. "Building Social Business Models: Lessons from the Grameen Experience." *Long Range Planning* 43 (2010): 308–325.

Zaltman, Gerald, and Robert Duncan. *Strategies for Planned Change*. New York: Wiley-Interscience, 1977.

Zappia, Charles A. "Academic Professionalism and the Business Model in Education: Reflection of a Community College Historian." *The History Teacher* 33(1) (1999): 55–66.

Zavelle, Michael. "The Bifurcating Higher Education Business Model." In *Change We Must: Deciding the Future of Higher Education*, edited by Matthew Goldstein and George Otte, 7–31. New York: Rosetta Books, 2016.

Zell, Deone. "Organizational Change as a Process of Death, Dying, and Rebirth." *The Journal of Applied Behavioral Science* 39(1) (2003): 73–96.

Index

AACC. *See* American Association of Community College's Pathways Project
AAS. *See* associate in applied science
AC. *See* Amarillo College
ACA. *See* Affordable Care Act
academic departments and majors: additions in, 154; challenges in, 153; economic and societal and technology shifts in, 154; enrollment decline impact in, 153–54; ethnic and gender studies in, 154; relevancy and efficacy evaluation in, 154–55
Accelerated Study in Associate Programs (ASAP) case study, 198; academic support services in, 170; career development in, 170; cohort experience in, 170; CUNY and New York Center for Economic Opportunity partnership in, 169; economic mobility in, 169; financial support in, 170; full course load in, 170; goal of, 169; intrusive and individualized advisement in, 170; results of, 169; student demographics in, 169; student outcomes in, 170–71; success and replication of, 171; transportation costs and books and wraparound support services challenge in, 169–70
ACCT. *See* Association of Community College Trustees
Achieving the Dream (ATD), 16, 44–45, 59, 189
adhocracy culture, 60–61, 65–66, 82, 85, 140
administration, 56, 158–59, 167–68, 182, 184, 196–97; abundance approach use of, 73–74; CCBM role of, 71–74; centralization and standardization in, 72; change pace determination of, 73; cultural dynamics understanding of, 72; definition of, 71; formalization and specialization in, 72; institutional culture accountability in, 73; investment building of, 74; organizational business and management approaches continuum in, 72; role of, 120; scale of change determination of, 73; strategic and operational principles introduction of, 73
administration and governance and leadership hypothetical case studies, 82; adhocracy culture example

215

216 *Index*

and questions in, 85; clan culture example and questions in, 84–85; hierarchy culture example and questions in, 86; market culture example and questions in, 86–87
administrative, educational, and student support units (AES), 156, 167
advising, 122, 124–25, 157, 160–61, 164, 170
Advocacy and Resource Center (ARC), 109
AES. *See* administrative, educational, and student support units
Affordable Care Act (ACA), 23
Amarillo College (AC) case study, 197; CCBM representation in, 112; culture of caring in, 108, 111; faculty and staff student success participation in, 110; greeters and secret shopper program in, 111; institutional values of, 110; No Excuses Poverty Initiative at, 108, 109; redesign decision at, 110; relationships and empathy in, 111; student knowing in, 108; student population at, 109; student success examination at, 109; SVP at, 111–12; Wisconsin HOPE Lab survey participation and results of, 109; Witherspoon's predictive analytics use in, 109–10; Zappos team challenge concept in, 110–11; Zappos value reframing example in, 110
American Association of Community College's (AACC) Pathways Project, 44–45, 59, 189
ARC. *See* Advocacy and Resource Center
Arizona State University, 35
ASAP. *See* Accelerated Study in Associate Programs
associate in applied science (AAS), 137
Association of Community College Trustees (ACCT), 75
ATD. *See* Achieving the Dream

basic needs insecurity, 102, 158, 165–66
Baumol, William J., cost disease of, 92, 181
business industry standard lifecycle phases, 20
butcher knife budgeting, 177, 184–85

career development, 170
CBE. *See* competency-based education
CCAM. *See* community college abundance model
CCBM. *See* community college business model
CCCOER. *See* Community College Consortium for Open Educational Resources
Central Piedmont Community College (CPCC), 137
Chronicle of Higher Education, 3
City University of New York (CUNY), 169, 198
clan culture, 60–61, 62–65, 78, 79, 82, 84–85
CMS. *See* course management system
community college abundance model (CCAM), 81
community college business model (CCBM), 34–35; adhocracy and clan culture in, 60–61; administration and governance and leadership hypothetical case studies in, 82, 84–87; administration in, 71–74; as anti-corporate business model, 41; assessment and evaluation importance in, 44; ATD and AACC commonality with, 45; business and finance dimensions in, 42; change process intentionality of, 41; concept of, 2; corporate model difference in, 5–6; cost containment and scalability in, 15; crosswalk table in, 9, *10*; culture type hypothetical case studies for, 62–68; design thinking in, 45; distributed leadership in, 80–82; educational experience as product

Index 217

in, 12; effective model development approach in, 91; empathizing as stage in, 46; flexible thinking and decision making in, 61; for-profit colleges' programs and services and processes relevance to, 15; four fundamental objectives in, 8; four pillars of, 88; goal of, 5–6; governance in, 71, 74–77; healthcare industry similarities with, 14; IIE models in, 44; inventory of tools use in, 42–43; key resource identification in, 11–12, 48, *49*, 115; language concerns about, 41–42; leadership in, 71, 77–80; mechanisms and processes and structures intentional connection in, 12–13, 48; operational innovation disruptive approach of, 44, 57–58; operationalized definition of, 9; organizational behavior and management and leadership literature incorporation in, 5; organizational effectiveness enhancing in, 13, 68; organizational effectiveness management techniques limitations in, *43*; primary function of, 8; primary stakeholder serving in, 11; product delivery in, 48, *50*; profit formula for, 13; resources and finances distinction in, 11–12; singular mission and set of values in, 41; social business model concept in, 8; social impact maximizing in, 195; solutions-oriented framework of, 46; student population consideration in, 11; student success and, 11, 43, 59, 102, 196; SVP as primary focus of, 11, 47, *47*, 108, 113, 195

Community College Consortia to Education Health IT Professionals in Health Care Program, 138

Community College Consortium for Open Educational Resources (CCCOER), 137–38

community colleges: access commitment of, 31; accidental business models use of, 6, 42; accountability requirements challenge in, 32; adaptability of, 22; administration responsibility in, 56; ATD and AACC student success redesign challenge to, 44–45; business model concept and definitions for, 2, 7–8; business model differences between for-profit colleges and, 7; business model framework questions and response in, 10, *10*; challenges of, 1; change in, 68–69; compliance documentation and, 33; compliance expectations change impact on, 33; culture types and factors and change in, 69; current environment reacting of, 19; demographic shifts proactive addressing of, 29; demography impact in, 27–29; design thinking in, 45, 59; disruption concept understanding of, 25, 196; disruptive innovations and examples for, 26–27, 59; educational business of, 5; enrollment and economic strength inverse relationship in, 28; expansion lifecycle of, 21; federal government accreditation impact in, 32–33; financial model of, 46–47; financial picture for, 31, 117; financial support waning of, 19; for-profit provider presence impacting, 34; founding lifecycle of, 20–21; framework in, 6; growth lifecycle of, 21; healthcare industry insight gain of, 25; high school graduates race and ethnicity percentages in, 29; human development and societal impact purpose of, 9, 41, 147, 179, 185, 195, 199; hybrid innovations and, 27; IIE use in, 44; industry characteristics and, 4; industry shakeout and decline stages similarities in, 21–22; innovation forms in, 25; institutional culture and subcultures in, 58; institutional planning forms in, 44; key resource categories of, 115, *116*; key resource identification in, 48, *49*; loose and tight coupling concept in, 56; maturity lifecycle of, 21; as open access institutions, 1–2; operational management value proposition focus in, 49; operations consolidation of, 25; organizational culture impact in, 53; performance-based funding push in, 32; pipeline shrinking and enrollment percentages in, 28; proactive and reactive decisions in, 6; product delivery in, 48, *50*; as professional bureaucracy, 56, 74, 196; profit formula need of, 175; prototypical operating practices problems of, 42; public disinvestment of, 30, 195; regulatory oversight of, 5; reinvention lifecycle of, 21; scrutiny growth on, 1; as social business, 9, 199; solutions development process strategies for, 46; stability of, 1; stakeholder serving in, 9; state low-cost business model use for, 30–31; state revenue competition in, 30; state spending on higher education and, 29–30; strategy purpose in, 43; student and community needs met in, 6–7; student learning and success redesign of, 4; student relationship with, 5; student success intentional design in, 22; student underserving of, 45; support structures and missions of, 5; sustaining innovation move to disruption in, 42; sustaining innovations and examples in, 25–26; SVP considerations of, 112–13; technology disruptive influence on, 34; three operational subgroups in, 56; traditional operational and management practices of, 15–16; transformation and redesign urgency for, 21; tuition increase in, 31; underserved populations in, 9; upheaval examples in, 22; volume to value in, 14

community outreach, hypothetical case study: community disconnect in, 106; needs addressing in, 107–8; political and social pressure in, 106–7; primary problems in, 107; SVP definition in, 107

competency-based education (CBE), 153

compliance, 33, 168, 183

Connecticut State Colleges & Universities Board of Regents, 22

cost containment, 15, 198; "administrative bloat" assumption in, 182; administrators increase in, 184; budgetary processes transparency and communication lack in, 186; butcher knife budgeting and denominator management in, 184–85; college culture in, 185; compliance personnel increase in, 183; cost cutting tactics in, 185, 186, *187*, 192; cost savings decisions in, 185; counseling staff and academic support personnel increase in, 183; culture type in, 185; expenditure-reduction model considerations and processes in, 185–86; faculty increase in, 183; grant staff increase in, 183; information examination in, 186; information technology staff increase in, 183; institutional research and planning staff increase in, 183–84; instructional space development in, 184; instruction as budgeting priority in, 182; leadership type in, 185; marketing and public relations and development staff increase in, 184; new academic and student support buildings establishment in, 184; online courses

hidden costs and recoupment in, 182–83; operational costs managing in, 184; partnerships in, 186; reactive budgeting in, 184; revenue decline and, 184; student population served in, 185; student support staff increase in, 183; technology building and support costs in, 184
cost disease. *See* Baumol, William J.
cost structure: Baumol's cost disease in, 181; cost and price difference in, 178; cost-driven and value-driven models in, 179; cost reduction necessity in, 179; direct and indirect costs in, 180; drivers of, 177; economies of scale and misuse in, 180; economies of scope in, 180; effectiveness-minded approaches and, 182; efficiency and productivity and resource deployment improvement in, 181–82; fixed costs in, 180; human labor in, 179; hybrid cost model in, 179; multiple subcultures and, 178–79; primary characteristics in, 179–80; production costs increase in, 181; productivity and efficiencies measures in, 181; productivity focus and, 180–81; variable costs in, 180
course management system (CMS), 134, 183
CPCC. *See* Central Piedmont Community College
crosswalk table, 9, *10*
culture of care, 64, 84, 108, 111, 123–24, 127, 189
culture type, 61; in community colleges, 69; in cost containment, 185; decision-making category and institutional orientation of, *60*; hypothetical case studies of, 62–68; leadership and, 78, *79*, 80; in revenue generation, 190
culture type hypothetical case studies: adhocracy culture example and questions in, 65–66; clan culture example and questions in, 62–65; hierarchy culture example and questions in, 66–67; market culture example and questions in, 67–68; in organizational change, 62
CUNY. *See* City University of New York
curriculum: change historical context in, 155; corequisite courses and, 155; faculty engagement in, 155; OER in, 156; online education and hybrid courses in, 156; self-paced developmental coursework in, 155

denominator management, 184–85
design thinking, 59; defining in, 45; empathizing in, 45; ideate in, 46; prototype in, 46; testing in, 46
distributed leadership, 80–82, *83*
dollars chasing, 189–90

economy of scale, 135, 180
educational and student support, 124, 133, 183–84; academic coaching and success coaches in, 164; advising caseload approach and high-impact practices in, 164; basic needs handling in, 165–66; career services function in, 165; college-wide adherence in, 164; counseling service utilization strategies in, 165; peer tutoring in, 165; SI use in, 165; staff member responsibility in, 164
educational experience support, 121; administrative element in, 158–59; advising as, 157; AES in, 156; basic needs support in, 158; college website in, 159; counseling and health services in, 157–58; critical functions of, 156; equipment and information technology in, 159; financial aid in, 158; internships as, 157; learning communities and cohort programs in, 158; library and

220 *Index*

learning resource as, 157; structure and space in, 159; student activities as, 157; student success importance in, 156; tutoring as, 157
educational pipeline, 28, 136–37
educational programming: CBE approach in, 153; collaborative process benefits in, 152; community programming in, 152; education and training difference in, 151; faculty in, 153; life experiences credit in, 153; new approaches in, 152–53; occupational programs in, 151–52; programming philosophies reevaluation in, 151–52; stackable credentials in, 153; workforce development programs in, 152
EHR. *See* electronic health record
electronic administrative systems, 167–68
electronic health record (EHR), 138
empathy, 45–46, 111
EMS. *See* enrollment management system
enrollment, 28, 124, 176, 188–89
enrollment management system (EMS), 134, 168
expansion lifecycle, 21

facilities, 91, 117; facilities range in, 128–29; facilities satisfaction degree tools in, 129; institutional integrity and, 129; open learning and communal space intentional design in, 129; physical space for student success design lack in, 130, *131*; question addressing in, 130; space utilization impact in, 130; SVP support in, 129
faculty, 74–76, 110, 119, 153, 183; academic skills focus of, 121; advisor and mentor and developer roles of, 122; commitment and dedication of, 120; curriculum engagement of, 155; educational experiences creation of, 121; engagement encouraging of, 121; full-time and part-time impact of, 122; higher-order learning focus of, 121; leadership opportunities considerations of, 123–24; positive student relationships of, 120; processes obligations of, 160–61; regular student interactions of, 121; student capabilities and abilities strengths-based approach of, 121; student outcome success considerations in, 122; supportive teaching and learning environment considerations in, 123; teaching adaptability of, 121
financial aid, 102, 158
financial austerity, 186–88
flipped classrooms, 163
food and housing insecurity, 97, 102, 104, 166, 169
founding lifecycle, 20–21

games and gaming, 163
George Mason University (GMU), 136
GI Bill, 21
GMU. *See* George Mason University
governance, 196–97; ACCT principles in, 75; board change support and roles in, 75; Board of Trustees in, 74; board proactive engagement in, 75–76; College Executive responsibilities in, 74, 76; definition of, 71; Faculty Senate CCBM involvement in, 76; Faculty Senate in, 74–75; primary groups responsible for, 74–75; shared process in, 76–77; student success shared responsibility in, 77; subculture collaboration in, 76; trust and respect in, 77
growth lifecycle, 21
Guided Pathways colleges, 16

HEA. *See* Higher Education Act
healthcare industry, 30; ACA and, 23, 24; CCBM similarities with, 14; change drivers in, 23; changes in, 14; community colleges insight from, 25; financial liability in, 24; financial resources generation in, 8; individualized medicine expansion in, 24; insurance providers and healthcare systems partnerships in, 23; modified business model of, 8; patient-centric value proposition in, 23, 24; patient outcome quality in, 23; patient value creation in, 8; population-based to value-based business models in, 14; significant disruption in, 22–23; as social business, 8–9; subacute care services experimenting in, 24; technology advances and market trends disrupting, 23; telemedicine introduction in, 23; underserved populations in, 9; urgent care clinics and ambulatory facilities use in, 23–24; value-based approach in, 24
hierarchy culture, 60–61, 66–67, 78, 79, 80, 86
higher education: adhocracy culture in, 60–61; Baumol's cost disease in, 181; business industry standard lifecycle phases and, 20; business model concepts to questions translations for, *10*; business models research and view and rejection of, 3, 19; business questions regarding, 4–5; changing and fluid dynamics in, 16; clan culture in, 60–61; cost-cutting and revenue-generating tactics and, 192; culture types in, 60–61; external influence immunity of, 19; federal government accreditation impact in, 32–33; financial austerity in, 186–87; for-profit providers and rise in, 6, 34; hierarchy culture in, 60–61; market force protection in, 3–4; organizational culture and, 59; ROI focus in, 32; state spending on, 29–30; student loan debt in, 32; teaching importance in, 161; technology influence examples in, 34–35
Higher Education Act (HEA), 33
Hope Center for College, Community, and Justice, 102
human resources, 91, 117, 197; academic preparation in, 118; clear goals in, 118; college plans in, 118; cultural capital in, 118; external demands managing in, 119; faculty and staff behaviors in, 119–20; graduates common characteristics in, 118–19; preenrollment characteristics in, 118; self-empowerment in, 119; skills and behaviors and attitudes in, 119; socioeconomically disadvantaged students in, 119; student validation in, 119; success desire in, 118–19. *See also* faculty; staff; students

integrated institutional effectiveness (IIE) model, 44, 167
intellectual resources, 91, 117, 197–98; partnerships as, 135–38; tacit knowledge as, 138–41
Iota College (fictitious name) real life case study: adhocracy model culture in, 140; explicit knowledge conversion at, 141; horse sense for leaders program and study in, 140–41; tacit knowledge and organizational success at, 140

Joliet Junior College (JJC), 20–21

Kaplan University, 35
key resources, 88, 91, 195, 197; CCBM identification of, 11–12, 48, *49*, 115; community colleges categories of, 115, *116*; corporations and social

businesses use of, 115; facilitated networks in, 117; finances managing distinction from, 116–17; key product development responsibility in, 115–16; resource deployment variations in, 117; solution shops in, 117; tangible or intangible, 115; understanding of, 141; value-adding process in, 117. *See also* human resources; intellectual resources; physical resources

leadership, 5, 161, 185, 190, 196–97; abundance practices in, 81–82; as action oriented, 77; autocratic leadership and hierarchy culture in, 78, *79*, 80; CCAM leaders responsibility in, 81; culture type understanding in, 80; definitions of, 71, 77–78; democratic and participative approach and clan types in, 53, 78, *79*, 82; distributed approach and CCAM in, 81; distributed approach principles in, 80–81; distributed leadership and subculture value in, 80; distributed leadership principles and practices for, 82, *83*; faculty opportunities considerations in, 123–24; laissez faire approach and clan types in, 78, *79*; situational type of, 78; styles and culture type alignment in, 78, *79*; as value neutral construct, 78
learning management system (LMS), 134, 168, 183
life experiences credit, 153
Lowery-Hart, Russell, 108, 110–11

market culture, 60, 67–68, 86–87
maturity lifecycle, 21
mechanisms, 12–13, 48, 92, 148, 198; academic departments and majors as, 153–55; curriculum as, 155–56; educational experience support as, 156–59; educational programming as, 151–53; institutional student ready analysis and questions in, 150–51; students' educational experience frameworks in, 150; teaching and learning experience in, 150
Mercedes Benz, 137

NAICS. *See* North American Industry Classification System
New York Center for Economic Opportunity, 169
No Excuses Poverty Initiative, 108, 109
North American Industry Classification System (NAICS), 4
Northern Virginia Community College (NOVA), 136

occupational programs, 151–52
OER. *See* open educational resources
Office of the National Coordinator for Health Information Technology (ONC), 138
open educational resources (OER), 138, 156, 183
open pedagogy, 163
organizational change, 196; adhocracy and clan culture type success in, 82; cultural factors inventory impact to, *64*; culture type hypothetical case studies in, 62–68; institutional history factor in, 61–62; institutional history methods impact in, *63*; internal subgroups role in, 53; major change initiatives responses in, 55–56; organization description in, 55; resistance to, 61; subculture values retreat in, 58
organizational culture, 68; CCBM subculture cohesion in, 57; in community colleges, 53; culture type by decision-making category and institutional orientation in, *60*; definition of, 57; disruption examples in, 59; emergent forces in, 58; institutional and subculture

values tension in, 56–57; institutional culture and subcultures in, *58*; organization and culture constructs in, 57; societal and higher education and college in, 59; subgroup continual influence in, 58; subgroup cultures in, 57

organizational effectiveness, 13, *43*, 68, 131

partnerships, 23, 186; CCCOER example in, 137–38; consortia arrangements and examples in, 137–38; CPCC example in, 137; educational pipeline and examples in, 136–37; external stakeholder connections in, 135; long-term relationships guiding principles in, 135–36; NOVA AND GMU example in, 136; ONC example in, 138; optimization and economy of scale in, 135; P-TECH example in, 136–37; resources and activities acquisition in, 135–36; in revenue generation, 190–91; risk and uncertainty reduction in, 135–36; shared values in, 135; Shelton State Community College example in, 137; students as primary beneficiaries of, 138; workforce development and examples in, 137

Pathways in Technology Early College High (P-TECH), 136–37

physical resources, 91, 117, 197; facilities as, 128–30; technology as, 130–35

Prince George's Community college, 136–37

Prince George's County Public Schools, Maryland, 136

processes, 12–13, 15, 48, 92, 148–49, 198; activities core of, 160; continuous evaluation of, 160; educational and student support in, 164–66; faculty and advisor obligations in, 160–61; how in, 159–60; leadership shared approach and, 161; organizational architecture challenge in, 161; as personal, 160; teaching in, 161–63

product delivery, 48, *50*, 88, 141, 195; challenging environment of, 149; economic factors impact in, 149; educational experience reimagining in, 171; financial solvency in, 149; lever categories in, 148–49; mechanisms in, 92, 148, 150–59; notion understanding of, 148; optimized educational experience in, 148; processes in, 92, 148–49, 159–66; revenue generation in, 171; social business model goal in, 147; structures in, 92, 149, 166–71; student expectations in, 149–50; three components of, 91–92; traditional understanding and modified description of, 147–48

profit formula, 13, 88, 195, 198; Baumol's cost disease in, 92; broad numerator-focused management practices, 177; broken business model in, 178; community college need of, 175; as corporate concept, 175; cost reduction and revenue increase determination in, 178; costs and revenue consideration in, 176; costs evaluation in, 177; cost structure drivers in, 177; cost structure in, 178–82; denominator-focused budgeting avoidance in, 177; enrollment view in, 176; financial resources and, 92, 116; financial strategy term in, 175; funds deployment in, 176; indiscriminate cutting in, 172; main purpose of, 176; resource generation in, 92; revenue generation in, 177, 186–92

P-TECH. *See* Pathways in Technology Early College High

Purdue Global, 35

\# RealCollege survey, 103
reinvention lifecycle, 21
resources. *See* key resources
return on investment (ROI), 32
revenue generation, 177, 198–99; college culture in, 190; culture of care and, 189; culture type in, 190; dollars chasing in, 189–90; enrollment increase tactic in, 188–89; financial austerity and rationale in, 186–88; financial stewardship in, 192; finite resources in, 189; grant funding in, 190; leadership type in, 190; major issue in, 188; partnership pursuit in, 190–91; product delivery and, 171; resource development considerations in, 190–91; stable funding era in, 188; student population served in, 191; student retention strategy in, 189; tacit knowledge use in, 192; tactics for, *191*; traditional approaches and, 192; tuition revenue reliance in, 188
ROI. *See* return on investment

science, technology, engineering and math (STEM), 137, 154
Shelton State Community College, Alabama, 137
SI. *See* supplemental instruction
SIC. *See* Standard Industrial Classification system
SIS. *See* student information system
social business model, 8–9, 115, 147, 199
social media, 163
Southern New Hampshire University, 34
staff, 110, 119–20; aspirations and secure commitment clarification of, 125; cocurricular services of, 124; college sensemaking function of, 125; comprehensive advisement approach of, 124–25; culture of care maintaining of, 124; development opportunities and considerations for, 126–27; educational and student support responsibility of, 164; enrollment management of, 124; learning and student support of, 124; out-of-classroom educational experience considerations in, 126; respected leader considerations for, 127; roles and responsibilities of, 124; social relationships creation of, 125; student demands balancing assistance of, 126; student educational experience impact of, 124; student success tactics of, 125–26; student welfare institution commitment and, 126. *See also* cost containment
Standard Industrial Classification (SIC) system, 4
Starbucks College Achievement Plan, 35
STEM. *See* science, technology, engineering and math
structures, 5, 12–13, 48, 92, 149; ASAP real life case study in, 169–71, 198; comprehensive strategic and operational planning process in, 167; continued improvement and enhancement in, 167; electronic administrative systems in, 167–68; EMS use in, 168; IIE use and growth in, 167; institutional compliance function in, 168; LMS use in, 168; philosophical and strategic and operational elements in, 166; regional accreditation bodies focus in, 168–69; SIS use in, 167–68; utilization growth of, 166–67
student demographics, 27–29, 169
student information system (SIS), 134, 167–68, 183
students, 4–7, 44, 119; academic support of, 128, 170, 183; ASAP case study and, 169–71, 198; ASAP real life case study and, 169–71, 198; CCBM and, 11, 43,

59, 102, 196; community colleges success intentional design for, 22; community colleges underserving of, 45; community development of, 128; cost containment and, 183–85; educational experience support of, 156–58; faculty and, 120–22; governance shared responsibility of, 77; loan debt of, 32; mechanisms and, 150–51; as partnership beneficiaries, 138; peer support benefits in, 128; peer-to-peer programming design and growth in, 128; peer-to-peer relationships importance in, 127–28; physical space for success design lack for, 130, *131*; product delivery expectations of, 149–50; resource and referral in, 128; revenue generation and, 189, 191; staff and, 124–26; technology support systems for, 133. *See also* Amarillo College; educational and student support

student value proposition (SVP), 12, 22, 26, 34, 88, 197; Amarillo College case study about, 108–12; basic needs insecurity in, 102; benefits and problems and needs by mission type in, *97*; business model and, 93; business serving questions for, 94; CCBM and traditional business model of, *47*; as CCBM focus, 11, 47, *47*, 108, 113, 195; community colleges considerations in, 112–13; consumer not customer in, 93; data collection and analysis in, 100; data usage and evaluation in, 100, *101*; different student populations expectations in, 95, *96*; direct beneficiaries in, 98–99; educational experience consideration in, 95; external pressures and, 108; facilities support of, 129; financial aid system jargon in, 102; food and housing insecurity report in, 102; indirect beneficiaries in, 99; institutional information systems enhancing of, *134*; operationalized definition of, 97; optimized educational experience in, 91; primary and secondary beneficiaries in, 94–95; service area needs in, 98; student learning and success in, 94; student needs and expectations in, 93; student populations in, 91; student segmentation construct in, 95; student subset focus hypothetical case studies on, 103–8; tacit knowledge central importance in, 138; tuition increase and underserved populations in, 100–102; value contextualizing questions in, 95; varied needs in, 94

student value proposition, hypothetical case studies: community outreach in, 106–8; traditional academic programs in, 103–4; workforce and continuing education programs in, 104–6

subcultures, 56–58, *58*, 76, 80, 178–79
subgroups, 53, 56–58
supplemental instruction (SI), 165
SVP. *See* student value proposition

tacit knowledge, 198; explicit knowledge difference in, 139; important features of, 139; major issue with, 139; organizational environment conditions for, 139–40; person and organization alignment in, 139; as powerful and underleveraged, 138; rareness of, 139; real-life explicit knowledge transformation example in, 140–41; revenue generation use of, 192; SVP central importance of, 138. *See also* Iota College real life case study

teaching, 121, 123, 150; flipped classrooms in, 163; games and gaming in, 163; higher education importance of, 161; individualized or personalized education approach in, 162; learning environment expectation in, 162–63; method examination in, 162; open pedagogy use in, 163; professional development opportunities in, 162; self-evaluation in, 161; social media integration in, 163; technology and expectation changes in, 162–63; technology-enhanced techniques in, 163

technology, 35, 159; academic departments and majors shifts in, 154; business model principles in, 132–33; challenges and opportunities in, 131, *132*; community colleges disruptive influence of, 34; computing equipment use in, 132; cost containment and, 183–84; as disruptive force, 130; educational experience enhancing opportunities in, 133, 135; healthcare industry and, 23; institutional information systems SVP enhancing in, *134*; intentional design in, 130–31; organizational effectiveness increase of, 131; references of, 130; student support systems in, 133; in teaching, 162–63

telemedicine, 23

traditional academic programs, hypothetical case study: needs addressing in, 104; primary problems in, 103–4; student value proposition definition in, 103

Truman Commission, 21

tuition, 31, 100–102, 188

tutoring, 157, 164–65

underserved populations, 9, 100–102

urgent care clinics and ambulatory facilities, 23–24

Wisconsin HOPE Lab survey, 109

Witherspoon, Collin, 109–10

workforce and continuing education programs, hypothetical case study: career-oriented programs and workforce development lack in, 104–5; needs addressing in, 106; primary problems in, 105–6; SVP definition in, 105

Zappos, 110–11

About the Author

Christopher Shults, PhD, is the dean of institutional effectiveness and strategic planning at the Borough of Manhattan Community College. As the chief planning officer, Dr. Shults is responsible for institutional effectiveness, planning, assessment, institutional research, analytics, and accreditation activities. Previously, he served as the executive director for planning and institutional effectiveness at Suffolk County Community College, as acting associate and assistant provost at Mississippi Valley State University, and as research associate at the American Association of Community Colleges.

Dr. Shults holds a PhD and MA in higher education administration from the University of Michigan's Center for the Study of Higher and Postsecondary Education. He earned his BS in psychology with honors from Morgan State University, where he was a four-time member of the Honda Campus All-Star Team and an inductee into six honor societies.

He has authored or coauthored more than one dozen books and journal articles; cocreated and coled leadership development programs for aspiring presidents and faculty; conducted professional development for colleges, universities, and regional accrediting bodies; and taught classes as an adjunct faculty member. Dr. Shults has also served as the university liaison to the Economic Development Council of Washington County (MS) and institutional representative to the Long Island Regional Advisory Council on Higher Education (NY). He recently served as vice-president for the Association of Higher Education Effectiveness and currently serves as an advisory board member for the EdD program in community college leadership at New Jersey City University.

Born to two United States Navy veterans, he has served as a lay minister in the United Methodist Church, a lead chef for a single mom's ministry, and as a big brother and mentor to teenagers and adolescents. Finally, and most importantly, he has been married to his best friend Keiva for twenty-two years and thoroughly enjoys the company of their three children—Niriel, Arianna, and Micah.

Made in the USA
Columbia, SC
29 May 2025